SECO

Patient

NO

Longer

RYAN

SECOND EDITION

Patient No Longer

How YOU Can Lead the Consumer Revolution in Healthcare

RYAN DONOHUE | **STEPHEN K. KLASKO, MD, MBA**

Foundation of the American College of Healthcare Executives, Chicago, Illinois

Library of Congress Cataloging-in-Publication Data
Library of Congress Cataloging-in-Publication Data is on file at the Library of Congress, Washington, DC.
ISBN: 978-1-64055-481-8

The paper used in this publication meets the minimum requirements of American National Standard for Information Sciences—Permanence of Paper for Printed Library Materials, ANSI Z39.48-1984. ♾ ™

Manuscript editor: Lori Meek Schuldt; Cover designer: James Slate; Layout: Integra

Found an error or a typo? We want to know! Please e-mail it to hapbooks@ache.org, mentioning the book's title and putting "Book Error" in the subject line.

For photocopying and copyright information, please contact Copyright Clearance Center at www.copyright.com or at (978) 750-8400.

ACHE Learn
A division of the Foundation of the American
    College of Healthcare Executives
300 S. Riverside Plaza, Suite 1900
Chicago, IL 60606-6698
(312) 424-2800

Contents

Preface

WHEN WE WROTE the first edition of this book in 2019, powerful trends were clear. Generations were shifting to a mobile, digital lifestyle, and healthcare needed to keep up. Further, people were struggling with the system. It was confusing, expensive, too often unsafe, and inequitable. It felt like a system set up to get paid, not to help. That's why we knew people would be "patient" no longer. In fact, many were confused, exhausted, and angry. As we demonstrate throughout the book, people do better when they are none of those things. All of us want to be treated as people, who wish to thrive and be happy without healthcare delivery getting in the way.

Even with these powerful trends already apparent in 2019, so much has happened to change healthcare as we know it in just a few short years. Today, those trends have been accelerated. We are writing this new edition during a phase we call "kinda after COVID," because COVID-19 hasn't gone away. But those early days of panic and lockdown have left their mark. As a result, every part of this book has been reconsidered for this second edition.

Sadly, the pandemic struck hardest those who could least afford it. But it also highlighted the consumer movement and the technology that will make it possible. The stories are now burned in memory:

> *Let's make it easy.* Consider the 94-year-old widow who now believes the best way to see a doctor face-to-face is onscreen. She won't go to an office. Indeed, she's not alone. People are

questioning why they have to travel to a hospital or office when new tools allow us to shift the locus of care to the home.

Let's give people the power to change their lives. Consider the teenage mom who used her smartphone to get birth control while on a city bus traveling from her job to visiting her newborn in the neonatal intensive care unit.

Let's bring clinicians into the home to see social determinants of health up close. Consider the physician whose virtual home visit revealed that the patient did not have a refrigerator, even as she managed medications that need to be kept cold.

And let's think about what it takes to create trust. Consider the husband who refused to set up a telehealth call when his wife contracted COVID, and who now blames himself that she died.

Even back in 2019, our call to action was loud, and we believe it was one that needed to be heard in every corner of the healthcare industry. Now we are calling louder, with even more conviction, on behalf of all healthcare workers, clinicians, and leaders who have been and remain on the front lines. We know we can act fast and be nimble. We know our consumers and patients can be our allies as we codesign the best healthcare for all. So much is possible. Let's make it happen.

Acknowledgments

I NEVER DREAMT this body of work would make such an impact on our critical industry of healthcare and ultimately spawn a second edition—one in which we could rethink and rewrite our findings for this perplexing post-COVID world. It's been an honor to receive another crack at these ideas and how to apply them.

I would like to again acknowledge my wife, Andrea, a wonderful woman who is always there for me and admirably stepped up to care for our children while I was consumed by the writing (and rewriting) process. And to my four children, Ryan Jr., Winnie, Maggie, and Rory—our youngest who didn't exist when this book was first published but has now more than earned his mention. Thank you for being four little sparks of joy and, perhaps most important, not being too hard on Mom while Dad was writing. I love you all.

I would also like to acknowledge my current and past colleagues and fellow associates at NRC Health and The Governance Institute for your fellowship and support. Especially Jona Raasch, who served as the keystone in holding this book together. Same goes for those I call "friends of the family" in the healthcare organizations in which I serve, the thought leaders who challenged me to push further, and the agencies and firms in which I collaborate and occasionally debate. Without you, *Patient No Longer* doesn't exist.

—*Ryan Donohue*

This book could not have been published at a more opportune time given the challenges and opportunities in American healthcare.

To my five grandchildren, Evan, Juliet, Berkley, Georgie, and Natalie, who expect and hope that those of us responsible for the healthcare ecosystem will finally get it right.

To my wife, Colleen, who allows me to keep the light on late at night when I work on books.

And my greatest thanks to the team who envisioned and assembled this book: Jona Raasch and Kathryn Peisert at The Governance Institute along with Ryan Donohue, and my colleagues Michael Hoad and John Ekarius.

In essence, this book is dedicated to all of you who seek what we all want for ourselves and our families—health assurance—the ability to thrive without having health get in the way.

—*Stephen K. Klasko, MD, MBA*

The original idea and encouragement to write the first edition of this book came from three individuals who have spent their entire careers building cultures that are, first and foremost, patient-centered: Richard Buck, MD; Michael Bleich, PhD, RN, FAAN; and Tamera Mahaffey, NP. We appreciate their early meetings with us, discussing how to build on the book *Through the Patient's Eyes*, a gift to our industry, by providing us with a way to understand and promote patient-centered care through the patient's eyes. We benefited greatly from their advice to do more than just update the book's content and show what, if any, progress the industry has made in improving the patient experience. To truly do what is best for patients, we need to change ourselves first and then move from a patient-centered industry to a consumer-obsessed industry. To do this, you must have human understanding. We knew the research would show that the eight Picker dimensions of patient-centered care are still as relevant and as important to patients today as they were 30 years ago. And we have taken the liberty to show how they are important to consumers.

None of this work would have been possible without Harvey and Jean Picker's insight into the need for research to create the original Picker dimensions and ensure that they were used to help drive improvement and not just measurement. Harvey was supportive and engaged in making sure the Picker work continued in the hands of NRC Health and internationally. We will be forever grateful for his ongoing encouragement and participation until his death in 2008. Gail Warden was also instrumental in continuing the Picker work with his role on the Picker Institute board and on the NRC Health board. We benefited greatly from his support, guidance, and insights into how great leaders lead and how you create a patient-centered culture that constantly develops leaders and providers who put the patient first while supporting and growing a community that understands the importance of how social determinants affect health.

We also would like to thank Dr. Stephen Klasko and Michael Hoad. We knew the minute we met Dr. Klasko that he was a forward-thinking and an innovative leader. We have benefited from our many interactions and enjoyed observing what a truly driven, positive, futuristic, and committed leader can do regardless of their address. Michael Hoad gifted us with his writing and brilliant advice for both the first and second editions.

We also thank all the associates at NRC Health, who are passionate about our mission and dedicated to helping our clients deliver not only patient-centered care but also human understanding. Finally, we are grateful to Mike Hays, our founder and CEO, who has insisted that we remain "outside-in," focused on what is right, and that we always make others successful and look for solutions.

—*Ryan Donohue, Jona Raasch, and Kathryn C. Peisert*
NRC Health, Lincoln, Nebraska

Finally, the authors would like to acknowledge the following individuals, who helped to update the stories in chapter 6 with their organizations' patient experience perspective post-COVID:

- Steve Meth, JD, MS, Vice President, Chief Patient Experience Officer, Johns Hopkins Health System and Armstrong Institute for Patient Safety and Quality
- Judith Wolfe, MD, Former Associate Chief Experience Officer, Enterprise Safety, Quality and Experience, Cleveland Clinic
- Stephanie Bayer, JD, Senior Director, Officer of Patient Experience, Cleveland Clinic

BC, DC, and KAC: An Introduction to the Technological and Human Aspects of the "New" Healthcare

Stephen K. Klasko, MD, MBA

WE TEND TO overstate "once in a lifetime" events, almost like the "trials of the century" of which there have been ten at last count in my lifetime. But no one will argue that the COVID-19 pandemic is exactly that for every aspect of the healthcare ecosystem. Rather than speculating whether this event was attributable to a bat or a lab or analyzing the number of cases still being hospitalized (on the rise again as of this writing), the goal of this book—written by a national thought leader in healthcare consumerism (Ryan Donohue) and an obstetrician, medical school dean, and academic medical center CEO (Stephen Klasko)—is to look past that event at what healthcare will look like ten years from now and what we should do today. Within the spirit of our first edition of *Patient No Longer*, we aim to dig deeper into what this means not just to "patients" but to "people" who want to be able to thrive without healthcare getting in the way. So, for the purposes of this introduction to the new edition, we ask our readers to view this timeline along with us as BC, DC, and KAC—before COVID, during COVID, and "kinda after" COVID! In case you haven't been following the news, we are now well entrenched in KAC, with generative AI and large language models (LLMs) being the hot topic of the day, and patients expecting healthcare to join the consumer revolution.

BC (before COVID), being a healthcare CEO used to be easy. Well, maybe not easy, but certainly easier! The metrics were relatively straightforward. Provide the best "sick care" possible with the least amount of errors and attempt to solve the "iron triangle" of access, quality, and cost. The iron triangle is a bit like a Rubik's Cube in that without some creativity, improving one aspect affects the other. Without "disrupting" the current system, improving access would mean that you needed to increase cost or reduce quality . . . and so on. Disruption is painful. By definition, disruption means threatening your existing product line and your past investments. In healthcare, those past investments involved building more "sick care" bricks and mortar, consolidating for leverage with commercial insurers, and talking (but not really doing much) about social determinants and health equity. Patients by and large were viewed as potential "sick people" who could come to our office, our urgent care center, our emergency department, or our hospital. As a physician, even talking about the patient as a "consumer" would elicit confused and, in some cases, derogatory looks from my senior colleagues.

While health system websites highlighted equity, community engagement, quality, safety, and whole-person care, most health system CEOs were incented based on EBIDA (earnings before interest, depreciation, and amortization), hospital census, U.S. News and World Report rankings, and the opinion of the hospital's specialists toward the CEO and administration. With the advent of accountable care organizations and "value-based care," primary care took on an expanded role and the pay gap between specialists (e.g., orthopedic surgeons, dermatologists, interventional cardiologists) and family medicine providers was astounding. As my chair of community medicine said, "You want me to be the quarterback, but you pay me like the kicker!" Population health, social determinants, and health equity were mostly philosophical and academic concerns. Not surprisingly, while individual fragments of many systems made individual health equity and gap reduction investments, zip code disparities remained virtually unchanged. In fact, when I was the CEO of Jefferson Health, my team changed our mission from being "the premier academic medical center in Philadelphia" to "we improve lives." A portion of my own and my senior team's incentives were based on reducing certain healthcare gaps in Philadelphia—a logical and necessary step that was viewed as revolutionary. Similarly, behavioral and mental health were viewed as "carve outs" by hospitals and payers, largely because they didn't fit into the relative value unit–based model that was largely dependent on specialty care, hospital visits, and surgery.

In healthcare marketing, there was almost no consumer segmentation. Billboards pronouncing a hospital's "patient-centered care" neglected to specify whether that care was centered on a 60-year-old athlete with an Oura Ring and an Apple Watch, a 30-year-old disconnected person, or a 75-year-old cancer patient who only uses Facebook to chat with her "unbelievably cute grandchildren!" Healthcare marketing for most health systems was a one-size-fits-all billboard and TV strategy with a dash of digital advertising—mostly mired in the past. No one really knew what it cost to acquire or retain consumers or prevent them from going someplace else. Few organizations even mapped out the care journeys consumers took to become their patients, with all the decisions they needed to make along the way. Consumers routinely felt that health system marketing efforts had zero impact on whom they chose as their provider or payer, or whom they returned to when they needed care again. Yet providers and payers continued to spend money on marketing campaigns that did not resonate with anyone outside the hospital C suite and marketing department.

Amazingly, despite healthcare expenditures rising dramatically and outcomes becoming more disparate, there was little impetus for change. When Jason Kidd, an NBA point guard, was traded to the Dallas Mavericks (who were 24–52 at that time), he supposedly said, "I'm going to turn this team around 360 degrees." That was the BC story of healthcare consumerism for the 30 years prior to the pandemic: lots of talk, but by and large, we always ended up where we started.

DC (during COVID), everything changed. The pandemic was a public health, financial, and equity Category 5 hurricane that accelerated the recognition of the broken, fragmented, expensive, and inequitable healthcare consumer system that had been tolerated for the previous three decades. Nowhere was that more evident than in the distributive win–lose model between payers and providers. Health systems and hospitals lost billions of dollars because people did not get care; payers made billions of dollars because people did not get care. It is fair to say that there is no other sector where consumer choice and payment models are more disconnected than when they are dealing with their most important asset—their health.

Supply chain breakdowns and unpreparedness as well as foreign outsourcing of hospital supplies and personal protective equipment went from "someday" concerns to the national healthcare crisis. With political and state-to-state inconsistencies in insurance models, public health and Medicaid expansion went from eccentricities to life-and-death concerns. Public health, in particular, transformed overnight from an ignored and academic discipline to a political hotbed. BC, how many people could name the director of the Centers for Disease Control or the head of the National Institute on Aging? But DC, doctors Anthony Fauci and Rochelle Walensky became household names, magazine covers, and political darlings or targets. On the ground, the system I ran encompassed several counties in two states, all with different "mandates" regarding vaccinations, hospital regulations, and consumer behavior.

Telehealth and "healthcare at any address" moved from Silicon Valley to Main Street and home (except for the underserved population who did not have broadband, access to virtual care, or appropriate health insurance). Many of the so-called COVID fatalities were collateral damage of our broken and inequitable system. People died at home not of COVID but of treatable heart disease, lung disease, diabetes, and other acute exacerbations of chronic conditions because they were afraid to go to the hospital. Consumers pulled back the veil that "healthcare was somehow different" and could not provide the same level of consumer- and home-oriented care, as this crisis forced providers and hospitals to recognize that telehealth and virtual care were not an "innovation luxury" but the lifeblood of a newly transformed healthcare system. Almost overnight, by March 2020 telehealth suddenly became the primary mode of seeking care. At my institution, the Jefferson telehealth team began calling themselves the "Night's Watch," a reference to the Game of Thrones border army. And they were right—telehealth tackled the first wave of the virus that causes COVID-19. Telehealth and virtual care expanded twenty-fold in our system, and by 2021 we were already seeing some claw-back because of payment and fragmentation concerns.

Many of our predictions back in 2021 in the first edition of this book regarding virtual care for consumers might have seemed radical, but they have become mainstream while others have struggled to gain traction—mostly because of payer–provider misalignment, health system inertia, and in some cases, consumer apathy. We will describe some of our predictions and what happened with them in the following paragraphs.

Digital tools for delivery of services must be robust and clearly communicated to customers and staff alike.

What we said: "For example, pregnant women are already afraid to visit hospitals for prenatal care. Whereas home pregnancy monitors used to be a luxury, they will now rapidly become part of a new mode of pregnancy: digital diagnostic tools combined with the wisdom of obstetricians and pediatricians, many times offered virtually."

The reality: While the technology exists for virtual pregnancy monitoring and electronic fetal surveillance, malpractice concerns and payment models geared toward patients getting care in the hospital have limited their use. Not surprisingly, creating these barriers to fetal and maternal care has resulted in the United States being one of the few countries (along with several third world countries) where maternal and fetal negative outcomes have *increased.*

A vast reskilling of service jobs will be needed in the world of artificial intelligence.

What we said: "In healthcare, we're now seeing thousands of physicians learning how to deliver sophisticated medicine through virtual visits. That kind of learning will occur in every industry."

The reality: Workforce became the number one issue for health systems around the country. Nurses joined unions and went on strike over staffing issues. As reported in Deloitte's online article "Addressing Health Care's Talent Emergency" (Medlock et al. 2022), an alarming number of nurses did not believe that the administration cared about them postpandemic. Contract nursing soared virtually, tripling the hospital's human resource budget. Along with inflation and supply chain issues, hospital net operating incomes plummeted as hospitals were one of the few industries that could not adjust pricing to expense increases. Relief is coming, however, in the form of LLMs and generative AI. For 18 cents an hour, these entities can talk to thousands of patients doing preop work, follow-ups, and other tasks and act as cobots (collaborative robots) for the nursing staff.

We must put people first.

What we said: "Ethics must not be an afterthought but rather considered at the beginning of new product development, before a new digital product goes to market. COVID-19 arrived during a crisis of trust; surveys by Edelman (2020) and others have found a deep mistrust of social institutions and traditional elites. Some of this mistrust is caused by the digital revolution itself—the fear that collected information may be used against oneself. We must earn trust at every stage."

The reality: We were right! The more sophisticated technology becomes, the clearer it is that trust is more important than technology. The excitement of the so-called Fourth Industrial Revolution in healthcare is tempered by the fear that genomics, generative AI, robotics, and predictive analytics will be used in nefarious ways in much the same manner as the evolution of social media.[1] It is more important than ever that we put the appropriate guardrails on AI so that we are not retrospectively regretting this unfettered technology.

We must reinvent how we protect the people who work for us.

What we said: "COVID-19 has shattered the gig economy and the jobs of hourly employees in the service industry, and it has even injured those with full-time employment. In every crisis of the twentieth century, business and government leaders worked to 'cover' employees by providing insurance for sickness, creating rules for employment status, and the like. The COVID-19 crisis demands similar leadership. The recovery of the economy in 2020 and beyond demands a new compact with those who do the work. This will be the single biggest concern of voters in the US elections of November 2020, and it will resonate throughout the world as the global economy rebuilds."

The reality: We were prescient. Social determinants, income inequality, and workers' rights will be dominant factors in the political races of the 2020s. Food insecurity, housing issues, and childcare have affected not only individuals but also the overall quality of life and health in many of our major cities. Workers' rights have really hit home in the healthcare industry as nurse shortages and a "turnover tsunami" have led to increased unionization and vastly increased labor costs, mostly based on staffing and security issues.

In summary, the pandemic did not teach us anything we didn't already know. Behavioral health and social issues affected millions of people and drove up social and healthcare costs, especially among adolescents and underserved individuals for which the healthcare ecosystem was unprepared. Population health, social determinants, and patient preferences around nutrition and exercise often have become the determinants of life and death. Broadband capability (no telehealth without broadband), homelessness and housing issues (it is hard to socially distance when several family members are in limited space), and increased supply chain costs accelerated food vulnerability. Most of the BC issues that we had swept under the rug came back out to bite us DC.

Technology in healthcare has done immeasurable good but also has caused immeasurable harm. When it's used to empower the patient and streamline the experience, the results have been impressive. When it's used as a surrogate for real human interaction, it has caused harm. Having ten different apps to manage while trying to figure out an already confusing industry is not what we call progress.

KAC (kinda after COVID), what did the pandemic teach us? That we could no longer pretend we had the best healthcare system in the world. For that reason, the KAC era would mean we could no longer ignore these issues and that, "patient no longer," we need to move toward a more consumer-driven healthcare system in the United States.

While the healthcare delivery story BC and DC is not pretty, there is room for optimism in the KAC era. Every sector of the healthcare ecosystem is under financial stress. While that does not sound optimistic, desperation often forces change. I believe as it relates to healthcare consumerism, we can enter a stage of "nondisruptive creation" as described by W. Chan Kim and Renée Mauborgne (2023). Nondisruptive creation represents a path to new industries, new jobs, and profitable growth but without the pain of shuttered companies, hurt communities, or lost jobs that come with disruption. It's a path beyond disruption, where business and society can thrive together. Nondisruptive creation is an alternative path to innovation and growth. Uber and Netflix were disruptive innovations—they won the competitions for taxi service and video content delivery, respectively, and Blockbuster lost. The development of Viagra is a great example of a nondisruptive creation. It created a market for a problem that had not had any easy or direct solutions. Obviously, the nondisruptive creation for healthcare consumerism in a fragmented, win–lose, and inequitable $4 trillion industry is no easy task.

The KAC world is ripe for nondisruptive creation and now looks like this:

- Health systems will be paid on total cost of care, access, quality, and user experience.
- Payers are not prepared for the latent illnesses that weren't seen DC.
- Founders' valuations are plummeting because digital health actually needs to be scalable and sustainable.
- Population health, social determinants, and health equity are moving from philosophical and academic concerns to the mainstream of clinical care and payment models.
- The old math of inpatient revenue, National Institutes of Health funding, and in-person tuition for academic medical centers will be commoditized. The new math will be value + innovation + consumer choice.
- Doctors and nurses will need to coexist and cooperate with robots and generative AI. For example, when online meets offline, what is the changing role for the human in the middle?

The opportunities for healthcare and healthcare consumerism KAC are enormous. Eight that we see as we write this second edition of *Patient No Longer* are the following:

1. We will need to select and educate humans to be better humans than robots instead of trying to compete with them on memorization and science. LLMs will replace 50 percent of what doctors do—but any doctor who can be replaced by a computer probably should be. What that means for consumers is that there is a better chance their doctor or provider will look like them and be more empathetic, creative, and communicative, and not just an amazing multiple choice test taker.

2. Radical communication, radical collaboration, and radical creativity will become crucial skill sets. For consumers, that means less fragmentation, more payer–provider alignment, and potentially a halt in some of the hospital-as-competitor wars, with a more nuanced "coopetition model" whereby hospitals work together in the population and community health arena. The lines are already being blurred. BC and DC, who would have thought that an insurer—United/Optum—would become the largest provider in the nation, or that traditional health systems would become large venture capital funds such as Northwell Ventures, Ascension, or Providence? Radical collaboration and communication will mean that the new healthcare marketing team will partner with product design and generative AI companies to create healthcare products based on *individual* consumer choices.

3. Nursing has gone from being commoditized and underappreciated and carrying out physician "orders" BC, to a short period of healthcare heroism DC, to being the most sought after "jewel" for a health system KAC. What this means for consumers is that collaborative robots and continuous data will allow for "healthcare at any address" and have people thrive without healthcare getting in the way. But when they need human interaction, there will be

nurses and physicians who can act as the "humans in the middle" when online meets offline.

4. Probably the greatest change for the healthcare ecosystem will be workforce transformation. As evidenced by the turnover tsunami, the pandemic and lockdowns created not only a need to develop flexible or hybrid models for the new workplace but also a need to address employee well-being and a need to foster inclusive and diverse leadership. Just as the patient experience is being rethought, healthcare employers are rethinking the employee value proposition and customizing worker experiences. Employees are seeking flexible work arrangements and the opportunity to develop fourth industrial revolution skills, be part of a shared sense of purpose and mission, and have the opportunity for personal development.

5. With the increase in genomics, predictive analytics, and data sharing, trust becomes more important than technology, and ethics need to be brought in at the beginning of these transformations. This will be even a bigger issue with LLMs for tuned-in consumers and will require guardrails around what is done with an individual's data. Unintended consequences are not unintended if you know they are going to happen. Abuses in data sharing, generative AI, and genomics *will* happen. How do we insert those in the beginning so that the social media revolution crisis does not get repeated in healthcare?

6. Regenerative medicine and bioprinting will increase longevity and revolutionize transplantation. Already there are developments in bioprinting lungs, breasts, and kidneys, and it is possible that ten years from now, the thought of someone having to take out their kidney to provide one to someone else will seem barbaric.

7. The revolution will help abolish the "episodic physical" (i.e., a person goes to a doctor only if something's wrong), and mental and behavioral health needs will be integrated into the whole-body primary care and specialty care experience. Right now, my car gets better care than I do. When I am away, it is sending continuous data and either self-correcting or telling me to go to the "car doctor." Humans who do checkups get a static exam from the neck down once yearly and, based on that data, are often told what to do for the next year. At best, mental, behavioral, and emotional health are part of a screening previsit questionnaire. KAC will bring a revolution of "intersentient" collaboration between the LLM, predictive analytics, liquid tissue biomarkers, and natural language processing. This collaboration will require human care providers with a different and more empathetic skill set who can deal with the whole body–and–mind dynamics of an individual in concert with the data and robots.

8. Healthcare will join the consumer revolution and embrace human understanding. First, we recognized that *people* don't want to be *patients* . . . they are *people* with diabetes, cancer, congestive heart failure, or some other condition. If all we do is treat them as sick people needing to come to our office, urgent care, emergency room, or hospital, we will be out of business. In some respects, this brings us "back to the future." *Through the Patient's Eyes* (Gerteis et al. 1993) is no longer theory. Although it was first published more than 30 years ago, the recognition that patient-centered care is not just a billboard but needs to be applied in an individualized, customized, culturally competent manner (e.g., consumer segmentation) is a very KAC concept. From a health system perspective, that means inspiring consumer loyalty by learning from the success of other industries, demonstrating value for

the money, giving consumers a single point of contact, and creating a seamless experience across the continuum. When Amazon disrupted the retail industry, Target and Walmart recognized their strength at providing service at their stores, but they also knew that to compete with Amazon, they would have to be in people's homes. Health systems and payers need to take that same "both/and" approach.

In 2020, we posited that healthcare consumers will be "patient no longer!" The good news is that we were right, and for the first time, consumers are being offered choices that were never true before. Innovative primary care models, retail care, and big tech entering the healthcare consumer market are all putting pressure on the traditional healthcare ecosystem. What no one can predict are the effects that generative AI, LLMs, machine learning, robotics, drones, and other fourth industrial revolution technologies will have on consumers and their health. As we write this book, it is unclear if those technologies will be *the* game changer and all positive and friendly like *E.T.*, or if they will be a stomach-destroying threat to humanity like *Aliens*, or if they will be something in between like *Close Encounters of the Third Kind*. One thing is for certain: my children and grandchildren will no longer have to be patient to receive customized, personal, and consumer-centric healthcare.

NOTE

1. The First Industrial Revolution (1784) introduced mechanization, steam power, and the weaving loom. The Second Industrial Revolution (1870) was technological, including mass production, the assembly line, and electrical energy. The Third Industrial Revolution (1969) was digital,

involving automation, computers, and electronics. The Fourth Industrial Revolution of today ushered in cyber physical systems, the internet of things, and networks (Wikipedia 2024).

REFERENCES

Edelman. 2020. "2020 Edelman Trust Barometer." Published January 19. www.edelman.com/trustbarometer.

Gerteis, M., S. Edgman-Levitan, J. Daley, and T. L. Delbanco (eds.). 1993. *Through the Patient's Eyes: Understanding and Promoting Patient-Centered Care*. San Francisco: Jossey-Bass.

Kim, W. C., and R. Mauborgne. 2023. *Beyond Disruption: Innovate and Achieve Growth without Displacing Industries, Companies, or Jobs*. Brighton, MA: Harvard Business Review Press.

Medlock, M., E. Radis, K. Abrams, J. Bhatt, E. Elsner, and R. Malhotra. 2022. "Addressing Health Care's Talent Emergency." Deloitte Insights. Published November 15. www2.deloitte.com/us/en/insights/industry/health-care/healthcare-workforce-shortage-solutions.html.

Wikipedia. 2024. "Fourth Industrial Revolution." Modified September 10, 21:55. https://en.wikipedia.org/wiki/Fourth_Industrial_Revolution.

PART I

History and Healthcare Context of Patient-Centered Care

CHAPTER 1

How We Got Here: A Brief History of Patient-Centered Care

IT WAS THE worst of surgeries, it was the best of surgeries. . . . Tim and Suzi had been married for 40 years and enjoyed good health and active lifestyles. Tim played golf, was caregiver to his four grandchildren, and did regular work tending to his sizable garden. Retired, he kept busy helping other family members and members of his church community in various ways.

Neither Tim nor Suzi had much reason to encounter the health-care industry in their more than 40 years of marriage. Their two children had been born with no complications and normal deliveries. Both Tim and Suzi saw a primary care physician and received medical screening tests and physicals recommended for their age.

But when Tim went in for his annual physical at age 62, his blood test showed an elevated prostate-specific antigen (PSA) score. It was slightly higher six months later, so his physician recommended he see a urologist. At the urologist appointment just a few weeks later, another blood test revealed that Tim's score on the Gleason scale was on the border of being considered cancerous. A biopsy showed cancer cells in 4 of the 12 samples, and the urologist encouraged Tim to have his prostate removed. The urologist pressed hard, saying that because Tim was active and in excellent health, he should make a complete recovery. Tim was reluctant, as his father had had his prostate removed 20 years prior, never regained normal control, and regretted having had the surgery.

Suzi questioned the urologist because she knew that the United States had more stringent recommendations for PSA testing and prostate surgery than other countries did, even though the number of deaths attributable to prostate cancer was no higher in other countries. Both Tim and Suzi expressed their concerns about Tim's father's experience. The urologist emphasized the many medical advances made in the past 20 years and explained that, with robotic surgery, he was confident there would be no problems. Tim and Suzi considered getting another opinion, but after Tim thought further about it, he decided he wanted to get it over with; he wanted to recover fully by January so that he would not have to miss marshalling at the PGA tournament in San Diego, a favorite activity of his that had become a cherished tradition.

Tim needed an electrocardiogram (EKG) and an additional blood test to get a sign-off from his primary care physician prior to surgery. He had to make these appointments on his own, all while thinking about the major surgery ahead of him. He didn't understand why another blood test was needed, as he had just had one prior to his urologist visit. During the EKG, Tim was asked when he had had a heart attack, even though he had never had one. After much discussion and further examination by his physician, he was sent to a local cardiology clinic to have yet another EKG to ensure that everything was OK prior to surgery. Finally, after further difficult testing that didn't make any sense to Tim and additional appointments, scheduling challenges, and great expense, he was assured that nothing was wrong with his heart and was cleared for surgery.

When the time came, Tim's surgeon explained to Tim and Suzi what to expect in the hospital and emphasized again that, because it was robotic surgery, Tim could expect a speedy and complete recovery. He was told the biggest inconvenience he would experience was having a catheter for seven to ten days after surgery.

Tim came through surgery with no problems. He was up and walking right away and quickly got accustomed to the catheter. He looked forward to going home. Hospital staff members were polite, but when Tim asked questions, they often replied, "Who is your surgeon? Oh, you have Dr. Jones. Well, he likes things done a certain way." This response made Tim wonder if his surgeon was different from most and how other surgeons did things, and it caused him some fear and anxiety. Also, depending on which nurse he asked, he received different answers to the same questions. There was no sense of teamwork or coordination.

Tim's first week home went according to plan, and he looked forward to his first follow-up visit to have the catheter removed. Everything checked out fine, and the physician seemed pleased with Tim's progress. But since Tim had expected to return to normal fairly quickly, and his physician had told him he was healing nicely, he became frustrated when he didn't regain his normal urinary control. Tim expressed this concern at his three-week follow-up visit and was told, for the first time, that it could take 9 to 12 months to get back to normal. This news came as a shock to both Tim and Suzi—this didn't sound like a "speedy and complete recovery" to them. It made them wonder what else they had not been told.

Around this time, Suzi began waking up frequently at night with what seemed to be stomach cramps. She thought she might be having a reaction to the acidic nature of all the fresh garden vegetables she and Tim had been enjoying recently. She also felt it might be stress caused by Tim's delayed recovery. But after about a month, the discomfort became longer and more intense and felt more like menstrual cramps, so Suzi scheduled an appointment with her obstetrician/gynecologist (ob-gyn). During the week she had to wait for the appointment, her pain became even more severe, lasting several hours at a time. Her ob-gyn scheduled an ultrasound for her. While driving back to work after the ultrasound, Suzi received a phone call from the technician, who said that the physician wanted to see her the next day in her office. At the visit, Suzi learned that her uterus was extremely enlarged—to 18 inches, compared to the normal uterus size of 3 to 4 inches. The increase in size concerned Suzi because, two years prior, she had had a dilation and curettage procedure to remove fibroids that were causing heavy bleeding and discomfort, and at the time the physician said her uterus was 14 inches. The consensus was that Suzi's uterus needed to be removed. Although Suzi's ob-gyn conducted a lot of hysterectomies, she wanted to consult with a specialist in a nearby city who conducted robotic hysterectomies; she wanted to see if he could do the surgery, as it would be a safer option in the event that cancer was involved.

Suzi was prescribed painkillers to help with the painful nights. A few days later, she and Tim met with the specialist and learned that the robotic procedure was in fact possible. The surgery was scheduled for the following week, and all necessary presurgical tests were handled and coordinated that day in the specialist's office. Tim and Suzi left with everything handled and scheduled for them. The only remaining challenge was managing the increasing pain until the surgery. On Sunday, the day before Suzi was to check into the hospital, her pain was so severe that she called the surgeon's office and spoke with the on-call physician. He recommended that she drive to the hospital and be admitted through the emergency department. There, Suzi was quickly set up with an intravenous morphine drip, which relieved her pain immediately. Soon thereafter, she was admitted the room she would occupy for the balance of her hospital stay. Once in her room, two nurses introduced themselves and explained that they were part of her surgeon's team. They confirmed that her surgery was scheduled for the next morning and explained that they were there to help manage the pain and prepare her for surgery the next day. That night, Suzi had her first hours of pain-free sleep in several weeks.

She came through surgery extremely well despite complications caused by the size of the uterus, and her surgeon had no concerns. Once back in her room, Suzi was up and walking and felt the best she had in over a month. Tim and her children had left by then, as it had been a very early morning and a long day. Suzi's nurses said she was doing so well that she would be ready to return home that evening or the next morning. Suzi decided to wait for Tim's planned return in the morning and not make him drive an hour back late at night. Everything was completely ready for her discharge the next morning. Suzi received full explanations of what to expect and when, and she was given options whenever possible.

Suzie's experience was extremely well coordinated, and all her health providers were members of the same team—Suzi's team. There was never any delay or waiting for answers. Everyone seemed focused on helping Suzi manage her pain and return home for a restful recovery. The team handled all appointments, always taking her preferences into consideration and making her feel like she was everyone's top priority. In contrast, Tim's experience was not at all coordinated. The burden was put on him to schedule, coordinate, call, explain and reexplain, and insist that his appointments be made in time for surgery. It was his responsibility to think of and ask every question possible, as the only information shared concerned the clinical process of the surgery. Tim was given neither time nor the opportunity to explore treatment options; in fact, he was given no treatment options other than surgery.

* * *

As an industry, healthcare can be mysterious. On the outside, it gives off a cold feel. It's a world you won't have to visit much, if you're lucky and healthy. That perception is not lost on its leaders. Healthcare CEOs, experts, and consultants have banged the collective drum to become more compassionate, more convenient, and more in line with the belief that care should be centered around the patient.

The past few decades have seen a lot of activity to improve the patient experience. Numerous factors have influenced this work, including legislative action, healthcare improvement initiatives, and the formation of quality improvement organizations that have helped create ways of quantifying, measuring, and reporting provider performance. Through such efforts focused on improving the quality of care, the healthcare industry has recognized that one key factor must be the patient experience, as it is intricately related to and affects overall quality.

Measuring quality began with the establishment of the Institute of Medicine (IOM) in 1970 by the National Academies of Science to help inform the nation on emerging healthcare issues. The IOM was responsible for developing the STEEEP acronym that is widely used today as a standard definition of quality in healthcare (safe, timely, effective, efficient, equitable, and patient-centered). The Agency for Health Care Policy and Research (AHRQ) was formed in 1989 under the Department of Health and Human Services. In October 1995, AHRQ launched the first Consumer Assessment of Healthcare Providers and Systems (CAHPS) program, based on the work of the Picker Institute at NRC Health. The initial focus was a multiyear initiative to support and promote the assessment of consumers' healthcare experiences in the hospital inpatient setting. The program now addresses a range of healthcare services to meet the needs of healthcare consumers, purchasers, health plans, providers, and policymakers (AHRQ 2023). The CAHPS program has two main goals:

1. To develop a standardized patient questionnaire to be used to compare results across sponsors and over time
2. To generate tools and resources that sponsors can use to produce understandable and usable comparative information for both consumers and healthcare providers

From 1995 to 2001, several other quality improvement initiatives, task forces, and sentinel event reports were initiated and published, including the two famous reports from the IOM, *To Err Is Human* (1999) and *Crossing the Quality Chasm* (2001). The latest charge for "patient-centered care" came in 2005, during a time when healthcare was coming to grips with rising costs and stagnating quality of care. The term *value-based care* was still not widely used or understood. The patient-centered charge made it all the way to Washington, DC, and politicians listened.

In December 2005, the Office of Management and Budget gave its final approval for the national implementation of the Hospital Consumer Assessment of Healthcare Providers and Systems (HCAHPS) surveys for public reporting purposes. When the Centers for Medicare & Medicaid Services (CMS) began tying a portion of hospital Medicare payments to survey scores in 2007, hospitals started to pay more attention. A widespread effort was put in place to give patients a voice and to improve healthcare for patients. The first public reporting of HCAHPS results occurred in March 2008 (CMS 2023a).

From 2007 to 2016, AHRQ expanded the CAHPS program to other areas beyond hospital care, including physician clinics, home health, hospice, and outpatient and ambulatory surgery. The CAHPS program is still regularly reviewed by CMS to ensure that the survey includes what is most important to consumers.

In 2014, CMS added HCAHPS scores to its Hospital Value-based Purchasing Program, tying those results to Medicare hospital reimbursements and thus elevating the importance of the CAHPS program. In 2019, the Medicare value-based physician payment system known as the Merit-based Incentive Payment System, which includes clinician and group CAHPS measures in its reimbursement calculations, was fully implemented. The US government's increasing emphasis on value-based payments is aimed at influencing other payers in tying the amount of reimbursement to the patient experience. These moves have placed the improvement of patient experience front and center for healthcare executives and board leadership.

After more than 20 years of efforts to improve the patient experience, what do we have to show for it? Has widespread measurement of the patient experience created actionable data and real-life improvement? Has the call to consider the patient's point of view shifted minds—and hearts—to what's most important in healthcare? Has an entirely new industry of patient-focused edu-cational and training tactics staffed hospitals with newer, kinder caregivers? To answer these critical questions, we must first revisit the most prolific study of patient-centered care in US history.

THE WORK OF HARVEY PICKER

Born into a healthcare-oriented family, Harvey Picker didn't set out to change the industry—at least not initially. Picker followed in his father's footsteps and took the reins of Picker X-Ray, a leading-edge X-ray technology company that aided Allied efforts during World War II (1939–45) and saved lives with small, nearly indestructible imaging machines that could be used almost any-where. Picker devoted three decades of his adult life to the business that bore his father's name. His wife, Jean, was a US ambassador to the United Nations, an acclaimed journalist for *Life* magazine, and a personal friend of Eleanor Roosevelt.

Picker spoke to a London *Times* reporter in 2006. According to the published article, "the couple's personal experiences of health-care changed everything. As president of Picker X-Ray, Harvey was in constant contact with the healthcare system. And Jean had regular stays in hospitals because of a chronic and incurable infec-tion of her neck and head" (Crompton 2006).

In his own time immersed in healthcare, Picker found health-care highly advanced in terms of technology but woefully under-performing in the way it treated patients. This observation intensified with Jean's experiences. As Picker recalled in the *Times* article (Crompton 2006):

> I am under no illusions that my wife and I were given above average attention in hospital. But while we were there we saw how other patients' needs were badly neglected. They were left unattended on stretchers in corridors for hours. This was happening all the time in the 1960s and 1970s, in

the U.K. as well as America. Now, of course, if it happens it gets far more publicity. Until the middle of the 20th century, if you became ill there were few things we knew how to cure, so patients got very personalised nursing care for almost everything, trying to pull the person through the illness. Then, with penicillin and the introduction of other medical technologies, there was a complete flip. Because you could cure people, personal care became less important and the attitude of healthcare professionals changed from looking at the person to looking at the disease. The pendulum had swung too far the other way.

In light of these experiences, Harvey and Jean Picker transferred the assets of their small family foundation to the Commonwealth Fund in 1986 and initiated the Picker/Commonwealth Program for Patient-Centered Care, which later became known as the Picker Institute (Kohler 1994). In Harvey Picker's words, "it was the first body to investigate scientifically not just what patients really wanted from healthcare but also how physicians and healthcare staff could improve the patient experience" (Kohler 1994). Harvey, Jean, and the rest of the team tackled their goal with great vigor and immediately began to interview patients firsthand.

Over the next seven years, the Picker/Commonwealth program conducted extensive academic research, including more than 8,000 interviews with patients and families, as well as focus groups composed of dozens of caregivers. This research showed that patients' preferences were too often neglected and that amenities, such as hospital food and access to parking, were given far too much significance in existing patient surveys (Kohler 1994).

The Picker Institute developed a wide range of survey tools that quickly set the standard for performance measurement in the healthcare field. In addition to its own research, Picker Institute staff members were part of a large team of investigators from across the country—joining researchers from Harvard Medical School, the Research Triangle Institute, and the RAND Corporation—who worked to develop the CAHPS surveys and reports to improve public accountability and support consumer choice. The CAHPS instruments have become the national standard for evaluating care across the United States and are now required by the National Committee on Quality Assurance as well as CMS. The Picker Institute's emphasis on standardized instruments and methods of data collection helped support the creation of comparative databases that could facilitate benchmarking and spur quality improvement (Gerteis et al. 1993). As demand for Picker surveys increased, the institute lacked the capability to run large-scale data collection, processing, and reporting, so in 1994 its survey instruments were acquired by the National Research Corporation, now NRC Health (Kohler 1994).

The Picker Institute was the first of its kind in that it existed solely to advance the idea of patient-centered care. It argued that what matters most in healthcare is not what physicians or administrators think but what the patient thinks. The bedrock of this argument was the idea that for patients to truly receive the best care possible, they must be involved in the process—and partnership—of care delivery. In short order, the Picker Institute was "considered a leader in promoting patient-friendly medical care" (Hevesi 2008). This unique approach not only created reams of useful (and at the time rare) patient data but also culminated in a project known as *Through the Patient's Eyes*. This patient-centered masterwork, laid out in a 1993 best seller of the same name (Gerteis et al. 1993), concluded that patients held a high bar in their expectations of a healthcare experience and that the industry had a mountain of work to do to better serve its primary audience.

EIGHT DIMENSIONS OF PATIENT-CENTERED CARE

Out of *Through the Patient's Eyes*, the Picker Institute outlined a plan for health systems and hospitals to improve. From more than eight years of interviews and reams of patient feedback, the Picker team identified the following eight dimensions of patient-centered care (Gerteis et al. 1993):

1. **Respect for patients' values, preferences, and expressed needs**
   - Respecting the values of each individual patient
   - Involving the patient in medical decisions
   - Treating the patient with dignity
2. **Coordination and integration of care**
   - Clinical care
   - Ancillary and support services
   - Frontline patient care
3. **Information, communication, and education**
   - Accurate information on the patient's clinical condition and prognosis and on the processes of care
   - Additional information to support patient self-care and autonomous patient decisions
4. **Physical comfort**
   - Pain management
   - Assistance with daily activities
   - A supportive hospital environment
5. **Emotional support and alleviation of fear and anxiety**
   - Alleviation of anxiety over physical treatment and prognosis
   - Alleviation of anxiety over the impact of the illness on the patient and family
   - Alleviation of anxiety over the financial effects of illness
6. **Involvement of family and friends**
   - Providing accommodations for family and friends
   - Involving family and close friends in decision-making
   - Supporting family members who take on the role of caregiver

- Recognizing the needs of family and friends, as well as of the patient
7. **Continuity and transition**
    - Providing understandable, detailed information on medications and continuing patient needs
    - Planning and coordinating timely and appropriate treatment and services after discharge
    - Offering continuing information on access to clinical, social, physical, and financial support services
8. **Access to care**
    - Information on the location of needed healthcare services, along with appropriate transportation support
    - Ease in scheduling appointments
    - Accessible specialists and specialty services

These factors proved most important to patients before, during, and after their journey of care. Many of them, such as involvement of family and friends, were novel and underappreciated at the time. "Visitors," as family and friends were often labeled, were not considered a part of the direct care provided to the patient even though their support had an immeasurable impact on the patient's attitude, well-being, and ability to recover. The dimension of emotional support is hugely important to patients and correlates most highly with a patient's recommending an organization to others; however, this aspect of care continues to be a challenge for most organizations.

More than a quarter century has now passed since that landmark study. What has changed in that time?

CURRENT STATE OF PATIENT-CENTERED EFFORTS

Undeniably, activity, resources, and energy have been spent on the mission of patient-centered care. The Picker-inspired movement created vast amounts of patient- and consumer-provided data. Over time, data sets have become faster to collect, easier to access and share, and more robust and meaningful. These data managed to infiltrate healthcare organizations all the way to the top—finally bringing the average patient's evaluation of the care experience to the CEO's desk and the boardroom. Large swaths of organizations have created initiatives to improve the care they deliver. They have broken down silos that benefited internal departments but not patients. They have tied executive compensation and incentives to patient-provided scores. They have attempted to uncover patients' preferences beforehand and to follow up after discharge to ensure that patients are recovering as planned.

But ask anyone who has had a recent patient experience, and it's clear there hasn't been enough progress. Overall HCAHPS scores increased only about 7 percentage points from 2008 to 2015 (Papanicolas et al. 2017). The COVID-19 pandemic halted much of this progress, resulting in reduced quality of care, increased mortality, and lower HCAHPS scores (Elliott et al. 2023). National publicly reported data indicate that the pandemic set HCAHPS back almost ten years. Looking at the benchmark data (CMS 2023b) for HCAHPS surveys administered by NRC Health tells a similar story: the average overall rating in 2022 (71.1 percent) was at a level not seen since 2014 (NRC Health 2024a).

One of the most dramatic changes has been the increased cost of care. In 2001, the average American family spent about 12 percent of its income on healthcare; in 2019, it spent between 15 and 30 percent, depending on whether the family had employee-sponsored coverage or an individual plan (Kaiser Family Foundation 2019; Sekhar 2009). US healthcare spending in 2022 grew by 4 percent, reaching $4.5 trillion, or $13,493 per person, representing about 17 percent of the nation's gross domestic product (CMS 2024). Supply chain disruptions, increased labor costs, and postpandemic inflation are doubling or tripling the costs of care, depending on the service line or market. Most Americans now find themselves unable to comfortably afford healthcare. Medical bills have become a leading cause of personal bankruptcy and divorce. Surprise bills have become the fodder of journalists at the national, regional, and local levels.

What do Americans think about progress? In general, most consumers are not familiar with healthcare and don't pay much attention to it until they or their family member needs it. When they do access healthcare, they come to it with expectations from other industries—food service, hospitality, financial—that they use far more often. Those industries have made leaps and bounds in improving the delivery of a consumer-friendly experience. Healthcare has not, leaving many consumers with a strong desire and incentive to stay away from it—even to their detriment.

Clearly, this widespread perspective would trouble Harvey Picker. Before he passed away in 2008, Picker was still hopeful that healthcare would improve. He often argued that improvement must come from within the rank and file of healthcare organizations themselves—and not only nurses and physicians but senior leaders, too. How and when will healthcare change? Harvey's answer, from a Picker Institute-sponsored Future of Patient-Centered Care Vision Summit in Baltimore in March 2004: "I've never seen an industry change until the fear of remaining the same is greater than the fear of change."

Outside the hospital tower, it became evident to consumers that they must own their health. Out of both necessity and stewardship of their own out-of-pocket expenses, consumers have become more aware of healthcare and are hungrier for better information and care options. Only recently, healthcare providers began to encourage their patients to take a more active role in their health. The industry began to move from volume-based care to value-based care and from being disease-focused to being health-focused.

But few people saw it coming: a global pandemic that invaded every corner of the world and challenged US healthcare organizations in nearly unfathomable ways. COVID-19 exposed the many shortcomings of the US healthcare system, including the observations of Harvey and Jean Picker. COVID cast a harsh light on the lack of care coordination, equitable access to care, and overreliance on a fraying frontline. Some of the Picker dimensions were paused or outright banned (especially emotional support and the involvement of family and friends—outside visitors were no longer allowed, and COVID patients died alone and in isolation). The demands of today's healthcare consumers long preceded the pandemic, but COVID heightened their call to deafening levels. In many ways, healthcare organizations rose to the challenge, but the necessary focus on managing the COVID crisis took attention away from the progress being made on the value-based, patient-centered care journey. Now consumers hold an important memory: it can be done. Their expectations for future care will continue to trend up.

CREATING A MORE CONSUMER-FRIENDLY HEALTHCARE EXPERIENCE

On other end of value is the healthcare consumer, and they don't want to pay too much for too little. Healthcare provider organizations have only just started to realize the full breadth of information that needs to be captured to effectively create a more consumer-friendly experience. Historically, providers have done a poor job of listening to their patients and consumers. While the government mandate of HCAHPS has provided a basic level of patient satisfaction information, truly listening to the consumer involves gathering information about their experience before and after the hospital stay, not just understanding what went wrong in the hospital. Although traditional surveys capture information about a single care encounter, they don't ask about the experiences that surround it, including booking an appointment, waiting to be seen, and coming to grips with the bill—all domains that are frustrating to patients and where retail clinics tend to excel.

Consumer desire for more accessible, convenient care has tipped the balance in favor of retail healthcare. In 2019, consumers were evenly split between those who felt positively about care in a retail setting and those who felt negatively. Now, about 60 percent view it positively (NRC Health 2024a). Why? To answer this question, we found that for those who have visited retail clinics in the past, 56 percent did so because it was much easier to get an appointment with them than with traditional providers (COSHC and IOM 2015). Furthermore, even if they managed to secure an appointment with a physician, almost one-third of patients reported unduly long wait times—and 20 percent said they would switch providers if they had to wait too long (Heath 2018). Also, 61 percent of patients found their bills confusing, and most of these people believed that providers were to blame (Gooch 2016; Heath 2018). It's not always the appeal of something new but rather the removal of an existing frustration that may entice patients to switch.

Patient feedback surveys focus on discrete episodes of care, which for most patients are many months or even years apart. As a result, the collection of patient data is inherently sporadic. Nearly half of provider organizations report an inadequate understanding of a patient's journey of care (Gooch 2016).

In 2007, the Institute for Healthcare Improvement (IHI) introduced the Triple Aim as a framework for optimizing health system performance. Underlying this framework is the belief that new care designs must be developed to simultaneously pursue improvements in three dimensions of care (Berwick, Nolan, and Whittington 2008):

1. Improve the patient experience (including quality and satisfaction).
2. Improve the health of populations.
3. Reduce the per capita cost of healthcare.

The Triple Aim placed even greater emphasis on patient-centered care as a central core of high-quality healthcare (IHI 2024).

However, we also referred to the three legs of this aim as an "iron triangle" in the introduction, underscoring the difficulties of improving all three legs in a fee-for-service healthcare system.

An important attribute of patient-centered care is the active engagement of patients in making healthcare decisions, because most medical decisions involve more than one reasonable path or option (Barry and Edgman-Levitan 2012). AHRQ's definition of *engagement* includes both activation and engagement: "Patient engagement is the involvement in their own care by individuals (and others they designate to engage on their behalf), with the goal that they make competent, well-informed decisions about their health and health care and take action to support those decisions" (AHRQ 2024). Patient engagement is a broader concept than patient satisfaction; patient engagement combines patient activation with interventions to increase activation and promote positive patient behavior, such as obtaining preventive care or exercising regularly (James 2013). It also involves shared decision-making in which clinicians help patients understand the importance of their own values and preferences in making the decisions that are best for them. When patients know they have treatment options, most will want to participate with their clinician in making the best choice (Barry and Edgman-Levitan 2012).

Patient engagement is one strategy to achieve the Triple Aim (James 2013). To facilitate patient activation and engage patients, an organization needs to put patients first and ensure that their care is individualized. This means treating the patient as the most important member of the healthcare team and understanding the entire journey through the patient's frame of reference. For example, an individualized approach considers how a patient with a chronic condition would like to communicate after the hospital stay. It may include providing resources such as online communities where patients with that particular condition can discuss their concerns with one another, ask questions of a physician or nurse, and participate in group education by healthcare professionals. It also ensures that the healthcare team knows about any barriers the patient is facing that might inhibit compliance with the treatment plan or willingness to engage in healthy behaviors, so that the healthcare team can partner with the patient.

Ultimately, the heightened focus on healthcare quality and patient experience has helped multiple stakeholders align around the same essential goals for change, made patients or consumers more aware of the important role they play in managing their own health, and allowed patients or consumers to see themselves as vital members of the healthcare team.

Unfortunately, the United States still has large leaps to make before all consumers can receive consistent, high-quality, patient-centered care in a provider system that is easy to understand and navigate. The healthcare profession needs to stop thinking about patients or consumers only during their times of illness and consider how to interact with them during their times of wellness, too. Consumers have demanded change and will go to great lengths to get what they expect from healthcare, whether they find it in a traditional or nontraditional setting.

PICKER'S RELEVANCE TODAY AND IN THE FUTURE

In the midst of all this, one might ask, is the Picker work still relevant today? The crux of this book is to answer that question. So much has changed. Notably, the original Picker work was experience based: Organizations had to prove they boosted their performance. Picker wanted people to transcend measurement and focus on how to actually *improve* their scores. That way, progress could be quantifiably discerned on the basis of internal benchmarks.

Rather than combine existing or third-party data sets, Picker and his team believed it was important to conduct primary research with actual patients—to ask them how their experience was and why they feel the way they do. After years of success,

NRC Health partnered with the Picker Institute in 1994 to expand and further promote the Picker process. NRC Health adopted the Picker dimensions of care and followed the Picker process to conduct direct patient research. Since 2000, NRC Health (2024b) has received patient feedback regarding 161,693,915 encounters. Through NRC Health's current offerings, the discipline continues to keep the mission to achieve patient-centered care going after all these years.

HCAHPS was a step in the right direction because it forced the issue of patient-centered care throughout the industry and all the way to the top of health system and hospital leadership. But the bottom line is that the progress we have made has come at great cost and slow speed. If he were here today, Harvey Picker might argue that we still haven't achieved anything close to the improvements that patients laid out for us in *Through the Patient's Eyes*.

Alas, Harvey and Jean Picker aren't here to tell us what they think. But their legacy endures. Harvey and Jean had a dream to transform the healthcare world into a place where caregivers provide effective and compassionate care to everyone and experience joy in their work. That constant striving for improvement is what matters most to patients and consumers; healthcare providers need to continuously learn and seek to better themselves in order to better the patient experience.

NRC Health is striving to continue the Picker legacy. Our mission of human understanding is the next step in the evolution of patient-centered care and a way to carry Harvey's torch. We know that teaching and measuring can go only so far; hospitals and health systems must believe in the work and carry it out every day. Increasingly, that means going outside the hospital tower or physician's office and delivering human-centered care to wherever humans are. What is human understanding? It is the enablement of healthcare organizations to understand what matters most to each person they serve, and to ease that person's journey.

We will now take a deeper look at where we are today and compare it to where we were 30 years ago—what we've done and what we haven't, and what we've learned and what we still don't know. We will take a close look at how the Picker work still holds up (or doesn't) in today's healthcare age. And what about the future? We will look at what might be happening in healthcare in another 5, 10, or even 30 years.

REFERENCES

Agency for Healthcare Research and Quality (AHRQ). 2024. "Symposium on Patient Engagement (District of Columbia)." Accessed August 23. https://digital.ahrq.gov/ahrq-funded-projects/symposium-patient-engagement.

———. 2023. "The CAHPS Program." Reviewed April. www.ahrq.gov/cahps/about-cahps/cahps-program/index.html.

Barry, M. J., and S. Edgman-Levitan. 2012. "Shared Decision Making: The Pinnacle of Patient-Centered Care." *New England Journal of Medicine* 366 (9): 780–81.

Berwick, D. M., T. W. Nolan, and J. Whittington. 2008. "The Triple Aim: Care, Health, and Cost." *Health Affairs* 27 (3): 759–69.

Centers for Medicare & Medicaid Services (CMS). 2024. "National Health Expenditure Data: Historical." Modified July 8. www.cms.gov/data-research/statistics-trends-and-reports/national-health-expenditure-data/historical.

———. 2023a. "HCAHPS: Patients' Perspectives of Care Survey." Modified September 6. www.cms.gov/Medicare/Quality-Initiatives-Patient-Assessment-Instruments/HospitalQualityInits/HospitalHCAHPS.

————. 2023b. HCAHPS Update Training. Published March. https://hcahpsonline.org/globalassets/hcahps/training-materials/2023-hcahps-update-training-slides.pdf.

Committee on Optimizing Scheduling in Health Care (COSHC) and Institute of Medicine (IOM). 2015. "Issues in Access, Scheduling, and Wait Times." In *Transforming Health Care Scheduling and Access: Getting to Now*, edited by G. Kaplan, M. H. Lopez, and J. M. McGinnis, 17–31. Washington, DC: National Academies Press.

Crompton, S. 2006. "Father of Modern Patient Care." *Times* (London). Published October 28. www.thetimes.co.uk/article/father-of-modern-patient-care-kfm2qlwg5b3.

Elliott, M. N., M. K. Beckett, C. W. Cohea, W. G. Lehrman, P. D. Cleary, L. A. Giordano, C. Russ, E. H. Goldstein, and L. A. Fleisher. 2023. "Changes in Patient Experiences of Hospital Care During the COVID-19 Pandemic." *JAMA Health Forum* 4 (8): e232766. https://jamanetwork.com/journals/jama-health-forum/fullarticle/2808746.

Gerteis, M., S. Edgman-Levitan, J. Daley, and T. L. Delbanco (eds.). 1993. *Through the Patient's Eyes: Understanding and Promoting Patient-Centered Care*. San Francisco: Jossey-Bass.

Gooch, K. 2016. "61% of Patients Confused by Medical Bills, Survey Finds." *Becker's Hospital Review*. Published July 14. www.beckershospitalreview.com/finance/61-of-patients-confused-by-medical-bills-survey-finds.html.

Heath, S. 2018. "Long Appointment Wait Time a Detriment to High Patient Satisfaction." *PatientEngagementHIT*. Published March 23. https://patientengagementhit.com/news/long-appointment-wait-time-a-detriment-to-high-patient-satisfaction.

Hevesi, D. 2008. "Harvey Picker, 92, Pioneer in Patient-Centered Care, Is Dead." *New York Times*. Published March 29. www. nytimes.com/2008/03/29/health/29picker.html.

Institute for Healthcare Improvement (IHI). 2024. "Triple Aim and Population Health." Accessed August 23. www.ihi.org/Engage/ Initiatives/TripleAim/Pages/default.aspx.

Institute of Medicine (IOM). 2001. *Crossing the Quality Chasm: A New Health System for the 21st Century*. Washington, DC: National Academies Press.

————. 1999. *To Err Is Human: Building A Safer Health System*. Washington, DC: National Academies Press.

James, J. 2013. "Health Policy Brief: Patient Engagement." *Health Affairs*. Published February 14. www.healthaffairs.org/ do/10.1377/hpb20130214.898775/full/healthpolicybrief_86.pdf.

Kaiser Family Foundation. 2019. "The Real Cost of Health Care: Interactive Calculator Estimates Both Direct and Hidden Household Spending." News release, February 21. www.kff. org/health-costs/press-release/interactive-calculator-estimates- both-direct-and-hidden-household-spending/.

Kohler, S. 1994. "Case 83: Picker Institute." In *Casebook for the Foundation of a Great American Secret: How Private Wealth Is Changing the World*, edited by J. L. Fleishman, J. S. Kohler, and S. Schindler, 238–39. New York: PublicAffairs.

NRC Health. 2024a. *Market Insights Surveys of Healthcare Consumers*. Lincoln, NE: NRC Health.

————. 2024b. Unpublished quantitative survey data.

Papanicolas, I., J. F. Figueroa, E. J. Orav, and A. K. Jha. 2017. "Patient Hospital Experience Improved Modestly, but No

Evidence Medicare Incentives Promoted Meaningful Gains."
Health Affairs 36 (1): 133–40.

Sekhar, S. 2009. "Family Health Spending to Rise Rapidly."
Center for American Progress. Published September 15.
www.americanprogress.org/issues/healthcare/news/
2009/09/15/6699/family-health-spending-to-rise-rapidly/.

CHAPTER 2

The Rise of the Healthcare Consumer

As much as patient-centered care has enjoyed the limelight in the past 30 years, healthcare leaders have begun to shift their focus "off campus" to those people who aren't in a hospital gown—yet. Consumers—and the movement of consumerism they represent—are asserting their influence on healthcare more forcefully. Enrollment in high-deductible health plans has increased from 20 percent of covered workers in 2013 to almost one-third of all covered workers in the United States in 2023, and premiums for all types of health plans for covered workers rose by about 48 percent from 2007 to 2023 (KFF 2023). As consumers continue to pay more for healthcare, they will naturally demand more from healthcare providers. In fact, in any given sector, consumers will ask: If I pay more, do I get more in return? In healthcare, this question weighs heavily on consumers' minds. Faced with skyrocketing out-of-pocket costs and mounting frustration from having little control over their care, consumers are sick of a field meant to keep them well. Armed with vast amounts of information and shrinking patience, consumers aim to change healthcare for the better by standing up for themselves and turning this consumer-challenged industry around. It's no small task.

Consumers have a rising passion to better their health—and their healthcare. Six in ten consumers feel personally responsible for managing their own health, and another 25 percent view their doctor as responsible but want to be consulted and included in decisions involving their care (NRC Health 2023b). Though most are personally invested, very few consumers understand how to navigate the complex system of healthcare choices and care delivery. Unlike in virtually every other sector, consumers lack a working knowledge of their own healthcare. Little experience, myriad choices, complicated service flow, lack of up-front price information, and many other factors combine to make healthcare difficult to navigate. Nonetheless, the expectation persists that consumers can manage these factors on their own.

Consumers' passion is matched by the increasing financial pressure they face. For example, the spread of high-deductible health plans has shifted an immense amount of financial risk from hospitals and insurers to the consumer household—yet at the same time, consumers are expected to successfully manage their own care and all its responsibilities. We know consumers can struggle to manage their personal and family finances, and the complexity of healthcare costs only increases the level of difficulty they face. Numerous studies have shown that while these high-deductible plans have made consumers more cost conscious (despite the ongoing difficulty of knowing what their care will cost up front), the results have been lower utilization *and* patients not seeking necessary care (including decreases in appropriate preventive care and medication adherence). Over time, this situation results in patients getting sicker and needing *more* care, not less, and ultimately driving up healthcare costs for everyone. Even worse, these studies have shown that lower-income households in these plans defer more necessary care than households at higher income levels do, thereby widening the disparities of access and affordability (Agarwal, Mazurenko, and Menachemi 2017; Kullgren et al. 2018).

As a result, consumers seek meaningful change in healthcare. They seek organizations that understand them and are committed to creating better experiences for families and communities.

As consumers continue to be drawn into healthcare decision-making and to play a larger role in their own care, they are less likely to support organizations that they consider part of the traditional healthcare model. Why pay more for the same old thing? Hunger for innovative and convenient new avenues to care (e.g., urgent care centers, home health, telemedicine, AI) is often fueled by a disdain for the current delivery model. Therefore, healthcare providers need to pause and consider the consumer in ways they never have before. Simply attempting to improve the traditional patient experience—which touches very few consumers at any one time—will not impress the "new payers" of healthcare.

HISTORICAL FACTORS LEADING TO TODAY'S CONSUMERISM MOVEMENT

The rise of the healthcare consumer can feel sudden, but its origins trace back decades. To understand today's consumerism, we must look back to a time when patients began to behave like consumers—the 1970s. Although it wouldn't be formally recognized until much later, the advent of health maintenance organizations began during the decade of disco. This shift was spurred by patients' need to understand the copayments and formulary prescriptions that arose from the structure of managed healthcare. Certain procedures, as determined by the insurance companies, required prior authorization by the healthcare plan before payment to the provider or hospital would be guaranteed. Procedures requiring a prior authorization could be declined, after a review by the health plan for medical necessity, with the full expense then shifting to the insured. Patients often felt caught in the middle, with the physician directing the care and the insurance company determining approval. It was a time fraught with frustration by physicians, who had been accustomed to being paid for the services rendered (fee-for-service) rather than a bundled payment amount. Hospitals and physicians began to create group practices and focus on delivering outpatient services to counter the impact of reduced reimbursement for patient hospital stays (National Council on Disability 2013).

At the turn of the millennium, laptops, tablets, and eventually smartphones emerged. It would still be years before these devices made any difference in how consumers accessed their healthcare, but behind the scenes, new technologies made electronic medical records (EMR) portable. The 2000s saw the advent of outcome-based reimbursement, with technological functionality that enabled clinical decision support, analytic solutions, and data warehousing. Most departments still operated in record-keeping silos (e.g., pharmacy medications, clinical care plans, and laboratory orders and results were often on different IT systems). However, EMR adoption was the start of a push for an integrated system to deliver seamless care and provide better communication among all members of the patient's care team (Grandia 2014).

From the EMR, computerized systems evolved to the electronic health record (EHR). While the EMR was used predominantly for patient diagnosis and treatment and not designed to be used outside the hospital or clinical practice, the EHR provided a more complete picture of a patient's overall health, documentation by multiple departments and specialties in the same system, and a platform that promoted healthier lifestyles and more frequent use of preventive care (USF Health 2024). By 2021, 96 percent of hospitals and nearly 80 percent of office-based physicians were using a certified EHR for better documentation of patient outcomes, communication between clinicians, and coordination of care (Office of the National Coordinator for Health Information Technology 2024).

Today, these technological advances have finally found the consumer. The smartphone has revolutionized how all data are shared, but specifically healthcare data. Consumers can download an app from anywhere and then use it to interact with their healthcare providers and access their own healthcare data. Historically, information was retained within the hospital or clinic walls, sent via fax, or obtained as paper copies by patients, who were required to contact medical records departments. These processes often left consumers feeling frustrated and made healthcare look outdated compared with other industries and experiences. This isn't to say healthcare has caught up to other industries with their consumer-first approaches, but strides have been made. For consumers, the use of telehealth has opened a powerful new door to healthcare: the screen. Consumers have longed for healthcare to come to them and thus grown increasingly comfortable with the idea of a virtual visit. This shift is especially true for consumers with difficulty accessing care (e.g., rural consumers). Telehealth has allowed smaller facilities to have access to resources like those available in cities by using technology to communicate. In intensive care units equipped with telehealth devices, mortality rates have been lower and discharge has been 20 percent faster (*Becker's Hospital Review* 2014).

Nothing gave telehealth a boost like COVID-19. Adoption of telehealth among providers (and consumers) had moved like a glacier before the pandemic—in 2019, only about 11 percent of consumers had ever experienced telehealth (NRC Health 2020). COVID-19 served as a force multiplier for telehealth, however, and by 2023, nearly 48 percent of consumers reported having had a telehealth experience in the past (NRC Health 2023b). That means that today a lot more Americans are walking around with a positive healthcare experience to recall. The growing familiarity with telemedicine is coupled with increasing enthusiasm and excitement. The percentage of consumers who are "very excited" to conduct a future visit with their physician over video has more than doubled—from 11 percent in 2016 to 25 percent in 2023 (NRC Health 2023b). Except for maternity, enthusiasm for future healthcare utilization is rare. Telemedicine has become a bright spot for healthcare's future.

PATIENT USE OF TECHNOLOGY AS AN ACTIVE CARE TEAM MEMBER

Like telemedicine, patient portals have also allowed consumers and patients to engage with their providers in new ways. With patient portal technology, patients can log on to an app or a website and access their medical records and interact with their caregivers, all outside an examination room. This interaction has allowed patients and their families to be more closely involved and better educated in their care (*Becker's Hospital Review* 2014).

Sensors, remote monitoring tools, and wearable technology have also fostered patient involvement. As technology advances, cost shifting has increasingly been placed on employers and consumers through higher premiums, copayments, and deductibles. Patients are also living longer and with more comorbidities. Monitoring patients in their own homes, known as the Hospital at Home program, not only provides convenience but also reduces cost and unnecessary utilization (Achanta and Velasquez 2021).

With the use of remote monitoring, healthcare organizations are seeing substantial decreases in hospital readmissions, as reported by the Agency for Healthcare Research and Quality (2021). The use of sensors and wearable technology has a similar advantage, allowing consumers and patients the freedom and affordability to remain in their homes while ensuring clinical oversight. Such programs have proven effective in reducing complications while cutting the cost of care by 30 percent or more, but widespread adoption has been slow because of physicians' concerns about patient safety and legal risk and because of payer reluctance to reimburse providers for delivering such services in the home (Klein 2024). To help accelerate wider adoption, the US government in 2023 provided $1.7 trillion in funding for various aspects of care, including telehealth and the Acute Hospital Care at Home program offered through CMS (2024).

After all these advances in the care delivery process, where did the consumer truly enter the picture? By shifting from an EMR to EHR computerized system, care teams brought greater clarity to preventive health and wellness through access to more complete information and a better view of longitudinal care. By taking the long view, care teams regarded patients in a new way.

For patients, care went from focusing on a specific encounter to understanding the value of preventive care and wellness—areas well outside the traditional care experience. The implications were clear: The patient experience needed to be redefined as something more robust. This patient-to-consumer sea change and the decades-long advancements that powered it have repositioned patients to be true consumers before they enter a hospital or seek care from a physician and long after the episode of care ends. Today's higher deductibles, copayments, and cost-sharing arrangements have created a powerful responsibility for consumers and their families. The result—and perhaps one of the most significant developments since the 1970s—is that consumers are elevating their role in healthcare and becoming more focused on where, how, and if they elect to seek care.

Consumers are not without resources as they shoulder this responsibility. With technology at their full disposal, consumers now go online or use apps to obtain pricing information and review online ratings; they use social media to find recommendations from their peers; and they want physician confirmation of information from the internet. They are open to consulting AI to round out their knowledge and aid their navigation of healthcare. Consumers are seeking collaborative relationships, more interaction and engagement, and easy-to-access services, not "cookie-cutter" medicine.

This shift in consumer behavior has resulted in healthcare organizations shifting their mindset to one of consumerism, and they are adopting metrics from outside the industry, such as the net promoter score, which looks at the percentage of individuals who promote an organizational brand, to understand the loyalty of their customer base. Entrants from fields outside healthcare have appeared with innovative ways of understanding potential consumers, their buying habits, and their spending patterns. Technology has changed how consumers engage with and access their medical team and information in new ways that will only become heightened in the future.

There is still a long way to go toward consumer-centric care. Perhaps the most important technique that providers can use along the way is engaging the consumer. To design a better relationship with consumers, providers must include their input. If providers build the future of healthcare *for* consumers—but not *by* or *with* consumers—both parties may end up with buyer's remorse.

THE TRIPLE AIM: CONSUMER EDITION

To reshape healthcare through the eyes of the consumer, leaders should start with consumers' core beliefs. No model represents an approach to healthcare in the past three decades like the Institute for Healthcare Improvement's Triple Aim (as defined in chapter 1: simultaneously improving the patient experience, improving the health of the population, and reducing the per capita cost of care). This concept is one of the most universally accepted and least controversial in healthcare. Perhaps an even more significant factor is that consumers agree with the importance and focus of the Triple Aim (NRC Health 2012).

But as much as consumers agree with the Triple Aim, they don't speak the language of healthcare. They don't discuss the importance of quality or safety or managing infection rates, and they don't possess much knowledge on how these benchmarks affect their care. They don't strike up a conversation about "accountable care organizations" while in line at the grocery store. Jargon is for insiders, and consumers are healthcare's outsiders. However, in their own language, consumers paint a compelling picture of what they want.

It's time to define the consumer's version of the Triple Aim. In so doing, we can juxtapose what consumers want with the standard the industry is attempting to achieve. Let's examine the Triple Aim from the consumer's perspective with three consumer-driven issues: access, engagement, and value (see exhibit 2.1).

Consumer Aim 1: Access

To providers, the term *access* may invoke scheduling strategies, physician referral patterns, or capacity challenges. To consumers, access starts much earlier in the care journey and revolves around a central question: How can I find you? It's a question

EXHIBIT 2.1: Institute for Healthcare Improvement Triple Aim and Consumer Triple Aim

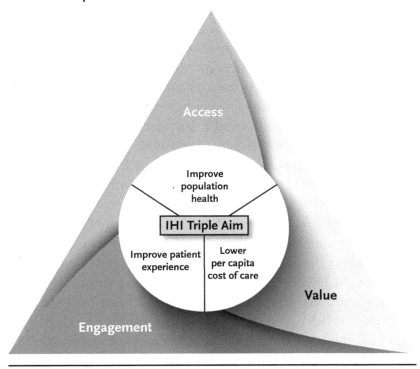

most consumers struggle to answer efficiently. Consumers want to be able to seek out a healthcare organization quickly via their preferred medium. For some consumers, that is still by phone, but for others it may be a website, an app, or even a text message. Some consumers simply want to walk into a provider location close to where they work or live. Consumers want to take the first steps of their journey in their own chosen ways and don't appreciate a one-size-fits-all approach to access.

Technology has changed the face of medicine—its many effects are chronicled throughout this edition of the book, and it continues to accelerate access in particular. According to NRC Health's *Market Insights*, the largest survey of healthcare consumers in the United States, consumers have heavily turned to technology to begin their journey of care. Two-thirds of healthcare consumers use social media as a source of information about their health, often seeking advice from their contacts and other connected consumers when they do. Six in 10 consumers have used a smartphone, computer, or other mobile device to access healthcare information in the past and also anticipate using these devices to access healthcare information within the next 12 months. Being informed is good, but guidance is better: 51 percent of consumers use online sources of information to educate themselves on their future options for seeking care (NRC Health 2023b). This tech-emboldened behavior is no longer limited to younger generations. Fifty-two percent of consumers aged 45–64 plan to go online to help decide future care destinations (NRC Health 2023b). Fifty-two percent of consumers aged 65 or older have viewed doctor ratings and reviews online as part of their decision-making (NRC Health 2023b). Screens aren't just for the young, especially when choosing care. Consider the average age of the decision maker for healthcare in US households: 48 years old (NRC Health 2023b). And these consumers, more often women than men, make decisions not just for themselves but also for their spouse, their aging parents, their newly insured children, and other family, friends, and fellow consumers they may interact with in person or online.

For consumers, it's not as much about healthcare's internal care delivery methodology as it is about their own ability to find their desired care provider quickly and easily. These crucial first steps will define the rest of the consumer and patient journey of care, and most often they occur outside the four walls of healthcare facilities. In fact, consumers' first steps may include more than one brand. As systems struggle to provide quick access to all services needed, consumers are increasingly comfortable seeking out urgent care, boutique physician groups, and unaffiliated surgery centers—if they go the brick-and-mortar route at all. While consumers prefer to receive all healthcare services under one roof—or healthcare brand—they are increasingly impatient with this disjointed experience and are willing to take on multiple brands to keep their journey moving.

Consumer Aim 2: Engagement

Long before providers started thinking longitudinally about episodes of care, consumers saw the long view in their own care. For regular, everyday people, *healthcare* has always been a journey— a string of episodes lasting months or years that eventually will end. Consumers are hopeful they will "get back to normal" and no longer need healthcare. When consumers are asked about *health* instead, a different story emerges. Consumers don't want engagement solely through a patient experience. To consumers, health is a container for many personal factors including nutrition, exercise, and overall well-being. To manage and improve their health, they need guidance—but perhaps not in the traditional healthcare way. Consumers don't want health*care* to hijack their own agency to live a healthy life. Most consumers want to be in control of their health—and their healthcare—but often feel they forfeit much of this control once they enter the world of traditional healthcare. Caregivers must balance their own strategies, processes, and responsibilities against consumers' desire to play a significant role in their own care. True consumer engagement (not simply patient engagement) will involve a significant organizational shift in how consumers' own desires are viewed and valued against healthcare executives' directives. (Indeed, an important part of the patient experience that results in better outcomes is patient *activation*, a component of engagement, as discussed in chapter 1. Perhaps consumers must be activated in a similar way before they become patients, which represents a strategic opportunity for healthcare organizations.)

The difference between consumer engagement and patient engagement is an issue of perception. When we focus on patient engagement, we often turn a blind eye to what happens to our patients before and after they receive treatment. Patient experience pertains to those who are on the receiving end of traditional care—whether experiencing a hospital stay, enduring a surgery, or anxiously awaiting their physician. While these hours or days are essential to all patients and their ultimate health, this time makes up only a small portion of their lives—many perceptions are formed and decisions are made before and after the traditional patient experience. Consumers, on the other hand, are out living their lives long before they become patients. They are working, driving, buying groceries, and generally doing everything but receiving healthcare. Once they sense an issue, they go online, research their options, and speak with like-minded consumers before they receive any actual treatment.

Further, once consumers are in a treatment room gown, they already have formed many perceptions that will influence how they receive care and assess it after the hospital stay or visit to the physician. Consumers will ask themselves: Were my expectations met? Consumers will form opinions about every facet of care they receive. They will take stock of their health and their journey to recovery. Their "patient experience" lens was widened by COVID—including testing, vaccinations, and accessing information about COVID online. Perhaps once considered ancillary, these actions have become part of or even all of the healthcare experience for consumers, who are more open-minded than ever about what constitutes a healthcare "experience." Engaging patients is vital, but it's only one segment of a vast and winding consumer journey of care. Engaging consumers means healthcare organizations are dedicated to focusing on and caring for people who haven't yet come through the door and following up with them after they have left.

Consumer Aim 3: Value

Once consumers have accessed their care and completed a patient experience, they will calculate value. Value continues to be misunderstood in the context of healthcare. Many executive conversations on value tend to gravitate toward care models, pricing strategies, and cost of care. To consumers, the cost of care (and being able to afford it) is important, but it's only one side of the value equation—a high-quality experience is on the other side. Quality and cost are the two halves that form a single whole. This yin and yang are often out of alignment for consumers.

For example, if the quality of an experience is poor and the cost is exceedingly high, consumers will feel that the overall experience lacked value. On the flip side, a high-quality experience for a low cost will be considered to be of high value. Many healthcare executives get stuck on the issue of cost and ask: Do consumers want the lowest-cost healthcare around? Not necessarily. NRC Health's Market Insights studied consumer perception of cost of care and found that, as in other industries, consumers will pay more if they perceive quality to be higher than that of similar products or services. This finding highlights the need to pair information on outcomes with information on pricing to allow consumers to determine value (NRC Health 2015).

The consumer desire to consider quality alongside cost is intensified by the direction of a particular variable: rising out-of-pocket costs. As mentioned earlier, consumers will eternally ask: If I pay more, what more do I get in return? Because costs have exceeded the rate of inflation (not an easy task in the United States) and defied common sense, consumers have concluded that the value of healthcare is low. Surprise billing, medical bankruptcies, and massive deductibles have wreaked havoc on wallets. The mounting pressure to pay has forced a large swath of consumers to opt out of healthcare altogether. As mentioned at the outset of this chapter, deferment of care—a consumer deciding to forgo necessary medical treatment—is a phenomenon NRC Health has been studying for years. In 2020, as the COVID-19 pandemic set in, 33 percent of US consumers were deferring necessary medical treatment, a new record (NRC Health 2020). For perspective, the previous high occurred during the throes of the Great Recession, during which 27 percent put off care in 2008 (NRC Health 2008). Following the COVID-19 pandemic, deferment has remained at Great Recession–type levels, with 25 percent of consumers still putting off care as the pandemic wanes (NRC Health 2024). Throughout this astonishing sixteen-year period of deferment, consumers have consistently deferred care to avoid their perceived cost of care.

The fear of medical costs is fueled by a crippling lack of transparency in healthcare. Going into an experience, most consumers have no idea what their treatment will cost, leaving them to inflate the figure in their heads, all while quality remains a mystery.

Healthcare pricing tools have been around for nearly 20 years, but very few consumers are aware they exist. Only one in five consumers are aware of Medicare's Hospital Compare website and subsequent price comparison tools (NRC Health 2023b). This is not due to lack of demand; most consumers are actively interested in knowing about cost and quality before they become patients. As deductibles and premiums continue to rise, the call for cost and quality transparency will become deafening. Consumers remain largely unconvinced by a growing glut of hospital awards and advertising. They require real evidence to prove not only that they can seek the care they want and need but also that they can afford it, and they would prefer this evidence up front (and given by the provider, rather than having to spend precious time searching for estimates online) so they can make decisions based on value and follow this assessment throughout their journey of care.

WHY IS QUALITY IN HEALTHCARE SO MYSTERIOUS?

The word *quality* is unfortunately overused in healthcare. The term has become so vague that, if you ask ten healthcare professionals what it means, you will receive ten distinct responses. Because there is so little consensus on what quality is and, by extension, so much confusion around how to achieve it, pursuing it can become a trap for providers.

For example, a committee might be put in place to define, measure, and improve quality. As discussed in chapter 1, it's quite valiant (and necessary) to pursue quality—it powers one of the three components of IHI's Triple Aim, after all, and we've learned through the history of measuring quality that it goes hand in hand with patient experience. So in our example, the committee members set forth on a righteous journey and begin by talking with one another and a few clinicians about "quality." They come up with their own definition that may not be congruent with that of patients or the larger consumer base the organization serves. They don't have an unlimited budget, so they tack a few questions onto an existing survey, or they do a small-scale project to measure their newly defined quality against actual patient outcomes. Perhaps they find they are measuring up, and they don't make any changes. Perhaps they aren't measuring up, so they reinvest in what they believe will improve quality (often doing more of what they've already been doing—more rounding, more surveys, more coaches, more training, and so forth). They will often find themselves burned out without much to show for their efforts. All the while, consumers who demand a personalized experience and define quality differently are left with unmet expectations and subpar experiences.

It's important to step back and see how massive the quest for quality has become for so many healthcare organizations. Quality is probably the most widely used measure of performance in healthcare today. Measuring quality began before the Hospital Consumer Assessment of Healthcare Providers and Systems (HCAHPS) and even predates the original Harvey Picker work (discussed in chapter 1). Though it originally came about as a tool for physicians to assess medical performance, quality has morphed into a larger, more nebulous concept to describe the overall performance of the organization, and even strength of the brand as perceived by consumers. Today, many healthcare leaders and healthcare improvement entities include patient experience and patient safety under the overall quality umbrella. More recent additions under this umbrella since COVID are equity and access. Improved patient experience is being increasingly linked with better care outcomes as well as better long-term financial performance for hospitals (Stepnick 2019). When patient experience is appropriately linked with quality, we believe organizations can do more to improve every facet.

But like patient experience, healthcare organizations still have a ways to go when it comes to improving quality of care. Conversations about quality often have excluded the employees who are tasked with delivering it. Much as HCAHPS felt forced onto physicians, nurses, and other frontline caregivers, the quest for quality became a corporate motto that didn't seem to stick in hospital hallways. Caregivers have often cited their own lack of resources and personal burnout as critical on-the-ground barriers to the larger organizational goals for quality (Vibberts 2018). It matters not what leadership says if managers and their direct reports—those who physically deliver care—do not feel engaged in the call for quality (Munch 2017).

Like healthcare professionals, ask ten consumers what quality means and you will receive ten distinct responses. Yet there is a deeper meaning that seems to emerge at the individual level. NRC

EXHIBIT 2.2: Independent Versus System Hospital Performance on HCAHPS

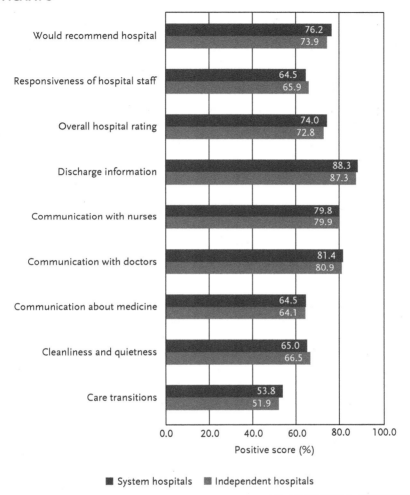

Positive score (%)

■ System hospitals ■ Independent hospitals

Source: NRC Health (2019).

Health's Market Insights sought to understand how consumers view this word and conducted two massive tests: a survey of 23,000 consumers in 2017 and a follow-up survey of 24,000 consumers in 2024. These studies revealed that consumers vary greatly in how they define *quality*. Yet both studies confirmed quality as the most important attribute a healthcare organization can possess and provide, according to its patients (see exhibit 2.3).

How can this be? In their own words, consumers could not articulate the importance of quality. However, when listed as one of many choices in a survey question, quality seemed to be the *most* important attribute to consumers.

The design of the question in exhibit 2.3 may point to a key clue regarding the importance of quality to consumers. Respondents were able to choose multiple metrics, and although quality was chosen more often than any other, most consumers chose at least one (if not two) additional metrics. In fact, the average consumer selected 3.6 factors. Why choose quality when there are other, more understandable metrics? Could it be that quality is seen as a proxy for these other metrics? When you consider the vast array of measures that can be drawn from a company's performance, you might consider the sum of those measures to indicate a high level

EXHIBIT 2.3: Healthcare Attributes Consumers Value Most

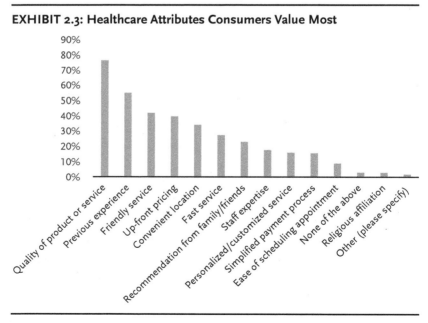

Source: NRC Health (2017).

of quality. When the organization falls flat on multiple factors, lower quality may be perceived. Consequently, everything from convenience to compassion ends up as a proxy for quality. Thus, it is up to healthcare leaders to define quality and demonstrate it to consumers through clear, understandable means. The difference between doing this well and doing it poorly (or not at all) could be the determining factor in whether consumers view a healthcare organization as a success or a failure. And that consumer determination is critical to future stability and growth. NRC Health broadly asked consumers what drives their loyalty toward a brand. The number one answer? You guessed it: quality (NRC Health 2024).

While the COVID-19 pandemic laid bare the long-existing disparities in care across socioeconomic or racial populations, many healthcare leaders are now realizing that their organization's definition of quality must use a broader, more consistent interpretation, one that is accessible to all patients and measured against something we can tangibly track and realistically improve. Quality, for many organizations, becomes a dream never truly realized, which, in turn, renders the consumer calculation of value an unsolvable equation.

THE CALL FOR CONSUMER-CENTRIC HEALTHCARE

Through its surveys, NRC Health tracks consumer and patient trust in healthcare roles and institutions. Across the board, NRC Health found that consumers professed more trust and confidence in healthcare entities in 2023 than they did in 2013. According to NRC Health (2023a), "None of the entities earned 'very high' trust among a majority of consumers, but doctors and nurses—representatives of the human teams out there providing clinical care—earn[ed] the highest trust and confidence" at 43.1 percent in 2023, up from 26.9 percent in 2013 (see exhibit 2.4). The key is maintaining and building trust over time. A legion of consumers can bolster an organization, serving as advocates more powerful than any marketing message. On the other hand, a critical mass of distrust can take a brand down.

While the healthcare field's quest for patient-centered care retains immense importance and meaning to those in healthcare, its translation to consumers reveals a different story. Consumers don't necessarily care how we model improvement in the industry; they care that it happens. To them, finding us (access), staying in touch both on and off campus (engagement), and being able to

EXHIBIT 2.4: Trust and Confidence in Healthcare Entities

Entity	Very High 2023	Very High 2013
Doctors/Nurses	43.1%	26.9%
Hospitals/Health Systems	29.4%	20.9%
Pharmacies	28.8%	22.9%
Hospice	27.2%	18.8%
Home Health Services	18.5%	7.5%
Long Term Care/Nursing Homes	16.7%	6.8%
Health Insurance Companies	16.6%	8.1%

● Very High 2023   ● Very High 2013

National Market Insights Study | 2013 n = 22,438 | 2023 n = 75,367

Source: NRC Health (2023a).

afford the high-quality experience they deserve (value) all coalesce into a simple theme, in consumers' own words: "Consider me. Include me. Listen to me. Know that I need you, but also know that I need you to be better. I'm not satisfied with healthcare and neither are you, so let's improve one step at a time, and let's do it together. For healthcare. For everyone."

REFERENCES

Achanta, A., and D. E. Velasquez. 2021. "Hospital at Home: Paying for What It's Worth." *American Journal of Managed Care* 27 (9). Published September 10. https://doi.org/10.37765/ajmc.2021.88739.

Agarwal, R., O. Mazurenko, and N. Menachemi. 2017. "High-Deductible Health Plans Reduce Health Care Cost and Utilization, Including Use of Needed Preventive Services." *Health Affairs* 36 (10). Published October. https://doi.org/10.1377/hlthaff.2017.0610.

Agency for Healthcare Research and Quality (AHRQ). 2021. "Hospital at Home Care Reduces Costs, Readmissions, and Complications and Enhances Satisfaction for Elderly Patients." Published April 7. https://psnet.ahrq.gov/innovation/hospital-homesm-care-reduces-costs-readmissions-and-complications-and-enhances.

Becker's Hospital Review. 2014. "10 Biggest Technological Advancements for Healthcare in the Last Decade." Published January 28. www.beckershospitalreview.com/healthcare-information-technology/10-biggest-technological-advancements-for-healthcare-in-the-last-decade.html.

Centers for Medicare & Medicaid Services (CMS). 2024. "Acute Hospital Care at Home Individual Waiver Only (Not a Blanket

Waiver)." Accessed January 30. https://qualitynet.cms.gov/
acute-hospital-care-at-home.

Grandia, L. 2014. "Healthcare Information Systems: A Look at the
Past, Present, and Future." Health Catalyst. Published May
20. www.healthcatalyst.com/insights/healthcare-information-
systems-past-present-future (content no longer available).

KFF. 2023. "*2023 Employer Health Benefits Survey* Section 8: High-
Deductible Health Plans with Savings Option." Published
October 18. www.kff.org/report-section/ehbs-2023-section-8-
high-deductible-health-plans-with-savings-option/.

Klein, S. 2024. "'Hospital at Home' Programs Improve Outcomes,
Lower Costs but Face Resistance from Providers and
Payers." Commonwealth Fund. Accessed January 30. www.
commonwealthfund.org/publications/newsletter-article/
hospital-home-programs-improve-outcomes-lower-costs-face-
resistance.

Kullgren, J., E. Cliff, C. Krenz, B. West, H. Levy, A. M. Fendrick, and
A. Fagerlin. 2018. "Consumer Behaviors Among Individuals
Enrolled in High-Deductible Health Plans in the United States."
JAMA Internal Medicine 178 (3): 424–26.

Munch, D. 2017. "Why Middle Managers Are the Key to Quality
Improvement Success." *Insights* (blog), Institute for Healthcare
Improvement. Published November 22. www.ihi.org/insights/
why-middle-managers-are-the-key-to-qi-success.

National Council on Disability. 2013. "Appendix B. A Brief History
of Managed Care." In *Medicaid Managed Care for People with
Disabilities: Policy and Implementation Considerations for State
and Federal Policymakers*, 161–64. Published March 18. https://
ncd.gov/publications/2013/20130315/20130513_AppendixB
(content no longer available).

NRC Health. 2023a. "Turbulence, Trust, and Loyalty." nSight. Published March 8. https://nrchealth.com/resource/turbulence-trust-and-loyalty/.

———. 2008, 2012, 2015, 2017, 2019, 2020, 2023b, 2024. *Market Insights Surveys of Healthcare Consumers*. Lincoln, NE: NRC Health.

Office of the National Coordinator for Health Information Technology. 2024. *2022 Report to Congress: Update on the Access, Exchange, and Use of Electronic Health Information*. Accessed August 26. www.healthit.gov/sites/default/files/page/2023-02/2022_ONC_Report_to_Congress.pdf.

Stepnick, L. 2019. *Patient Experience Is Quality: The Role of Healthcare Leaders in Improving Outcomes and Building Loyalty*. Lincoln, NE: Governance Institute.

USF Health. 2024. "Differences Between EHR and EMR." Updated January 8. www.usfhealthonline.com/resources/key-concepts/ehr-vs-emr.

Vibberts, M. 2018. "Caring for Frontline Staff Impacts the Bottom Line (with Patient Satisfaction Scores)." *BeekSpeak* (blog), Beekley Medical. Published November 16. https://blog.beekley.com/caring-for-frontline-staff-impacts-the-bottom-line-with-patient-satisfaction-scores.

CHAPTER 3

Building a Consumer–Provider Relationship

Now THAT WE have chronicled the rise of the healthcare consumer, we can see why the industry must adapt to a shifting, consumer-driven landscape. Consumers have laid out their needs, and providers must be prepared to deliver. If they don't deliver, they risk alienating their future patients: the ultimate determinants of their success or failure. In response to this pressure, can't consumer-minded providers simply start crafting relationships with their own patients? Can't they reach out and engage these consumers somehow? As is true in much of healthcare, it's not that simple. Many barriers, each formidable in different but not entirely dissimilar ways, stand firmly between the provider and the consumer.

SIX DEGREES OF SEPARATION

Perhaps you recall the fame game of the 1990s, "Six Degrees of Kevin Bacon." The game informally posited that every human on the planet is only six people away from knowing the famed *Footloose* actor. Bacon was the friend of a friend of a friend of a friend, if you will. Think of Kevin Bacon as a proxy for our healthcare consumer. In extensive, decades-long research, NRC Health's

Market Insights has identified six distinct barriers that often keep providers and consumers from engaging and establishing meaningful relationships. For providers, the six degrees of separation are strategic and operational gaps. Understanding what they are and why they keep consumers away is the first step toward realizing a true consumer–provider relationship.

Degree of Separation 1: An Industry Ignored

Separation between consumer and provider often begins in the mind. NRC Health's research reveals a universal truth: Consumer perceptions create market realities. Many paradoxes characterize how consumers think about healthcare. Consumers generally avoid thinking about healthcare and often do not consider it a high priority in their lives until a health issue emerges. Healthcare then becomes their top, and often only, priority until the issue is resolved. Yet, as much as consumers usually keep their present and future healthcare needs at the back of their mind, a general sentiment about the industry creeps to the center: Healthcare is broken. NRC Health's Market Insights surveys have revealed that while most consumers don't actively think about healthcare, they do have strong opinions about it. In general, they believe that healthcare needs a serious overhaul, though they are unable to describe exactly how they want such reform to unfold. Many consumers admit they simply don't know enough about healthcare—and don't even realize how little they know—until they are thrust into a journey of care.

This much is clear: The intersection between healthcare consumers' limited knowledge and their negative sentiments toward the industry undergirds the journey of care and begins long before health issues surface. This unintuitive blend of emotion and knowledge (or lack thereof) ensures that most consumers set off on the wrong foot, and it explains why their journey is plagued with confusion and a lack of confidence as individuals try to navigate an industry that seems out of focus—made worse by the dark cloud hanging over it all.

Consumer confusion and lack of understanding are exacerbated by the lack of outreach *to* consumers *by* providers. Healthcare organizations tend to understaff their marketing departments and often rely on antiquated methods of advertising (Greystone. Net and Klein & Partners 2016). For example, a healthcare marketer may continue to place outdoor advertisements because an influential physician demands to see his face on a billboard as he drives into his practice. A healthcare business development executive might run into the boardroom sentiment that hospitals really don't (or shouldn't) need to compete for patients, a position that doesn't align with the competitive realities of healthcare. These stubborn notions create an environment in which consumer engagement gets bogged down or mothballed entirely by provider politics. In his book *Joe Public Doesn't Care About Your Hospital*, healthcare marketing expert Chris Bevolo (2011) explained that so much of what reaches consumers by way of marketing initiatives, especially advertising campaigns, is driven not by sound marketing strategy but in response to internal political pressure.

NRC Health has been testing advertising efforts by healthcare organizations, in quantitative and qualitative settings, for more than a decade. During that time, insights point to an industry filled with healthcare brands struggling to define themselves. Nearly every healthcare organization's advertisements attempt to convey their compassion *and* advanced technology, while also talking up their physicians, slipping in their latest awards, and layering classical music over the top with a splash of blue or green in the logo. This crowded-but-bland approach adds confusion to consumers' already loose grasp of their healthcare options. Even as captive audience members in a research setting, consumers struggle to assign the correct brand name to recently viewed ads. Many of these ads fail to break through in consumers' minds, which are already barraged by thousands of ads every day. This onslaught of ads leaves people with "brand blur" and little ability to distinguish between providers for care in the future (NRC Health 2019). This blur was made worse by the unified messaging of the COVID-19 pandemic. The need for hospitals, health systems, local health departments, and even local politicians to unite and communicate the same important directives to their markets left everyone saying the same thing: "unprecedented times," "six feet apart," "abundance of caution," and so on. According to NRC Health, only one in five consumers noticed differences in local messaging (NRC Health 2022). Out of the clutter of COVID communication, consumers are as open as ever to hearing something new and different from healthcare brands. As we formulate a new brand narrative, consider a long-standing truth about healthcare consumers: When we don't consider the consumer, they don't consider us. Healthcare is a two-way street, and a lack of understanding can travel both ways.

Degree of Separation 2: The Bright Light

What could cause consumers to know little about healthcare but think the industry needs to change? The "healthcare is broken" narrative has been written by many authors, but perhaps none with a stronger pen than the national and local media. In the never-ending quest for clicks, journalists have had a field day parading healthcare's deficiencies to all.

This bright light is never more searing than when the topic turns to the rising costs of care. The belief that healthcare costs have careened out of control—and providers are largely to blame—remains a media focus. "Hospitals, doctors, and nurses all charge more in the U.S. than in other countries, with hospital costs increasing much faster than professional salaries," claims one report (Investopedia 2023). Another reason cited is that hospitals are able to sustain profits and high prices because of their market power (Gee 2019). It's hard to fathom any industry's billing process being breaking news, but hospital bills are often front-page fodder and gripping national news narratives (Terhune 2018). What consumers must pay, down to the line item, became the topic of a popular *Time* magazine article by Steven Brill (2013) titled "A Bitter Pill," as well as a *New York Times* best-selling book, *America's Bitter Pill* (Brill 2015). Brill wrote of how industry pricing models are set up to benefit virtually all care stakeholders—from pharma to health plans to physicians—at the expense of the patient. More recently, physician and Institute for Healthcare Improvement founder Donald Berwick warned of the existential threat of greed in US healthcare, asserting that "the grip of financial self-interest … is becoming a stranglehold, with dangerous and pervasive consequences. No sector of US healthcare is immune from the immoderate pursuit of profit, neither drug companies, nor insurers, nor hospitals, nor investors, nor physician practices" (Berwick 2023). A guest essay in the *New York Times* was entitled, "Why Are Nonprofit Hospitals Focused More on Dollars Than Patients?" Readers didn't need to look any further without the damage already being done, regardless of the degree of truths cited (Navathe 2023).

These are searing narratives against hospitals, and they don't end there. Industry-roiling scandals such as the EpiPen price gouge; the Ebola public relations fiasco in Texas; the conviction of "Pharma Bro" Martin Shkreli; the embroilment of our doctors and nurses, and medical science at large, into the controversies and divisions created by COVID; and whatever negative story might hit the news next week have all given everyday consumers plenty of reason to believe healthcare is a harsh, troubled, and even corrupt world.

This negative coverage is missing a response from the healthcare industry. The American Hospital Association might issue a press release, and local providers may push back via an employee memo or their social media feeds, and there will surely be grumbling among board members, but often there is no substantial counternarrative in the media from healthcare organizations at large. Do we simply hope consumers are wearing earmuffs? We know, through research, that consumers are listening, and healthcare organizations would be wise to issue an appropriate response. A counternarrative and swift consumer-facing response is standard in other industries.

Consider what happened in the airline industry. Nothing saps the magic from Christmas like air travel, especially if you tried to fly on Southwest Airlines in December 2022. Long admired as a brand and considered different from the rest of the pack ("Bags Fly Free!"), Southwest found its highly touted customer service facing the ultimate test: an airline-wide meltdown. A perfect storm of actual bad weather, outdated tracking technology, and a stressed-out workforce caused the airline to cancel 16,900 flights, leaving more than 2 million passengers stranded over the crucial travel period of Christmas to New Year's Day (Rose 2023).

The meltdown cost the airline more than $1 billion, but it wasn't the financial fallout that most concerned leaders. Would Southwest's sterling reputation be ruined? CEO Bob Jordan was swift to apologize, issue refunds, and dole out points from its Rapid Rewards program to any and all passengers affected. In a media statement, Jordan declared, "We have spent the past year acutely focused on efforts to enhance the customer experience." Prior to the 2023 Christmas travel season, he went so far as to promise that "it will never happen again" (Rose 2023).

Since the meltdown, the airline has spent $1.3 billion and countless hours to overhaul its operational systems and upgrade the technology that failed both its employees and its passengers, tying the audiences together in its statements. "We disrupted thousands and thousands of customers at a critical point in time and really made a mess here for our employees. ... I really can't apologize enough for that. I own that," Jordan said (Wilen 2023). Dollars aside, Southwest seemed to understand the real metric of recovery: passengers trusting them enough to book future flights. A year later, Southwest reported a higher percentage of seats booked for Christmas 2023 than the previous year (Hernandez 2023).

While many passengers won't soon forget the Christmas meltdown, they will respond to clear action: apologies, refunds, and perhaps most important, a commitment to be better. There is no room for saving face, pointing fingers, or issuing halfhearted apologies. And as important as travel can be, it often pales in comparison to the high stakes of healthcare.

Public relations success stories such as these are commonplace in most industries, except healthcare. When healthcare organizations don't respond to negative publicity, consumers don't hear the full story and cannot make an informed judgment. To bridge this informational gap, providers must be willing to tell their side of the story to the media.

Degree of Separation 3: Follow the Money

The cost of care in this country drives the most negative narratives told today. It's too big to miss. Healthcare spending constituted 17 percent of the US gross domestic product in 2019, triple what it was 50 years earlier (Statista 2023). It's hard not to notice when almost one of every five US dollars is spent on a single industry, especially when more of those dollars are coming out of the wallets and purses of consumers via sky-high deductibles and rising insurance premiums—money flowing to an industry consumers often ignore and largely try to avoid.

In a typical calendar year, consumers' first exposure to healthcare is often defined by a lack of affordability. For the 179 million commercially insured individuals in the United States (KFF 2024), their "year of healthcare" begins with the open enrollment period. Unfortunately, for many people, the only choice is between high-deductible and *higher*-deductible plans (even PPO [preferred provider organization] plans have higher deductibles than they used to). Given the nearly unfathomable reality of individual and family deductibles ranging from $6,000 to more than $10,000 (Ward, Duren, and Roughley 2024), it makes sense that consumers are responding by deferring healthcare (as discussed in chapter 2) because they simply cannot afford it.

When care is essential, cost remains top of mind. Seventy percent of consumers believe that cost will make a difference in where they'll go for care in the future (NRC Health 2024). As we discussed in chapter 2, in consumers' search for value, their attempts to find cost and quality information remain frustrating. The effort is most maddening to consumers with high-deductible health plans. Historically, these consumers search for pricing more often than their counterparts with lower-deductible plans do (NRC Health 2015), but answers often elude them. Vital pricing information is not readily available to consumers. Providers have been slow to step in and, in some cases, defiant to offer anything of substance to their would-be patients. To counter this provider resistance, in January 2021, the Centers for Medicare & Medicaid Services (CMS) began requiring US hospitals to provide clear, accessible pricing information online about the items and services they provide, as a comprehensive machine-readable file with all items and services, and also as a display of shoppable services in a consumer-friendly format (CMS 2023). It took most hospitals a couple of years to figure out how to comply with this regulation; many went along with the change only begrudgingly.

As more consumers enter the high-deductible arena and pay for their own care, the frustration with price opacity will only grow, and providers will face increasingly agitated consumers. As famed US economist Milton Friedman (2004) laid out in his "four ways to spend money" theorem, we spend other people's money differently from how we spend our own. Gone are the days of $100 deductibles. The role of consumer as payer is distinctly different from the role of consumer as patient. The mystery of pricing and the pain of paying for healthcare are deterring patients, creating more anxiety for those already sick, and blocking healthcare brands from forming a stronger relationship with those they serve.

Degree of Separation 4: Infinite Information

In today's age of ubiquitous digital information and more screens than US citizens, consumers have an incredible wealth of information at their fingertips. Google gave consumers instant access to libraries of information. Facebook and other apps gave consumers the ability to instantly share information within their own social networks. Mobile technologies, chiefly smartphones, gave consumers the ability to participate in these activities virtually anytime and anywhere. Now AI is offering to do the work *for* consumers.

These connections cut across all consumer demographics. As mentioned in chapter 2, consumers are highly connected, and when they need healthcare, like any other service, they expect it to be a few clicks away. But even in times of lesser need, consumers appear to be going online—for healthcare information, more often. Forty-four percent of those surveyed by NRC Health (2024) recalled a recent visit to a hospital website (up from 33 percent in 2017); one in five said they have used social media to find, follow, or interact directly with a healthcare provider; six in ten access healthcare information via mobile device. Even when not seeking out healthcare information, three in ten US consumers are physically connected to their own health data via a wearable device everywhere they go (Chandrasekaran, Katthula, and Moustakas 2020). When you consider a connected consumer, you may still picture a Gen Z twentysomething bopping around. But it's not just younger consumers—Americans of all ages are increasingly going online for health information and drawing from a diverse set of resources (NRC Health 2024). In fact, the average age of consumers who specifically use social media as a source of healthcare information is 41 years old and rising (NRC Health 2024).

What about their level of trust in all the information they find? Historically, consumers trust social media five times more than they do advertisements (NRC Health 2015). Fifty-two percent are likely to prefer a healthcare brand after engaging in a positive online interaction. For consumers, these interactions are a modern version of the house call. The days of consumers having to travel to an appointment may be waning, as technology enables providers to bring the experience to the consumer. This hospital-to-consumer approach, an inversion of the last century of consumer-to-hospital care delivery, could convert our information age from a barrier to a bridge.

Degree of Separation 5: Greener Grass

Consumers' expectations for healthcare remain higher than those for any other industry (see exhibit 3.1). Getting nearly 68 percent of Americans to agree on much of anything is difficult, but when it comes to healthcare, the response is nearly unanimous: Consumers want their expectations met or, better yet, *exceeded*, or they may walk away dissatisfied. Why the high bar for healthcare? Rising out-of-pocket costs have raised consumer expectations faster than those for other industries. Also, healthcare is different in that its main purpose is to save lives—not many industries can claim that level of importance. The fact that healthcare can be a matter of life or death tends to propel expectations even higher.

EXHIBIT 3.1: Industries That Should Meet or Exceed Consumer Expectations, 2024

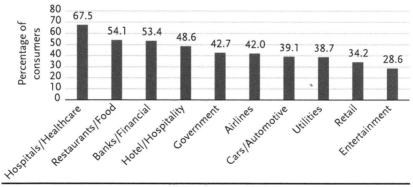

Source: NRC Health (2024).

The average consumer lives most of their life without wearing a hospital gown—buying groceries, eating out, traveling, and so forth. They pursue many more non–healthcare-related services than healthcare-related services. As such, consumers engage with service industries on a day-to-day basis in ways that they have come to expect everywhere. Uber delivers rides in minutes, Southwest Airlines gives points to incentivize repeat travel, and the myriad on-demand streaming platforms for TV shows and movies have changed the entertainment viewing experience for consumers, negating the need for long and frustrating phone calls with the cable company. (That said, these platforms are resulting in increased fragmentation and multiple digital front doors for consumers to keep track of, which is something healthcare is struggling with right now, too. We will discuss this issue of fragmentation more in later chapters, along with proposed solutions.) These positive experiences become instilled in consumers who then expect access, engagement, and value that, as we established in chapter 2, they rarely realize in healthcare.

Many healthcare organizations have shielded their offerings from comparisons with other industries, such as airlines, banking, and food service. The defenses are plenty: Healthcare is more regulated than other industries, healthcare faces limitations because of its responsibility to protect patient health information, healthcare isn't something you just order up, or perhaps healthcare is simply different. This defensiveness blocks us from comparing ourselves with other industries and learning how our patients determine their expectations. For consumers, healthcare should not measure up to other service industries—it should surpass them. And consumers would ask any healthcare provider whose chief concern is with the patient experience: How do you hope to provide an experience that meets my expectations if you don't know what they are?

Healthcare has little hope of meeting consumer expectations if it can't learn from other industries along the way. In the sections that follow, let's take a look at three nonhealthcare companies and what they have done to meet—and exceed—consumer expectations: Hilton, Uber Eats, and Amazon.

Hospitality: Hilton Introduces the Digital Key

While expectations typically aren't as high as in healthcare, hospitality is an industry that faces heavy competition among established brands such as Marriott and Hilton as well as from start-ups like Airbnb. A growing number of travelers demand a perfect experience from their hotels and are willing to pay more per room to satisfy these demands (Sheinman 2018). Parallels exist between hotel and healthcare brands with respect to how consumers want to access and engage with these industries.

Hilton Hotels is in the thick of the competition to be the preferred destination for travelers, but until the late 2010s, not much had changed in travelers' arrival experience. Every traveler dreads a long, slow-moving line to check in to the hotel. Even shortcut lines for rewards program members can slog along. Everyone in line has a reservation—they just need their room key. Hilton decided to give its guests a way to bypass the line by using a digital key. This technology allows a hotel room to be unlocked by a guest's smartphone—no plastic key card or 30-minute wait in line required (Grosvenor Technology 2017; Wiredcraft 2022). Changing door entry systems and building app-based technology that could consistently deliver such a special experience entailed a significant investment by Hilton. But the bet Hilton is making isn't a technology bet, it's an access bet. Skipping the line and going straight to their room allows guests to get where they want to go faster. It also works within the Hilton app, which behooves travelers to join the Hilton Honors rewards program if they haven't already. Consistent access can lead to increased loyalty over time.

Uber Eats: Convenience Personified

There was a time when food delivery was culinarily confined to pizza or only found in large urban centers. If we as hungry consumers wanted our go-to meal from our favorite restaurant, we had to *go to* a physical establishment. Uber Eats, along with other upstart, app-based food delivery services, chose to challenge these confinements and offer virtually every connected consumer a chance to turn the tide and have their favorite food come to them. As magical as this sounds, it wasn't a new idea: Meal and grocery delivery flashed brief potential during the dot-com era of the late 1990s. But that era didn't benefit from the versatility of the smartphone and the familiarity with any product showing up at your door à la Amazon. Uber Eats is also a brand extension of Uber, the company known for bringing transportation to your door via an easy, trackable, cashless app that was familiar to users and nonusers alike. Uber Eats immediately capitalized on brand value and an existing—and very mobile—workforce. If you didn't want to travel out to your favorite restaurant, Uber Eats offered to bring that food, drink, and spirit of the experience to you. As COVID forced consumers to bring products and services inside their home, the Uber Eats business model made perfect sense: Why venture out to a restaurant when the food can come to you? Seemingly everything else does. And through a familiar app. Even in the "kinda after COVID" period today, the sky seems the limit for Uber Eats and other delivery services that now drop off groceries, office products, pet food, and even pizza. That's right—the largest pizza chain in the United States, Domino's, now uses Uber Eats to deliver its pizza (McColl 2024).

Retail: Amazon Evolves from Bookseller to Go-To Source for Everything

Who would buy diapers from a bookseller? That's exactly what today's consumers do, and their favorite source is Amazon.com. Long before it boasted 100 million subscribers to its Prime membership service (Green 2019), Amazon started as an online bookseller competing with Barnes & Noble and a host of other physical bookstores. Amazon's virtual store advantage slowly attracted more and more customers as consumers opted to have their literary entertainment delivered to their door instead of visiting brick-and-mortar storefronts. The virtual bookstore bet worked, and most of Amazon's bookselling competition has since gone out of business.

Amazon has long since transcended the bookstore scene and now offers a website full of almost every product imaginable, all available within a day or two—or in some cases, a few hours—via Prime. It's not just about being fast and easy. Amazon's customers enjoy the ability to instantly calculate value. While searching for products and scanning their options, consumers can sort on the basis of price, composite reviews from consumers who bought the product, and similar products with similar prices and ratings. Gone are the days of asking a family member or neighbor about a product when you can consult hundreds of previous buyers and read their feedback boiled down to a single rating on a five-star scale.

Any way you slice it, consumers appreciate the full transparency that Amazon delivers—so much so that they will pay more to be members of Prime than they will the alternative memberships offered by big-box retailers. Consumers decided a while back that value is more about finding the product that fits their needs in terms of quality and cost than it is about doing what they have done in the past. Amazon and other innovators have won big by rejecting existing business models to deliver what consumers want.

* * *

No other industry is exactly like healthcare, but when studying consumers, looking at their behavior outside healthcare is important. Every other industry seems to have faced a consumer-led revolution, from banks wrestling with tellers versus ATMs in the 1980s and 1990s, to airlines adjusting to the transparency of online travel booking sites in the first decade of the twenty-first century, to Kodak inventing the portable digital camera but continuing to invest in its film business until its bankruptcy in 2012 (Dan 2012). What cuts across industries is the idea that those who listen to the consumer tend to know where things are going next, and those who cling to existing business models tend to get left behind.

As more and more consumers are wowed by other industries, the pressure on healthcare brands will only be ratcheted up. Even those few healthcare brands that consistently deliver an exceptional experience need to realize that there is pressure to *continue* to exceed consumer expectations. Those expectations are rising and, unless the cost of care goes down, they will continue to climb for some time. Meeting high expectations isn't easy, but the alternative is to risk not existing anymore.

Degree of Separation 6: The Rise of Choice

Our first degree of separation focused on the minds of consumers and their lack of knowledge about healthcare while being tasked with the responsibility to navigate the system on their own. This last degree of separation brings us full circle: the barriers in the minds of healthcare providers.

Healthcare has spent as much time dismissing consumerism as it has trying to adapt to it. Time and again, healthcare leaders ask: Do consumers really have a choice? Don't they listen to their physicians or just follow their networks? Speaking of networks, shouldn't we consider health plans our customers? Questions such as these were more valid in the days of $100 deductibles. Consumers are now paying more than ever before and asking: What have you done to be better than before? Why are you valuable enough for me to be your patient? Unfortunately, many providers struggle to answer these questions. Fewer than half of hospitals in the United States conduct consumer research other than administration of the Hospital Consumer Assessment of Healthcare Providers and Systems (HCAHPS) survey (NRC Health 2019). Even though reporting is mandated, it took until 2015 (nine years after fielding began) for a majority of hospital boards to report that they reviewed HCAHPS information at least once a year (Peisert 2015). Even when the data are in front of us, it can still be too easy for healthcare organizations to tune out the consumer in favor of more insular priorities.

On the other hand, we know consumers also can tune out providers. When they do pay attention to healthcare, plenty of tools are available to them. Yet, even though consumers can go online and find answers, the information typically isn't sufficient, and it isn't from their own healthcare providers.

When consumers don't have a ready go-to source, they often choose a do-it-yourself approach. As we know, they can opt out of healthcare services in favor of an alternative route to health and well-being. Most consumers want control of their journey of care, and that journey often starts with health. The health and wellness industry has grown immensely since the mid-2010s, and consumers' openness to receiving wellness information has also grown. As the wellness movement bloomed into a serious financial business, NRC Health Market Insights surveys found that if a hospital or health system hosted a wellness event to engage consumers, 53 percent would be likely to attend, which is up 10 percent since 2015. Six in ten consumers surveyed said they would submit to a health risk assessment or other screening if they could receive a readout of their results or receive other rewards or benefits for their participation (NRC Health 2024). More than information, consumers yearn to be involved in their own journey: they are eager for wellness education, preferring cooking classes and fitness training to online healthcare articles or health trackers alone. However, there are limitations to do-it-yourself health, and consumers can't—and shouldn't—go it alone. The United States is wrestling with what happens when consumers don't have the guidance they need: the opioid crisis, the childhood obesity epidemic, increasing prevalence of diabetes and prediabetes across the population, and the growing mistrust of information shared online. Consumers can't do it alone—so who will help them?

Consumer activation is contingent on the behavior of healthcare providers. If providers continue to ignore or underplay consumerism, or vacate their natural role as educators and influencers to anyone willing to fill the void, then consumers will remain information rich and knowledge poor, unable to realize their full potential and frustrated by the reality of having less control and self-confidence than they had hoped for in their journey of care.

Consumers need someone they can trust to help them make sense of the healthcare information they have—someone who is invested in them, in their community, and in their future. Despite the appeal of digital offerings, the reality still comes down to local healthcare organizations and their flesh-and-blood providers all stepping up and respecting the consumer's point of view, and the idea that consumers do in fact have some choice in where they go for healthcare services. Without this respect, it is hard to imagine any healthcare provider's offerings truly connecting with consumers.

THE DANGER OF THINKING LIKE A CONSUMER

Once we begin to consider the consumer's point of view, it can be easy to insert yourself or your family members and friends (or even fellow colleagues or board members) as proxies for consumers in your area. Your experiences and those of people around you can give rise to sweeping notions of who consumers are and what they want. If you are in a healthcare profession, pause before you try to walk in the shoes of a consumer. You know much more about how healthcare works than the average person does. If you talk about "continuum of care" or debate "meaningful use," you're too close to the fire and too far from consumers.

This proxy approach is well-meaning but can end badly. For example, a CEO may believe that they know local healthcare and therefore decide not to conduct any research directly with consumers. Or a vice president of marketing may conduct a survey, but the VP's own biases and assumptions end up distorting the data collected. When someone in healthcare tells a story of their own experience as a patient, they may even say something along these lines: "Thank goodness I had someone at the hospital I could call." That is a warning sign because the average healthcare consumer has no one there to call. Even when our intentions are good, we really can't understand consumers without asking them. There is no substitute.

THE INVASIVE SPECIES OF HEALTHCARE

Not all healthcare competition is coming from the world of e-commerce or Silicon Valley. Very real threats exist in every community in the form of retail chain giants that already possess quasi-healthcare brands. A 2024 NRC Health Market Insights survey asked consumers to consider receiving care in physical retail locations outside their current patterns of care. In some cases, the scenario was hypothetical only. The results were fascinating. While many healthcare-adjacent brands were tested, Walmart, for example, performed incredibly well. For basic healthcare needs (flu shot, blood pressure check, etc.), only 22 percent of consumers would "never consider" going to Walmart, whereas a whopping 57 percent would "somewhat" or "strongly" consider it (NRC Health 2024). For a more serious test or procedure (e.g., magnetic resonance imaging), 37 percent would "somewhat" or "strongly" consider heading to America's largest retailer (NRC Health 2024). Their willingness grows when consumers consider pharmacies like Walgreens, CVS Health, Rite Aid, and more, with 59 percent of consumers indicating they would visit a pharmacy for basic healthcare needs, and 48 percent saying they would visit a pharmacy for a more serious test or procedure (NRC Health 2024). It remains difficult to picture a patient receiving an MRI inside a Walmart, yet what is clear is that retail brands offer consumers convenience and affordability—two absolute rarities in today's healthcare delivery system. Consumers are hungry for something different, and not just coming out of COVID.

It's why they flocked to urgent care at the turn of the millennium and why there are now more than 2,000 such clinics in the United States. If consumers don't know the value of their local healthcare providers, they will consider other options. And if those options happen to be well-known brands that offer them better access and perceived value, consumers just might choose them.

So, why has it taken so long for these "retail alternatives" to devour the consumer aspects of traditional healthcare in a manner similar to what Amazon was able to do to the retail sector or Warby Parker accomplished with eyewear? In fact, just in 2024, Walmart announced that it was closing 51 of its health centers across five states as well as its much vaunted "virtual health" initiative (Hut 2024). When Haven healthcare was announced on January 30, 2018, traditional healthcare stocks were rattled. How can a venture combining Amazon, JP Morgan, and Berkshire Hathaway not create a seismic disruption to the fragmented payer–provider–consumer jumble? In fact, when Haven was announced, Dr. Klasko was asked, as the CEO of a health system, if he was terrified of the future. He responded, "It's like the Loch Ness monster. If I ever saw it, I'd be scared, but I don't think I will see it in my lifetime." Haven announced it was closing its operations on January 4, 2021.

The answer to why Walmart, Walgreens, CVS, Amazon, and others have not had the effect on the healthcare delivery system that one might expect is not that complicated. There is a fundamental disconnect between consumer expectations and their willingness to pay for the service. Put another way, the American healthcare system has managed to disarticulate the consumer from the business aspects of their healthcare unlike any other transactional part of their life. When a consumer looks for a karaoke machine on Amazon, they can easily compare features with price, convenience, and ease of use (as well as filtering for only those that fit within their budget). Healthcare financing has traditionally served to benefit the purveyors—hospitals, insurance companies, pharmacy benefit managers, pharmaceutical companies—which has served to allow consumers to by and large obtain their needed healthcare and let the providers, insurers, and pharmacy-related services fight it out. When Walmart or Amazon tries to fit that fragmented, inconsistent payment model into its direct care for patients, the math does not add up (and they are certainly not willing to accept the pitiful margins that not-for-profit healthcare systems do for their all-in care.)

The following sections discuss four new disruptors to the industry since the first edition of this book was published; disruptors that will significantly impact the consumer experience: (1) non-contiguous consolidations, (2) creative partnerships, (3) venture capital firms diving into the hospital and health system market, and (4) private equity gobbling up lucrative national specialists and specialties.

Noncontiguous Consolidations

With retail outlets such as Walmart, Amazon, and CVS cherry-picking profitable health provision through mergers and acquisitions (One Medical, Village MD, etc.) and with an increasingly difficult Federal Trade Commission (FTC) stance on health system consolidation, the traditional hospital ecosystem is "fighting back" with noncontiguous consolidation. The advantages of that are yet to be seen, but generally the FTC has no right to stop these consolidations because the geographic diversity solves the "market power" issue. Aurora–Advocate, Intermountain, Common Spirit, and others are allowing hospital systems to potentially reduce administrative costs and dilute the costs of IT expansion.

Creative Partnerships

Combating the rise of for-profit insurers, retailers, and big tech, competing directly for primary and specialty care with traditional hospital systems are a new wave of cross-industry partnerships aimed at rebalancing the scales. Most recently, Kaiser Permanente (based in California) acquired Geisinger Health (based in Pennsylvania) to create a new company called Risant. The plan is to acquire four or five systems (Cone Health in North Carolina signed on in June 2024), with the goal of achieving annual revenues of $30–$35 billion. The attraction for the acquirees is Kaiser's vast resources as well as its experience in implementing profitable value-based care in a consumer-friendly manner.

An even more unlikely model exists in Central Florida, where the nation's largest senior community, The Villages, has created a consumer-centered, primary care–driven model in partnership with several payers; it is owned by the same developer that created the consumer-centric living model. This partnership has expanded and now boasts some of the best outcomes among seniors as well as top decile medical loss ratios, risk adjustment factors, and consumer satisfaction metrics in the nation (net promoter scores in the 90s). The Villages are applying state-of-the-art AI tools as well, tracking patient needs using KAID Health's Whole Chart Analysis AI platform to project potential care plan gaps. They built a paramedic-at-home program that will dispatch a paramedic to help with home-based continuity and challenge identification. The care plan is consistent, from the primary care office to the patient's home, with everyone having access to the same plan. There is real-time communication as the paramedics are considered an extension of the healthcare team. Moving the program upstream required insights beyond awaiting a specific failure to drive intervention, so they crosswalk their data, derive insights, and then invite the patient to participate. Results have included reductions in utilization as well as improvements in adherence to care plans (AiThority 2022).

Venture Capital Firms Diving into the Hospital and Health System Market

General Catalyst (GC), the largest healthcare venture capital firm in the United States, has hundreds of "healthcare transformation" companies under its investment portfolio, including Livongo, AIDoc, Hippocratic AI (2024), Paradigm, and Commure. It has taken a bold step by creating "health assurance partners," a group of 20 hospitals that view GC as a strategic partner in moving from volume to value and moving toward financial stability.

At the same time, GC is working on an initiative called HATCO (health assurance transformation company), which announced plans to purchase and own a health system as an example of "responsible innovation and transformation," as inspired by the book *UnHealthcare: A Manifesto for Health Assurance* (Taneja, Maney, and Klasko 2020). In 2023, GC announced its intention to acquire Summa Health, a health system and integrated delivery network in Ohio, to create a blueprint for healthcare delivery transformation that can be applied to other health systems nationwide (General Catalyst 2024).

Both of these GC examples represent noncontiguous consolidations and creative partnerships largely outside the traditional tentacles of regulation that contiguous mergers or acquisitions would face.

Private Equity Gobbling Up Lucrative National Specialists and Specialties

In areas such as orthopedic surgery, urology, cardiology, and women's health, private equity firms are consolidating specialists across the country. There are several factors leading to this development. Specialty physicians feel as though they have lost autonomy when herded into large hospital-owned multispecialty groups. Private equity firms recognize that they are better than physician practices at finding efficiencies and creating new revenue. Also, for many specialists, given the move from hospital to "healthcare at any address," they have recognized that their financial needs and their patient-consumers' clinical needs do not necessarily align with the sick-care inpatient/outpatient mentality of their hospital partners' leadership.

In Philadelphia, for example, the Rothman Institute, a private group of more than 100 orthopedic surgeons, served as Jefferson Health's academic orthopedic group. Over a period of ten years, these surgeons moved many of their surgical cases to a single-specialty hospital they created (and in which Jefferson later coinvested) and then eventually to private equity–backed outpatient centers. Private equity and nonhospital system ownership of physician groups now represent more than one-third of the national market share, a 600 percent increase from 2012 to 2021 (Gamble 2024). These firms have limited regulatory oversight regarding quality of care and patient experience. When this kind of change in ownership takes place, in some cases, systems have had to renegotiate patient referrals with physicians who were previously integrated with their hospitals (Condon 2023).

These creative partnerships and noncontiguous consolidations have a lot to prove when it comes down to that iron triangle of outcomes, quality, and cost. Just as with contiguous mergers and acquisitions, their stated mission is to be a positive transformation in an industry that sorely needs that kind of disruption. It will take time and objective data to overcome the naysayers who are taking a "show me" mentality that these actions will have lasting power (unlike Haven and Walmart) and that they will not just increase costs and further fragment care, as has been the case in many traditional hospital or payer mergers and acquisitions. On the private equity side of the equation, there have been reports of the quality of patient care suffering at the expense of cost cutting and profit taking in some of these acquisitions by firms that may be entering this space for the wrong reasons.

***

Many of these disruptors, while providing consumer-centric solutions, are doing so in silos and are very narrowly focused. Often these solutions are further separating hospitals and doctors from each other and also from other stops on the care continuum. The data they generate exist in spaces that are not connected to any other systems, much less a single, integrated platform. They have the potential to cause more consumer confusion, despite their focus on ease and convenience, because their fragmented nature leaves consumers unable to follow a common thread in their journey of care.

These new entrants, consolidations, and creative partnerships are not going away, nor should they. The not-for-profit, mission-based legacy health systems and payers have allowed a broken, fragmented, increasingly expensive, and inequitable healthcare delivery system in which consumers are looking for alternatives. Which of these disruptors are true game changers and not just profit generators for their parent organizations will take time to discover. For now, the legacy systems have much to do to counter these disruptors, address the fragmentation, and create a seamless, integrated consumer experience focused on improving health.

REFERENCES

AiThority. 2022. "The Villages Health Partners with KAID Health to Optimize Clinical Efficiency and Care Quality." Published June 23. https://aithority.com/medical-apps/healthcare-management/the-villages-health-partners-with-kaid-health-to-optimize-clinical-efficiency-and-care-quality/.

Berwick, D. M. 2023. *"Salve Lucrum:* The Existential Threat of Greed in US Health Care." *JAMA* 329 (8) 629–30. https://jamanetwork.com/journals/jama/fullarticle/2801097.

Bevolo, C. 2011. *Joe Public Doesn't Care About Your Hospital.* Nashville, TN: RockBench Publishing.

Brill, S. 2015. *America's Bitter Pill: Money, Politics, Backroom Deals, and the Fight to Fix Our Broken Healthcare System.* New York: Random House.

————. 2013. "A Bitter Pill: Why Medical Bills Are Killing Us." *Time.* Published April 4. https://time.com/198/bitter-pill-why-medical-bills-are-killing-us/.

Centers for Medicare & Medicaid Services (CMS). 2023. "Hospital Price Transparency." Modified November 2. www.cms.gov/priorities/key-initiatives/hospital-price-transparency.

Chandrasekaran, R., V. Katthula, and E. Moustakas. 2020. "Patterns of Use and Key Predictors for the Use of Wearable Health Care Devices by US Adults: Insights from a National Survey." *Journal of Medical Internet Research* 22 (10). Published October 16. https://doi.org/10.2196/22443.

Condon, A. 2023. "Optum Strikes Patient Referral Deal with Virginia Mason." *Becker's Hospital CFO Report.* Published June 28. www.beckershospitalreview.com/finance/optum-virginia-mason-strike-referral-medicare-advantage-deal.html.

Dan, A. 2012. "Kodak Failed by Asking the Wrong Marketing Question." *Forbes.* Updated May 5. www.forbes.com/sites/avidan/2012/01/23/kodak-failed-by-asking-the-wrong-marketing-question/.

Friedman, M. 2004. "Liberty Quotation: Milton Friedman on the Four Ways to Spend Money." Libertarian Party of Maryland. Published July 9. https://lpmaryland.org/liberty-quotation-milton-friedman-four-ways-spend-money/ (content no longer available).

Gamble, M. 2024. "PE-Backed Physician Groups Grew 600% in a Decade." *Becker's Hospital Review.* Published March 5. www.beckershospitalreview.com/hospital-transactions-and-valuation/pe-backed-physician-groups-grew-600-in-a-decade.html.

Gee, E. 2019. "The High Price of Hospital Care." Center for American Progress. Published June 26. www.americanprogress.org/issues/healthcare/reports/2019/06/26/471464/high-price-hospital-care/.

General Catalyst. 2024. "Our Acquisition of Summa Health." Published January 17. www.generalcatalyst.com/perspectives/our-acquisition-of-summa-health.

Green, D. 2019. "A Survey Found That Amazon Prime Membership Is Soaring to New Heights—but One Trend Should Worry the Company." *Business Insider*. Published January 17. https://markets.businessinsider.com/news/stocks/amazon-more-than-100-million-prime-members-us-survey-2019-11027877518 (content no longer available).

Greystone.Net and Klein & Partners. 2016. *The State of Digital Marketing in Healthcare Moving Toward 2017*. Published November. www.greystone.net/docs/default-source/surveys/the-state-of-digital-marketing-in-healthcare-in-2017.pdf.

Grosvenor Technology. 2017. "Knock, Knock, Knocking on Hilton's Door." Published August 11. www.grosvenortechnology.com/2017/08/knock-knock-knocking-hiltons-door/ (content no longer available).

Hernandez, J. 2023. "It's Been a Year Since Southwest's Epic Meltdown. What's Changed?" *All Things Considered, National Public Radio*. Transcript published November 14. www.npr.org/2023/11/14/1213008566/its-been-a-year-since-southwests-epic-meltdown-whats-changed.

Hippocratic AI. 2024. "Hippocratic AI Announces Collaboration with NVIDIA to Develop Super-Low-Latency 'Empathy Inference' for One of the World's First Generative AI-Powered Healthcare Agents." News release, March 18. www.globenewswire.com/news-release/2024/3/18/2848236/0/en/Hippocratic-AI-Announces-Collaboration-with-NVIDIA-to-Develop-Super-Low-Latency-Empathy-Inference-for-One-of-the-World-s-First-Generative-AI-Powered-Healthcare-Agents.html.

Hut, N. 2024. "Closures of Walmart's Health Centers Reflect the Widespread Financial Constraints in U.S. Healthcare." Healthcare Financial Management Association. Published May 7. www.hfma.org/payment-reimbursement-and-managed-care/payment-models/

closures-of-walmart-health-centers-reflect-the-widespread-
financial-constraints-in-us-healthcare/.

Investopedia. 2023. "6 Reasons Healthcare Is So Expensive in the
U.S." Updated September 26. www.investopedia.com/articles/
personal-finance/080615/6-reasons-healthcare-so-expensive-us.
asp.

KFF. 2024. "Health Insurance Coverage of the Total Population:
2022." Accessed May 29. www.kff.org/other/state-indicator/
total-population/.

McColl, B. 2024. "Domino's Pizza Posts Strong Results on Loyalty
Program, Uber Eats Marketing." Investopedia. Published April
29. www.investopedia.com/dominos-pizza-posts-strong-
results-on-loyalty-program-uber-eats-marketing-8640263.

Navathe, A. S. 2023. "Why Are Nonprofit Hospitals Focused
More on Dollars Than Patients?" *New York Times*. Published
November 30. www.nytimes.com/2023/11/30/opinion/
hospitals-nonprofit-community.html.

NRC Health. 2015, 2019, 2022, 2024. *Market Insights Surveys of
Healthcare Consumers*. Lincoln, NE: NRC Health.

Peisert, K. C. 2015. *21st Century Care Delivery: Governing in the
New Healthcare Industry*. Biennial survey report. Lincoln, NE:
Governance Institute.

Rose, J. 2023. "Southwest Will Pay a $140 Million Fine for
Its Meltdown During the 2022 Holidays." *All Things
Considered*, National Public Radio. Transcript updated
December 18. www.npr.org/2023/12/18/1219906471/
southwest-airlines-2022-meltdown-fined-faa.

Sheinman, A. J. 2018. "Hotel and Air Prices to Rise Sharply in 2019,
per GBTA/CWT Research." *Meetings & Conventions*. Published July
24. www.meetings-conventions.com/News/Hotels-and-Resorts/

Hotel-and-Air-Prices-to-Rise-Sharply-in-2019-Per-GBTA/
CWT-Research/.

Statista. 2023. "U.S. National Health Expenditure as
Percent of GDP from 1960 to 2022." Published
December. www.statista.com/statistics/184968/
us-health-expenditure-as-percent-of-gdp-since-1960/.

Taneja, H., K. Maney, and S. Klasko. 2020. *UnHealthcare: A
Manifesto for Health Assurance.* Self-published, Lulu.com.

Terhune, C. 2018. "Life-Threatening Heart Attack Leaves Teacher
with $108,951 Bill." *Morning Edition*, NPR. Transcript
published August 27. www.npr.org/sections/health-shots/
2018/08/27/640891882/life-threatening-heart-attack-leaves-
teacher-with-108-951-bill.

Ward, L., J. R. Duren, and T. Roughley. 2024. "How Much Does
Health Insurance Cost in 2024?" *CNN Underscored Money.*
Published February 15. www.cnn.com/cnn-underscored/
money/how-much-is-health-insurance.

Wilen, H. 2023. "Southwest Airlines Plans Billion-Dollar
Investment to Upgrade Technology." *L.A. Business First.*
Published January 30. www.bizjournals.com/losangeles/
news/2023/01/30/southwest-airlines-holiday-operations-
recovery.html.

Wiredcraft. 2022. "Unlocking New Guest Experiences with Hilton's
Digital Key." *Wiredcraft* (blog). Published November 16. https://
wiredcraft.com/blog/unlocking-new-guest-experiences-
with-hilton-s-digital-key/.

CHAPTER 4

Organization, Culture, and Leadership

WE HAVE NOW established that consumer expectations for healthcare are incredibly high. We also know that the barriers to meeting these expectations are formidable. To have any hope of meeting those expectations, we must turn toward our greatest resource: the leaders and doers within the field. We need to ask ourselves point-blank: Are we up for the challenge? Can we make it through the gauntlet of consumer and patient expectations laid down for us? We need to take stock in who we are before we get caught up in what we must do.

CHOOSING HEALTHCARE

The antidote to much of what's ailing healthcare's workforce can be found by going back to the point of origin for virtually all healthcare workers: Healthcare is a calling. Talk to just about anyone in the field and they will say they specifically chose this industry to make a difference in the world. It is rare to find an industry so central to everyone's existence. We lose sight of how healthcare is woven into the fabric of our being. Most of us were born in a hospital, and many of us will die in one. Healthcare guides us from the cradle to the grave and during many of our most important moments in between. We rely on nurses and physicians during our most vulnerable and memorable life events. Inside the world of healthcare, infants are born, heights are checked off, and life is lived from beginning to end.

People drawn to healthcare desire to make the world a better place. Physicians aren't the only ones who ascribe to the Hippocratic oath: First, do no harm. We all want to make people better. And we all know that healthcare isn't perfect, so we want to make it better, for patients and for ourselves. In fact, our patients expect it. The question is this: As an industry and as a people, how do we get there?

The answers to this question are harder now than they were when we wrote the first edition of this book. COVID-19 set off an unmatched agitation in the US labor market. Pervasive job losses in the first year of the pandemic resulted in constricted labor markets in 2021, driven by the so-called Great Resignation. The Pew Research Center found that low pay, lack of advancement opportunities, and feeling disrespected at work were the top reasons Americans quit their jobs during this period (Parker and Horowitz 2022). Healthcare workers were impacted by this even more so, knowing that every day when they showed up to their "essential" job, they could contract a potentially deadly disease. The industry was already facing significant shortages in physicians and nurses along with problems of burnout from long and difficult shifts. Some physicians were feeling frustrated by increasing regulatory oversight and less autonomy to practice as a result of evidence-based care protocols and health systems' attempts to standardize care to increase quality and lower costs (Salvatore, Numerato, and Fattore 2018).

COVID only compounded these challenges. In 2021, 117,000 physicians left medicine (Devereaux 2022). During the pandemic, 70 percent of physicians reported symptoms of depression, and one in eight acknowledged suicidal thoughts (NIOSH 2024). One emergency room doctor left her career after 20 years. The last straw for her? After 18 months on the front lines of the pandemic, when she asked her leadership for an unpaid leave of absence, the answer was no—because "everyone else would want one too" (Phelps 2022). Even nonclinical staff left for local Amazon warehouses where the hourly pay was better, with equal benefits and a significantly less stressful workplace. Despite being healthcare heroes in 2020, in the years since COVID appeared, healthcare workers have faced increasing violence in the workplace, primarily from frustrated and angry patients. Today, healthcare workers are five times more likely to experience workplace violence than employees in any other industry (US Bureau of Labor Statistics 2024).

As the previous chapters have laid out, the challenge is massive. It is fair to question whether progress has truly been made in advancing patient-centered healthcare. Many patients still feel let down and describe an industry that is falling short of expectations. These patients are, on average, sicker and sadder than they were in 2019 when we wrote the first edition of this book. Scores on the Hospital Consumer Assessment of Healthcare Providers and Systems (HCAHPS) survey have not led to improved care and experience to the degree originally expected. The cost of healthcare has spiraled out of control, even with expanding (albeit slow) investment in value-based purchasing. It is now vitally clear that healthcare leaders must also address the experience and well-being of their care providers to meet this challenge. Our call to action today includes returning the practice of medicine to the calling that it once was. The following paragraphs demonstrate some of the barriers that must be removed as we continue our journey forward.

MEASUREMENT OVERLOAD

While many observers have expressed doubt about improvement in healthcare, there is little dissent in one area that has seen a remarkable activity spike since the first decade of the twenty-first century: measurement. We have measured ourselves to the nth degree. If we could be flies on the wall of healthcare organizations, we'd have heard *measurement* a million times. The term has been bandied about in board meetings, at executive retreats, and among employees. Entire businesses have been erected to focus on measuring the patient and consumer experience. In fact, an entire "culture of measurement" has been created in nearly every corner of the field.

Although there is consensus that we measure much more of the patient experience than we did in the time of Harvey and Jean Picker, there is also much debate about what all that measurement has taught us (see exhibit 4.1). For example, a big focus of HCAHPS was to shrink the large number of patients who were not willing to recommend a hospital after a care experience. In 2008, at the outset of HCAHPS public reporting, 33 percent of patients across the United States did not recommend a hospital (NRC Health 2008). In 2024, after 16 years of HCAHPS measurement and billions spent on improvement, 28 percent of patients were not willing to recommend a hospital after a care experience, a percentage that has remained at the same level since 2016 (NRC Health 2016, 2024). Considering the money and effort spent, we do not consider this reduction to be a victory.

EXHIBIT 4.1: The System Is Designed to Deliver Metrics, Not Better Experiences

Percentages of patients reporting a positive overall experience for all hospitals and hospitals in the Value-Based Purchasing (VBP) program, 2008–14

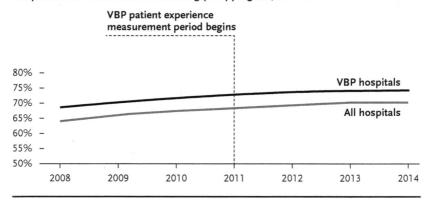

Source: Papanicolas et al. (2017). Reprinted with permission.

In defense of measurement, it is impossible to know if an industry has changed—especially one as complex as healthcare—without systematic and widespread gathering of information. Evidence is especially important in an industry in which memories are long and anecdotes abound. To prove things have changed in healthcare, every organization must ponder, devise, and deploy an intensive measurement program that covers all facets of care across the organization and digs into enough detail to yield meaningful insights. The complex experiences within the ecosystem of healthcare require it. But we argue that healthcare has now reached a point where our next challenge is to determine how to measure what truly matters most.

An essential but often overlooked component to systemic measurement is direct patient feedback. An antidote to anecdotes, asking patients to describe their experience in their own words is vital to understanding how the industry is performing. To address gaps in performance, we must include the voices of consumers and patients, or improvement plans might miss the mark with respect to future experiences.

Much of Harvey and Jean Picker's work (discussed in chapter 1) rests on the idea that patients should not only be included in the assessment of care, they should be the *focus* of improvement. The Picker work often cites the negative impact of excluding patients and the downstream effect of having changes made by leaders who fail to include their most important audience: the patients who receive their care. Even with respect to measurement, it can be easy to misinterpret results and drown out the patient's voice in the echo chamber of the C suite. Therefore, every measurement plan under consideration by leadership must not only include the patient's voice, it must place it front and center.

As documented in earlier chapters, HCAHPS became the direct, mandated intervention to ensure that patient feedback was being put first. However, what was the impact of HCAHPS *inside* healthcare organizations? The idea of having activity mandated puts a whole new spin on efforts to improve patient experiences.

When a large outside entity requires you to do the work you were inspired to do on entering the profession (and perhaps thought you were already doing successfully), the process can be an adjustment. While working to embrace this mandated form of measurement, healthcare leaders must take a balanced approach. How do you make the mandate your own? How do you ensure that employees are actively engaged in the mission and not just complying? How (and why) do you create your own measurement plan without it feeling reactive? How do we build a culture where everyone involved in care is motivated to hold ourselves more accountable than anyone else? These questions place a great imperative on the shoulders of senior leaders: Tap into your workforce's natural passion and ambition or face a crowd of skeptics.

TOP DOWN

The move to improve the patient experience landed with a bang in the C suite of every healthcare organization. As HCAHPS demanded more and more executive attention and became bound to reimbursement, the C suite and CEOs in particular seemed to move measurement strategies higher up the priority list to increase excitement and employee engagement. To avoid the risk of HCAHPS being perceived as a "checkbox" initiative, many executives pushed patient-centered care as a transformative effort worthy of top priority in the strategic planning process (Penso 2017).

How did things go early on? It is unclear whether HCAHPS led to much improvement in patient care in its first few years. When the Affordable Care Act (ACA) was enacted in 2010, it stole some limelight from the HCAHPS movement. But HCAHPS and the ACA were intertwined. Many saw HCAHPS as a way to measure and add value to the new experiences of patients under expanded forms of healthcare coverage.

Driven by the ACA and the greater movement to reform healthcare, the shift to value-based purchasing (VBP) occurred in 2012. Born out of frustration with rising costs and middling patient satisfaction, the idea was to move from volume and fee-for-service models that created incentive to overtest and overcharge patients (Porter and Teisberg 2006) toward a model that relied on care demonstrated to be clinically necessary and the ability to keep a population healthy over time in order to receive full reimbursement and even bonuses from the Centers for Medicare & Medicaid Services (CMS 2024). At the time, VBP was described as a bold step with the aim of "transforming Medicare from a passive payer of claims to an active purchaser of quality healthcare for its beneficiaries" (Borah et al. 2012). On inception, VBP quickly moved to the forefront of the greater reform movement and transcended HCAHPS as the focus of efforts toward improving the patient experience (Japsen 2015).

Whether you lived through these quick-hitting eras or not, you can feel empathy for healthcare leaders trying to keep up with the latest change. For many, the sole constant was an aspect of the measurement movement in which they were entangled: executive compensation tied to HCAHPS scores. Many healthcare leaders have some form of compensation or bonuses tied to organizational performance on the HCAHPS survey. SullivanCotter's 2023 executive compensation survey shows that 42 percent of total direct compensation is now composed of performance-based incentives (up 10 percentage points since 2019!). Seventy-two percent of organizations use patient experience metrics in their annual incentive performance scorecards, while 22 percent now incorporate a measure of patient access (SullivanCotter 2023). This form of compensation can become a double-edged sword in the minds of executives. If everyone is measuring the patient experience, determining what to fix and moving in lockstep to accomplish it, then a just reward for all these efforts would be a bonus at the end of the year. However, if results aren't great—or at least not good enough to hit the organization's goal—then HCAHPS could become a source of frustration and elicit doubt regarding whether the data are painting a true picture of performance or the system is rigged. As Dr. Robert Wachter of the University of California, San Francisco, lamented, "The focus on numbers has gone too far. We're hitting the targets but missing the point" (Wachter 2016). The point, Dr. Wachter argued, is that while measurement is a good idea, it has become a fad that has spun out of control. Physicians and executives alike are chasing their own ratings and losing focus on their patients. Dr. Wachter also argued that computerized systems such as electronic medical records have robbed physicians of true patient interaction, and that hitting numbers has replaced satisfaction derived from providing real human care. "Our businesslike efforts to measure and improve quality are not blocking the altruism, indeed the love, that motivates people to enter the helping professions," he explained. "While we're figuring out how to get better, we need to tread more lightly in assessing the work of the professionals who practice in our most human and sacred fields" (Wachter 2016).

Dr. Wachter is not the only one to have noticed this sweeping problem. The movement toward measurement has become a culture of overmeasurement, confusion about what to measure, and disdain for survey tools and the leaders who pushed them. A general feeling surfaced that the surveys seem geared toward what patients want out of an experience rather than actual medical outcomes, and that physicians may be engaging in inappropriate medical practices (e.g., prescribing unnecessary drugs to complaining patients) to avoid negative comments on surveys (Zgierska, Rabago, and Miller 2014). This feeling has pushed healthcare leaders to question, if not disagree with, the HCAHPS approach altogether.

One question we have asked is whether one person in an organization can influence the composite HCAHPS score of that organization. To better understand this issue, we need to look at the structure of the typical healthcare organization.

SYSTEMNESS

"Systemness" is an organizational trend that has changed the healthcare landscape. In 2005, The Governance Institute defined *systemness* as health systems attempting to "look and act more like a single, integrated organization rather than a collection of independently functioning pieces" (Bader et al. 2005). The days of mostly independent hospitals have drawn to a close. As of 2024, 67 percent of hospitals were part of a system that consists of two or more acute care hospitals (American Hospital Association 2024). Most consumers support the idea of a system, with the majority (61 percent) preferring to choose a hospital that is part of a system rather than one that is not, driven largely by the hope that a system will offer more coordinated care (NRC Health 2024). Consumers have other reasons for shifting toward the system concept, including the belief that systems can eliminate confusion and simplify their care journey by tying together the disparate episodes of treatment they will receive. Independent hospitals often struggle to provide comprehensive care and don't always have the resources available to better coordinate care. (Of course, many healthcare systems also struggle to provide the coordinated care consumers long for.)

Things look different on the inside of a system. Typically, a system office is established to better oversee the operations of multiple hospitals and the larger footprint of care sites, as well as to project impartiality among all employees. But the leaders inside these system offices often spend more time with one another than they do at the many care sites under their corporate umbrella. Managing disparate care sites can be difficult; the idea of one-size-fits-all metrics and standardized measurement and reporting processes is the ultimate aim of most systems.

Assigning only a handful of people to oversee an entire system's metrics usually results in executives reviewing a dashboard of ten or fewer metrics. We have seen three notable effects of this reduction in metrics. First, most of the HCAHPS survey has become trivial compared with those few metrics that are considered dashboard worthy: willingness to recommend, physician and nurse communication, and overall rating. Second, when those few metrics are not sufficient or the findings are disappointing, leaders tend to continue focusing on them and fail to look at the interconnectedness of the entire survey and the other, ancillary metrics that need to be tracked to drive greater improvement (such as room cleanliness and noise level, comprehension of medication instructions, and postdischarge clarity and confidence). Finally, this maddening focus on such a sliver of the overall survey, coupled with the tie to executive compensation, has caused many observers to lament the entire movement toward patient-centered care (Johnson 2014; Quick Leonard Kieffer 2016).

This effect of "measurement madness" has increased since the mid-2010s and created an ironic reality: We seem to be unable to focus on measurement at a time when patient expectations and consumer costs have heightened the call for better quantification of our performance (Moore 2019). For example, take a typical hospital that used to measure 5 or 6 concrete metrics, such as patient infection rates or average length of stay. Now, it is flooded with 36 patient experience metrics, 22 employee engagement key performance indicators, and 8 organizational culture indicators. From the outside, the organization may seem to be highly committed to quantifying its performance, but from the inside, executives and managers are likely suffering from data disorientation. When too much is being measured, it is difficult, if not impossible, to understand what matters most to patients. The patient voice can easily be drowned out in the cacophony of corporate performance measurement.

Inside the swirling storm of measurement, a question remains: Who hears the patient's voice? Who is aware of the HCAHPS metrics within and throughout the organization? Who actually sees the metrics? Typically, a leader in quality "owns" the patient's voice and oversees the ins and outs of the survey process. This person or team can report out to other leaders—or not. What if some metrics aren't rosy? What if they are going in the wrong direction and the cause is unknown? Does the quality leader or team want to share these results with the CEO and board now, or are they more likely to wait a month or two and see where the numbers are at that point? Without clear lines of responsibility and a strong push for reporting, it can be easy to gloss over HCAHPS and leave employees in the dark regarding their own performance.

Even when regular reporting is achieved, communicating the findings to employees is a challenge. Whereas CEOs may issue an all-employee memo, and senior leadership may be well briefed on the numbers, middle managers are the key to employees understanding the performance measurements (Munch 2017). Without a dedicated focus on middle management—an often overlooked layer in a complex healthcare organization—it is easy to imagine a nurse or a security guard having little understanding of HCAHPS or hearing only a distorted version of what leadership is trying to accomplish. When communication isn't clear or a topic is poorly explained (whether intentional or unintentional), healthcare employees, like most people, will fill in the blanks and form their own conclusions, which can result in substantially different realities from those intended by senior leadership.

Despite these challenges, are systems better able to achieve patient-centered care? The benefits of system membership and consolidation translate to potentially greater access to capital, ability to consolidate overhead and support functions, and ideally improved and more standardized system-wide performance. But while the financial benefits of system development and consolidation have been clearly demonstrated, the promise of improved quality and patient experience across health systems has lagged. A comparison of HCAHPS performance in independent hospitals and systems shows that systems perform better, but only slightly (NRC Health 2019).

NRC Health (2023) has seen slow and steady improvement, the most substantial being 7 points on any given composite HCAHPS score from 2008 to 2015. Moreover, there has been no improvement in HCAHPS scores since 2017 (COVID halted progress on improving quality and patient experience scores across all US hospitals, but it is notable that the improvement plateaued several years prior to the onset of the pandemic). Although these findings may not seem promising, when we consider that they pertain to 4,000 hospitals that see about 3 million patients a year, an annual improvement rate of only 1 percent would result in 30,000 patients receiving improved care.

The Governance Institute, a subsidiary of NRC Health, pursued research in 2021 and 2022 to determine whether health systems have been able to demonstrate improved quality metrics (including HCAHPS) consistently across hospitals (Pugh 2022). This research combined system-level rollups of CMS Star Ratings and corresponding system-level rollups of NRC Health's Market Insights Overall Quality Scores to capture the consumer perception of quality and patient experience in these health systems. Through both iterations of this research, the findings showed that very few systems had consistently high performance across every hospital within the system.

Whether it is measurement overload or the challenge of growing systems, these issues are at the heart of healthcare. Are we providing the best possible patient experience? How do we know it's the best?

THE STRUGGLE TO SUSTAIN RESULTS

Even when success is achieved, sustaining results can be difficult. As much as we have measured and measured over the past few decades, still little is known about how to sustain success. And when an organization reaches the top, there is not much room left to improve.

A change in leadership opens up the risk of a decline in quality and the patient experience (Sfantou et al. 2017), and many healthcare organizations have experienced this during the Great

Resignation as their CEOs decided to resign or retire early. As much as leaders try to share their approach and build a team effort, the CEO can often be a single point of failure for any given initiative driven by senior management. From a measurement perspective, this possibility highlights the need for a CEO to have a deeper understanding of their role as a quality champion, as well as sharing metrics widely (i.e., beyond the board and C suite) to ensure smoother transitions when a leader exits.

Many external factors need to be considered as well. The calls from hospitals to modernize HCAHPS have grown increasingly louder (Bean 2019). To answer those calls, CMS is making some key changes that will take effect in 2025. The most impactful of these changes for consumers and healthcare leaders include the ability to complete the survey online, which will increase response rates; patients' family members will be able to complete the survey on their behalf; and hospitals will be required to collect information about what primary language a patient speaks (Bean 2023).

Industry turbulence has kept big financial concerns dangling over healthcare leadership. The consistent challenges to the ACA and what may or may not replace it also create a moving target for those pursuing value. Population health efforts also are constantly up against public health trends and a wide swath of aging Americans who are only going to get sicker.

These headwinds must be faced by engaged leaders who have well-communicated visions, along with a sense of urgency to implement and sustain a consumer-centered delivery model that also addresses the well-being of care providers, so that everyone's focus, above all else, can remain on their patients. In the following chapters, we present our updated research on the Picker dimensions and explore what matters most to patients today. We also present case examples and a solution framework for healthcare leaders to consider to build and sustain a true consumer-centric culture for the future of healthcare.

REFERENCES

American Hospital Association. 2024. "Fast Facts on U.S. Hospitals, 2024." Updated January. www.aha.org/statistics/fast-facts-us-hospitals.

Bader, B. S., E. A. Kazemek, R. W. Witalis, and C. Lockee. 2005. *Pursuing Systemness: The Evolution of Large Health Systems*. White paper. San Diego, CA: Governance Institute.

Bean, M. 2023. "6 Changes Coming to HCAHPS in 2025." *Becker's Hospital Review*. Published August 9. www.beckershospitalreview.com/patient-experience/6-changes-coming-to-hcahps-in-2025.html?oly_enc_id=6577B0117745B1Z.

———. 2019. "Hospital Groups Propose HCAHPS Modernization: 5 Things to Know." *Becker's Hospital Review*. Published July 25. www.beckershospitalreview.com/patient-engagement/hospital-groups-propose-hcahps-modernization-5-things-to-know.html.

Borah, B. J., M. G. Rock, D. L. Wood, D. L. Roellinger, M. G. Johnson, and J. M. Naessens. 2012. "Association Between Value-Based Purchasing Score and Hospital Characteristics." *BMC Health Services Research* 12: 464.

Centers for Medicare & Medicaid Services (CMS). 2024. "The Hospital Value-Based Purchasing (VBP) Program." Modified September 10. www.cms.gov/medicare/quality/value-based-programs/hospital-purchasing.

Devereaux, M. 2022. "Physicians Left Their Jobs by the Hundreds of Thousands in 2021: Report." *Modern Healthcare*. Published October 20. www.modernhealthcare.com/physicians/physicians-left-their-jobs-droves-2021-report.

Japsen, B. 2015. "Value-Based Care Will Drive Aetna's Future Goals." *Forbes*. Published May 15. www.forbes.com/sites/

brucejapsen/2015/05/15/value-based-care-may-drive-aetnabid-for-cigna-or-humana/ (content no longer available).

Johnson, C. 2014. "The Promises and Pitfalls of Healthcare Quality Performance Measures." Published December 29. www.chrisjohnsonmd.com/2014/12/29/the-promises-and-pitfalls-of-healthcare-quality-performance-measures/.

Moore, L. G. 2019. "Are We Collapsing Yet? Over-Measurement Is Part of the Hemorrhage in Healthcare Delivery." *Inside Angle* (blog), 3M. Published August 19. https://insideangle.3m.com/his/blog-post/are-we-collapsing-yet-over-measurement-is-part-of-the-hemorrhage-in-healthcare-delivery/.

Munch, D. 2017. "Why Middle Managers Are the Key to Quality Improvement Success." *Insights* (blog), Institute for Healthcare Improvement. Published November 22. www.ihi.org/insights/why-middle-managers-are-key-quality-improvement-success/.

National Institute for Occupational Safety and Health (NIOSH). 2024. "Health Worker Mental Health." Reviewed May 3. www.cdc.gov/niosh/newsroom/feature/health-worker-mental-health.html.

NRC Health. 2023. *Moving the HCAHPS Needle*. Lincoln, NE: NRC Health.

———. 2019, 2024. *Market Insights Survey of Healthcare Consumers*. Lincoln, NE: NRC Health.

———. 2008, 2016. *Patient Experience Survey*. Lincoln, NE: NRC Health.

Papanicolas, I., J. F. Figueroa, E. J. Orav, and A. K. Jha. 2017. "Patient Hospital Experience Improved Modestly, but No Evidence Medicare Incentives Promoted Meaningful Gains." *Health Affairs* 36 (1): 133–40.

Parker, K., and J. M. Horowitz. 2022. "Majority of Workers Who Quit a Job in 2021 Cite Low Pay, No Opportunities for Advancement, Feeling Disrespected." Pew Research Center. Published March 9. www.pewresearch.org/short-reads/2022/03/09/majority-of-workers-who-quit-a-job-in-2021-cite-low-pay-no-opportunities-for-advancement-feeling-disrespected/.

Penso, J. 2017. "A Health Care Paradox: Measuring and Reporting Quality Has Become a Barrier to Improving It." *StatNews*. Published December 13. www.statnews.com/2017/12/13/health-care-quality/.

Phelps, M. 2022. "COVID Taught Me That I Don't Matter as an ER Doctor: So I Quit." *San Francisco Chronicle*. Published November 21. www.sfchronicle.com/opinion/openforum/article/COVID-doctors-burnout-17589985.php.

Porter, M. E., and E. O. Teisberg. 2006. *Redefining Health Care: Creating Value-Based Competition on Results*. Cambridge, MA: Harvard Business School Press.

Pugh, Michael. 2022. "The Governance Institute Health System Quality Honor Roll 2022." *E-Briefings* 19 (6). https://cdn.ymaws.com/www.governanceinstitute.com/resource/collection/14082583-FA83-45CD-9EFA-D9F250246B38/E-Briefings_V19N5_November_2022.pdf. Published by The Governance Institute.

Quick Leonard Kieffer. 2016. "The Problem with Patient Satisfaction." *QLK* (blog). Published December 11. www.qlksearch.com/blog/problems-with-patient-satisfaction.

Salvatore, D., D. Numerato, and G. Fattore. 2018. "Physicians' Professional Autonomy and Their Organizational Identification with Their Hospital." *BMC Health Services*

Research (18): article no. 775. Published October 12. https://
doi.org/10.1186/s12913-018-3582-z.

Sfantou, D. F., A. Laliotis, A. E. Patelarou, D. Sifaki-Pistolla,
M. Matalliotakis, and E. Patelarou. 2017. "Importance of
Leadership Style Towards Quality of Care Measures in
Healthcare Settings: A Systematic Review." *Healthcare* 5 (4): 73.

SullivanCotter. 2023. *Health Care Management and Executive
Compensation Survey Report.* Chicago: SullivanCotter.

US Bureau of Labor Statistics. 2024. "Injuries, Illnesses, and
Fatalities." Accessed May 29. www.bls.gov/iif/home.htm.

Wachter, R. M. 2016. "How Measurement Fails Doctors and
Teachers." *New York Times.* Published January 16. www.
nytimes.com/2016/01/17/opinion/sunday/how-measurement-
fails-doctors-and-teachers.html.

Zgierska, A., D. Rabago, and M. Miller. 2014. "Impact of Patient
Satisfaction Ratings on Physicians and Clinical Care." *Patient
Preference and Adherence* 8: 437–46.

PART II

Dimensions and Stories

CHAPTER 5

Defining a Conceptual Framework: The Dimensions of Patient-Centered Care

THE FOCUS OF this chapter is the Picker Institute's original eight dimensions of patient-centered care, viewed in the context of consumerism. We want to understand the extent to which these eight dimensions are still relevant to today's patients, and how perceptions of the patient experience have changed over time. We then provide examples of how to apply these dimensions to healthcare in the future.

To review, the eight dimensions of care are as follows (see chapter 1 for the complete definition of each of these dimensions):

1. Respect for patients' values, preferences, and expressed needs
2. Coordination and integration of care
3. Information, communication, and education
4. Physical comfort
5. Emotional support and alleviation of fear and anxiety
6. Involvement of family and friends
7. Continuity and transition
8. Access to care

To assess the continued relevance of these eight dimensions of patient-centered care and the extent to which patients' ratings of their experiences have changed over time, we conducted both qualitative and quantitative research from 2018 through 2019. Both types of research covered the same general topic areas, such as organization of care, communication, courtesy, wait time, trust in hospital staff, emotional support, pain control, the discharge process, and overall impressions about the care received.

STUDY METHODOLOGY

Qualitative Methodology

We conducted qualitative research in three distinct ways. First, focus groups led by a professional moderator were conducted in an online format, with each group composed of eight participants from across the United States. All participants were aged 18 or older and had reported a nonmaternity overnight stay at a hospital in the past 12 months. Participants were recruited in collaboration with an organization that maintains a panel of individuals who have opted to share their thoughts and opinions through periodic surveying and focus group participation. Eligible participants received an e-mail invitation to participate in exchange for a small financial incentive.

The second source of qualitative information was a comparison of comments written on patient experience surveys administered during two time periods. The historical perspective was provided by approximately 11,000 open-ended comments on paper surveys administered after inpatient stays between 2001 and 2005. A more recent perspective was provided by approximately 12,500 open-ended comments on paper surveys administered after inpatient stays in 2016 and 2017. We used natural language processing (NLP) to assign themes and sentiments (positive, negative, neutral) to each comment. NLP is a query-based algorithm that uses key word searches to categorize and summarize large quantities of qualitative feedback. The NLP results were then compared between the historical and recent surveys, and similarities and differences were measured.

The third source of qualitative information was open-ended comments included at the end of a quantitative survey conducted in 2019 in preparation for the first edition of this book (quantitative survey methodology detailed in the next section). Using this format, we were able to assess qualitative feedback from more than 3,000 patients. Various open-ended questions were asked. "If you could do it all over again, what would you change about your actual patient experience?" "Is there anything we haven't asked about? What else is on your mind about your patient experience?" These results were hand coded to summarize the findings and identify trends and themes.

Quantitative Methodology

After the focus groups were conducted and the qualitative historical comparisons were completed, we designed a quantitative survey. The quantitative survey was primarily a replication of Cleary and colleagues' 1993 study, which was one of several studies that informed *Through the Patient's Eyes* (Gerteis et al. 1993). In addition to historical questions fielded to replicate the original study, the survey was informed by the results of our qualitative research, and several more survey questions were designed and included.

In their study, Cleary and colleagues (1993) surveyed 3,076 medical and surgical patients from ten participating hospitals. Interviews were conducted via telephone between February and May 1992. Our replication of that study, conducted between July 26 and July 29, 2019, included responses from a total of 3,004 individuals who reported having a nonmaternity overnight stay at a hospital within the prior 12 months. The sample was nationally representative in terms of distribution across the four major geographical regions of the United States.

Similar to recruitment of the focus group participants, respondents to the 2019 quantitative survey were recruited in partnership with a panel provider. Respondents received an e-mail invitation to participate in the online survey in exchange for a small financial incentive.

RESULTS

Qualitative Results

Several common themes arose from the three sources of qualitative information (focus groups, comments written on historical and recent patient experience surveys, and open-ended comments included on the 2019 quantitative survey). Most prominent among the dimensions of patient-centered care were access to care (especially wait time), emotional support, and physical comfort.

Participants in the focus groups confirmed that the needs and desires of patients today are in line with those of patients outlined by Gerteis and colleagues in *Through the Patient's Eyes*. While medical and information technology have advanced since publication of that book, our findings suggest that not much has changed in terms of what is important to patients. According to participants in our focus groups, access to care and emotional support are crucially important to the patient experience and largely determine whether an experience is positive or negative. Although the dialogue included elements of the other dimensions of care, these two concepts were discussed most frequently.

The open-ended comments on the 2019 survey corroborated the focus group findings. When asked about their recent hospital experience, most respondents commented about access to care; information, communication, and education; emotional support; respect for patient preferences; and physical comfort. One interesting finding was a preponderance of patients who indicated that they wished they had advocated more for themselves while in the hospital and undergoing treatment. Respondents indicated that if they had to do it over again, they would "be more assertive," "speak up for myself," and "advocate for myself," and they wouldn't "blindly agree to what [providers] say." These comments speak to the continued importance of the dimensions of respect for patients' values, preferences, and expressed needs and of information, communication, and education.

Our comparison of comments on historical (between 2001 and 2005) and recent (2016 and 2017) patient experience surveys not only confirmed the continued importance of the eight dimensions of patient-centered care but also allowed us to understand how the relative importance of the dimensions may have evolved over time. Emotional support and physical comfort were the topics discussed most frequently on the historical and recent surveys. The distribution of comments across the dimensions was remarkably stable in the two study periods. However, as shown in exhibit 5.1, patient feedback categorized as emotional support and respect for patient values increased slightly over time, while feedback categorized as physical comfort and access to care decreased slightly.

Some excerpts from the qualitative feedback include the following:

> "I did feel like I had to wait a long time to go to my room and they never explained to me why."

> "I felt very trusting of the doctors because of the way they spoke and treated me like they really cared."

> "The staff was slow, taking hours to give me the medication needed or said they already gave it to me when they didn't. They were never on the same page of what was going on. The hospital was constantly noisy, so I could never sleep between the pain and the noise. They never even gave me enough medicine to handle my pain and take the edge off. They never

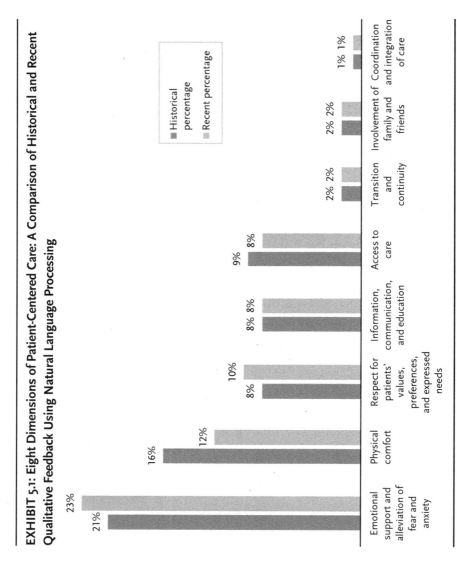

EXHIBIT 5.1: Eight Dimensions of Patient-Centered Care: A Comparison of Historical and Recent Qualitative Feedback Using Natural Language Processing

Historical percentage
Recent percentage

Dimension	Historical	Recent
Emotional support and alleviation of fear and anxiety	21%	23%
Physical comfort	16%	12%
Respect for patients' values, preferences, and expressed needs	8%	10%
Information, communication, and education	8%	8%
Access to care	9%	8%
Transition and continuity	2%	2%
Involvement of family and friends	2%	2%
Coordination and integration of care	1%	1%

Source: NRC Health (2019).

offered to help me get out of bed. I couldn't go for walks outside when I was healing and instead had to try to walk in the busy hallways instead of going at my own pace. They didn't explain much of anything."

"They talked to me while they were taking my information down but ignored me after they left."

"I was given different information from the doctor on duty at night than from the doctor I saw in the day."

"I feel doctors decide on tests and then only reluctantly listen to patients."

"I needed more communication during the stay as I did feel at times very lost about what was going on and what was next."

"I wish family members could stay overnight and until you are released from the hospital."

"I think follow-up is vital and the hospital totally dropped the ball in coordinating my after-surgery care needs."

"I just want to feel like a valued customer."

Looking at the cumulative results of the qualitative research, we find that the eight dimensions of patient-centered care are as relevant and accurate today as they were 30 years ago. All the dimensions were represented in all forms of patient feedback, indicating that the patient experience is still rooted in and measured by these eight basic needs. Moreover, these qualitative results were confirmed by the quantitative findings.

Quantitative Results

The purpose of the quantitative research was to determine whether perceptions of the patient experience have changed since publication of the study by Cleary and colleagues (1993). To accomplish this objective, we compared the results of the 2019 study with those of the 1993 study.

Cleary and colleagues presented their results in the form of "problem scores," meaning that scores represent the percentage of respondents who selected the least optimal (most negative) response option or set of response options. We applied this method to our analysis of the 2019 results to enable comparison. Problem scoring can be useful for quality improvement efforts because it creates a sense of urgency by highlighting areas for improvement. Since the publication of Cleary and colleagues' 1993 article, however, the industry has largely moved away from problem scoring in favor of "positive scoring" (the percentage of respondents who selected the most optimal response) because of its alignment with the Consumer Assessment of Healthcare Providers and Systems (CAHPS) initiatives as well as its ease of use.

It is important to note that the information from the 1993 study was gathered via telephone interviews, whereas the 2019 study was fielded via an online survey. Research has shown that survey modes can impact results (Centers for Medicare & Medicaid Services [CMS] 2008) and that web-based responses tend to be slightly less favorable than those gathered via telephone interviews (Keeter 2015). Additionally, whereas the original research was conducted with patients who had been recently discharged from one of ten US hospitals, the 2019 study was conducted with panel participants who self-reported a recent hospitalization. Because of these differences in both mode and population, results derived from direct comparisons of scores should be interpreted with caution.

Based on these differences in study methodology, it is not surprising that the 2019 scores tended to be less favorable than the 1993 scores. The average problem score in the 1993 study was 11 percent, while the average problem score across the same items in the 2019 study was 16 percent, indicating that the percentage of patients reporting negative experiences had increased by 5 percentage points on average. If, however, the change in scores over time could be attributed solely to methodological differences, we would expect to see similar changes in each item score (i.e., a change of approximately 5 percentage points for all items). However, the results show that the magnitude of the change over time differs across items and dimensions. These findings suggest that there may be meaningful differences unrelated to methodological effects.

The largest item-level changes (10 percentage points or more) are listed in exhibit 5.2. Note that all represent more negative experiences over time except for one item in the dimension of Continuity and Transition: "No one on hospital staff told patient when she could resume usual activities, such as when to go back to work." Scores for this item improved over time (the problem score decreased from 29 to 18 percent). The items with the largest changes are part of the following dimensions: physical comfort (three items); coordination of care (two items); emotional support and alleviation of fear and anxiety (two items); respect for patient's values, preferences, and needs (one item); continuity and transition (one item); and information, communication and education (one item). Historical and current item scores are listed in exhibit 5.2.

EXHIBIT 5.2: A Comparison of Historical and Recent Quantitative Feedback, by Dimension Level

Dimension	Item	Historical problem score	Recent problem score	Change over time
Physical comfort	Patient waited more than 15 minutes, on average, after requesting pain medication.	7%	41%	34%
Physical comfort	Patient felt much of his pain could have been eliminated if hospital staff had acted more promptly.	8%	37%	29%

(continued)

Dimension	Item	Historical problem score	Recent problem score	Change over time
Emotional support and alleviation of fear and anxiety	Patient did not get as much help as she would have liked with questions about hospital bill.	2%	31%	29%
Coordination of care	Physician and nurse have conflicting responses to patient's questions.	16%	36%	20%
Physical comfort	Patient waited more than 15 minutes, on average, for help after using call button.	5%	23%	18%
Information, communication, and education	Patient felt physician/ nurse was withholding information.	7%	24%	17%
Respect for patient's values, preferences, and needs	Physicians or nurses sometimes talked in front of patient as if he wasn't there.	9%	25%	16%
Emotional support and alleviation of fear and anxiety	Patient did not get desired help from hospital staff in figuring out how to pay his hospital bill.	19%	33%	14%
Coordination of care	Scheduled tests and procedures usually or always delayed.	4%	14%	10%
Continuity and transition	No one on hospital staff told patient when she could resume usual activities, such as when to go back to work.	29%	18%	−11%

Sources: Data from Cleary et al. (1993); NRC Health (2019).

Next, we calculated dimension scores by taking the mean of the item scores within each dimension. At the dimension level, we can see that the largest difference between the current and historical scores is in the physical comfort dimension (problem score increased from 12 to 27 percent, indicating more negative experiences over time), followed by coordination of care, emotional support, and respect for patient values (exhibit 5.3).

Although we expected to find differences between the historical and current problem scores (with less favorable scores in the 2019 study resulting from methodological factors), some differences exceeded that which we could reasonably attribute to methodology. Those items primarily related to physical comfort, coordination of care, emotional support, and respect for patient values. These results indicate that despite decades of work, improvements in the patient experience are small at best, and, in some cases, patients' care experience seems to be getting worse.

HOW PICKER DIMENSIONS SUFFERED DURING COVID

For this second edition of the book, we looked at the dimensions of patient-centered care that were paused or diminished (intentionally or not) during the COVID-19 pandemic and how that impacted patient experience and HCAHPS scores. In terms of scores, national publicly reported data indicate that the pandemic set HCAHPS back almost ten years (CMS 2023). Looking at the benchmark data for HCAHPS surveys administered by NRC Health tells a similar story: the average overall rating in 2022 (71 percent) is at a level not seen since 2014.

A cohort study of HCAHPS-participating hospitals found that patient experience scores declined from 2020 to 2021 by as much as 5.6 percentage points (Elliott et al. 2023). The most affected measures from this study were staff responsiveness and cleanliness, possibly reflecting high illness-associated hospital

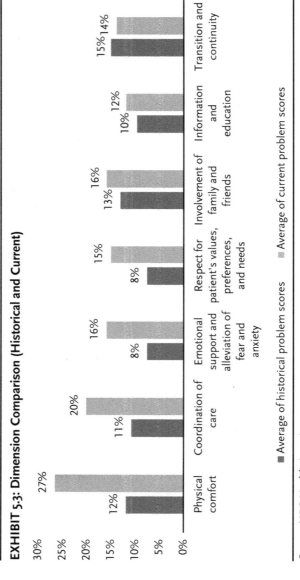

EXHIBIT 5.3: Dimension Comparison (Historical and Current)

Physical comfort: 27% / 12%
Coordination of care: 20% / 11%
Emotional support and alleviation of fear and anxiety: 16% / 8%
Respect for patient's values, preferences, and needs: 15% / 8%
Involvement of family and friends: 16% / 13%
Information and education: 12% / 10%
Transition and continuity: 15% / 14%

■ Average of historical problem scores   ■ Average of current problem scores

Source: NRC Health (2019).

workforce absenteeism. Staff responsiveness and delays in services impacted several dimensions of care, from respecting patients' expressed needs to coordination and integration of care, physical comfort, and continuity and transition. It is important to note that several of these dimensions also translate directly to negative patient safety events, which also increased during the pandemic (Muoio 2022). Patients suffering from long COVID have reported being dissatisfied with their healthcare teams. Negative effects have included social distancing, disruptions to care, difficulties accessing healthcare services, anxiety, loneliness, and worries about their own family members' health (Baránková et al. 2022; Neyra 2023).

The third dimension—information, communication, and education—was impacted as well. For COVID patients requiring direct care in US hospitals, communication with patients and nurses suffered, as did patient education (Drapeaux, Jenson, and Fustino 2021; Muoio 2022). However, in the sole positive example from our many COVID lessons, hospitals and health systems across the country excelled in more broadly communicating to and educating their communities about how to access vaccines and testing, and the importance and efficacy of each. On this front, hospitals and health systems effectively stepped up to amplify public health messages and were integral in accelerating vaccination rates in many places across the US (Ellis 2021; Fiks, Nekrasova, and Hambridge 2021; French 2022; Irvin et al. 2023).

The eighth dimension, access to care, was impacted across all patients and service lines as people were told to "stay home" and not to seek care unless absolutely necessary. Telehealth expansion alleviated this issue to a significant degree, but not in the first few months, and as we have discussed previously, some patients in rural and underserved communities were never able to access telehealth. Americans today are still recovering from delays in care (for example, long-term postponement of planned surgeries), and we have documented "COVID-related" deaths of people who did not access care when they should have because of their fear of contracting COVID (Byrnes et al. 2021). Appointment availability is still problematic across much of the US. More generally, access to care varies widely, from less than 5 percent in some zip codes to more than 70 percent in others. The top differentiators related to access are insurance coverage, location, and appointment availability, much more so than cost or system affiliation (NRC Health 2022).

The most significant impacts fell on the fifth and sixth dimensions: emotional support and alleviation of fear and anxiety, and involvement of family and friends. Before vaccines were widely available, COVID patients were isolated, and their families and friends were not allowed to come to the hospital. The human interactions these patients experienced were with physicians and nurses in sometimes alien-looking outfits—multiple layers of personal protective equipment, faces covered, and hands encased in gloves and more gloves. The "healing of hands" was virtually impossible, much less the ability to make meaningful eye contact with patients. These documented feelings of isolation and the need to self-cope impacted patients' ability to heal (Elliott et al. 2023). The most significant fallout of this period occurred in the tragic form of the patients who died alone, unable to say goodbye to their loved ones.

Two key points are critical to mention at this stage. First, we must not forget the significant strain the pandemic placed on healthcare workers. Caregiver burnout is directly connected to a diminished patient experience as well as negative safety outcomes (Mazer 2021). Therefore, in large measure our solution to deliver a more consumer-centric healthcare experience needs to include making the giving of care a better experience for our caregivers (we will discuss this more in chapter 8). Second, the impacts of COVID on the Picker dimensions serve as the most recent and real-life indicators that Harvey Picker's research and these dimensions of patient-centered care continue to matter to patients today and are integral, more than ever before, in our ability to deliver high-quality, effective healthcare.

STUDY CONCLUSIONS

Evidence from both the qualitative and quantitative studies suggests that the eight dimensions of patient-centered care, developed more than 30 years ago, remain relevant despite the myriad changes that have occurred in healthcare. The qualitative research shows that when given an open forum, patients continue to provide feedback that spans all eight dimensions. However, no evidence of new dimensions was found in the qualitative data. Technology was more often a topic of current feedback than of historical feedback, but rather than manifesting as an additional dimension, it was a common thread throughout all eight dimensions. Many incredible advancements in healthcare-related technology have taken place in recent years: telehealth, the ability to book appointments online, healthcare-related smartphone apps, electronic medical records, robotic medicine. These advancements have created many benefits and led to challenges for patients, and they are tied in their own ways to each dimension. For example, telehealth has led to improvements in access to care as many patients are now able to reach their care providers virtually. On the other hand, one challenge in the area of emotional support is the feeling of being ignored as providers type seemingly endless notes into their computers.

Further evidence of the relevance of the eight dimensions can be found in the way in which the patient experience is measured today. Real-time patient feedback often is obtained immediately following a healthcare visit by means of automated Interactive Voice Response calls or online surveys. Few patients are now willing to fill out long-form paper surveys received via regular postal mail. With this evolution in feedback behavior and newer modes of information collection, the questions asked of patients have needed to change. Fewer, shorter, and more targeted questions are asked to minimize dropouts and maximize responses.

NRC Health partners with hospitals and healthcare systems to collect feedback from their patients using its dynamic Experience

Platform. While healthcare organizations leveraging this solution have ultimate flexibility in the questions they choose to ask patients, NRC Health offers a standard set of questions per care setting, based on decades of research and expertise in the area of patient experience. These recommended questions are rooted in the rich heritage of the eight dimensions but streamlined and modernized for the needs and wants of patients and healthcare organizations in today's consumer-centric world. NRC Health used correlation analyses to discover the topics most important to patients and, in turn, identify the key driver of patient loyalty in each dimension. Simple, targeted question-and-response text was then developed, with simplicity and clarity a top priority. Decades of patient data show the statistical relationship of the eight dimensions with patient loyalty, which is further evidence of their continued relevance.

Healthcare organizations partnering with NRC Health can opt to use the standard set of questions or devise their own questions based on their needs and what they deem most important to their patients. Since 2019, approximately 84 percent of healthcare organizations have opted to use part or all of the standard set of dimension-based questions, suggesting that they, too, believe that these are the most important aspects of the patient experience.

DEFINING THE EIGHT DIMENSIONS OF PATIENT-CENTERED CARE THROUGH THE EYES OF THE CONSUMER

We now understand that the dimensions established 30 years ago remain relevant today. The importance of each dimension has not changed, but how organizations are performing against them has (i.e., patient ratings have largely become more negative over time). When we look at each of the dimensions from a consumer perspective, it becomes clear that there are specific things healthcare organizations can do to ensure that they are meeting the needs of their consumers.

1. Respect for Patients' Values, Preferences, and Expressed Needs

Patients want to be informed regarding their medical conditions and involved in decision-making. They indicate that they want hospital staff to recognize and treat them as *individuals*, as noted earlier. To help meet these needs, healthcare leaders should think of population health from a consumer's perspective—patients are looking at your organization's involvement in their lives long before they enter its four walls. In response, some organizations provide on-site food, pharmacies, grocery stores, and cooking classes to remedy food desert conditions in their communities; others offer a gym and wellness programs. Consumers also want to know that they, their families, their values, and their culture will be respected when they are ill. Convey to patients that your organization is committed to helping them, as unique individuals with unique families, values, and cultures, live their fullest lives by getting them back to where they were before their illness (or as close as possible) through improved wellness-focused offerings. They will reward you greatly: NRC Health's research on human understanding (discussed in more detail in chapter 7) shows that people who feel as though they are treated uniquely as an individual are significantly more likely to rate an organization's overall image or reputation as "excellent."

2. Coordination and Integration of Care

People feel vulnerable and powerless in the face of illness, but proper coordination of care can ease these feelings and help patients navigate the often confusing healthcare system. To achieve better coordination, providers need to consider every interaction with consumers and keep in mind that they want to be treated as unique individuals. Organizing support groups for patients who have similar conditions is one way to accomplish this; such groups enable patients to attain a feeling of connected-ness. Going one step further and having a physician or nurse lead these groups allows patients to connect with their care providers, which is another deep-seated consumer desire. The desire for connection is even stronger as consumers emerge from COVID and long for a clear, coordinated re-introduction into the world of healthcare.

3. Information, Communication, and Education

In considering a healthcare system, consumers look for information transparency. Information alone is not enough, and as we discussed in chapter 3, too much information can be a serious detriment to consumers. Seventy-seven percent begin their healthcare search online, and when consumers search for something online, they are looking for specific information: (1) a convenient way to pay their bill and (2) provider ratings and reviews. Forty-six percent of consumers read online reviews before scheduling an appointment; one in three say that doing so is their first step in searching for a new provider; and 72 percent trust online reviews as much as a personal recommendation (NRC Health 2020). To help consumers find what they are looking for, providers can offer an easy-to-access website with transparent information. When consumers search for online reviews and don't find any, they often feel as though the organization is hiding something, which ties in to patients' often expressed fear that information is being withheld from them or they're not being completely informed about their condition or prognosis.

4. Physical Comfort

As noted earlier, patients' level of physical comfort has a tremendous impact on their care experience. Consumers are looking for a place they know will make them and their families comfortable; they like to see new, clean hospital facilities. Even when a new building is not an option, however, patients' needs for physical comfort can still be met by providing amenities such as additional privacy, comfier beds, shower supplies, and access to respite rooms so patients and their families can be made comfortable within the four walls of the organization. Also consider that prior to the pandemic, many consumers had no idea about their level of risk of acquiring an infection inside the hospital and now may be warier of this risk.

5. Emotional Support and Alleviation of Fear and Anxiety

Consumers with high-deductible health plans are becoming the largest payer in healthcare, second only to CMS. Accordingly, they are fearful not only about what could be wrong with them and how physically debilitating it might be but also about whether it will debilitate them financially. Unsure of the cost of care and whether they will be able to cover it, one-quarter of consumers are still delaying necessary care (NRC Health 2024b). The healthcare future these consumers are demanding involves greater price transparency. They understand that there might be price ranges rather than an exact price, but having a general idea of the cost of care would help ease their fears. Barcode scanners, which some hospitals use to keep track of medications and services, also can create stress if there is little or no communication about the scanner's purpose. Providers need to communicate with patients and explain how measures such as these are meant to ensure that the right care is being given to the right patient. Even a heightened focus on the most basic communication about what will happen next and when can have a huge, positive effect on alleviating patients' fear and anxiety during their hospital stay.

Emotional support also means understanding health that isn't often visible: mental health. The US is engulfed in a mental and behavioral health crisis, made worse by COVID. According to NRC Health (2024a) HCAHPS figures, the proportion of people who reported "excellent" or "very good" mental health dipped from 65 percent in 2013 to 60 percent in 2023. Depression in healthcare workers has also increased since the pandemic, as reported by the Centers for Disease Control and Prevention (CDC 2023). A greater commitment to emotional well-being is necessary to reverse the mental health crisis, one patient at a time.

6. Involvement of Family and Friends

Consumers involve family and friends from the beginning of their care selection process. As noted earlier, they look for patient ratings and reviews, and these include recommendations from family members and friends. Patients also heal more quickly when family and friends are involved in their treatment, so the more that healthcare organizations can accommodate loved ones, the better the healing environment will be. Providers need to allow family members and friends to spend time with the patient and help them find appropriate ways to advocate for and support their loved one. Those family members and friends designated by the patient as caregivers should be included in clinician-led patient discussions; they also should be kept well informed about the patient's condition and what to expect after discharge.

7. Continuity and Transition

Consumers want to be sure that if they are admitted to a hospital, they will be able to return home as soon as possible. They want to recover completely and are often nervous that if they go to the hospital, they won't come home or won't know what to do when they go home. Only about half of discharged patients report top marks on the HCAHPS transitional care dimensions, and NRC

Health research shows only four in ten discharged patients receive a follow-up call after departing a facility (NRC Health 2023). Contacting patients once they are home instills confidence and ensures the ability to administer self-care, which has demonstrated significant improvements in outcomes.

Accordingly, the more information made available online and outside the actual care environment (e.g., discharge instructions, follow-up appointments needed), the better. In addition to being educated about various conditions, consumers love to see evidence of the hospital's focus on wellness, such as recipes and organized support groups for individuals with their conditions. When these types of "off campus" resources are made available to patients, they will be less nervous about their diagnosis or about receiving care "on campus."

8. Access to Care

When most healthcare leaders think of access, they think of wait times in their hospital or visitors' ability to park at and navigate the hospital campus. In their minds, they likely see their own buildings, intake systems, and throughput dashboards. When consumers think of access, they see a screen. As discussed in chapter 2, first steps are often first clicks as consumers peruse hospital and health system websites to find care. They mean business, as "how to find a physician" and "patient ratings/reviews of doctors" rank as the top two useful pieces of information on a website (NRC Health 2023). Convenient access is a particularly strong competitive separator: Convenient locations, easy access, and proximity are the top differentiators cited by consumers when asked what sets one healthcare brand apart from the rest, slightly outpacing insurance acceptance, compassionate care, use of advanced technology, and other important attributes (NRC Health 2024b). Consumers are open—even looking forward—to new care opportunities and settings. As mentioned in chapter 1, consumers have come around on receiving care in retail settings because of convenience, but they are even more interested if these settings are convenient *and* connected: three in four are excited to use urgent care while two in three are excited about the opportunity to use a retail clinic or office in the future, if offered by a hospital or health system they know and prefer (NRC Health 2024b). Does this mean they no longer desire to be seen at the doctor's office or in a more traditional setting? Not necessarily, but the bottleneck has become unbearable. Coming out of COVID, and in an industry of constricted resources and workforce, not having to wait months to receive care is becoming an increasing luxury for many consumers and only underpins the importance of timely and convenient access. Simply getting an appointment is vital to the entire care journey: when NRC Health asked recent patients when they considered their most recent journey of care to truly begin, "making an appointment with my doctor" was the most popular answer (NRC Health 2023). Internal customers, such as the physicians on the other end of that appointment, like being able to show ratings and reviews to patients when making a referral. When it comes to being guided by fast and reliable data, physicians and their patients are not all that different.

To better understand what is most important to consumers, providers have to ask the right questions at the right time. LaVela and Gallan (2014) found that the mode, timing, and frequency of feedback solicitation can influence survey scores. We found that e-mail was the optimal modality (55 percent of patients preferred this mode, more than five times the percentage who preferred postal mail [10 percent] or telephone calls [11 percent]). Regarding timing, consumers want to provide feedback on a regular basis: four in ten stated their preference to give feedback after every episode of care—but consumers also want surveys to become available quickly: 25 percent would prefer to give feedback either during the event or a few minutes after, 15 percent would prefer to give feedback within just a few hours, 28 percent (the most common answer) would prefer to give feedback a few days after the event, and only 7 percent preferred to wait a few weeks (akin to the typical CAHPS survey timeline); further, it should be noted that 25 percent did not wish to provide feedback (NRC Health 2024b). For the majority of consumers who do, however, healthcare is woefully slow in soliciting and receiving their feedback.

Chapter 6 examines how top-performing healthcare organizations across the United States are using the eight dimensions to create a consumer-centric culture.

REFERENCES

Baránková, M., K. Greškovičová, B. Strnádelová, K. Krizova, and J. Halamová. 2022. "Let Us Take It into Our Own Hands: Patient Experience During the COVID-19 Pandemic." *International Journal of Environmental Research and Public Health* 19 (21): 14150. Published October 29. https://doi.org/10.3390/ijerph192114150.

Byrnes, M. E., C. S. Brown, A. C. DeRoo, M. A. Corriere, M. A. Romano, S. Fukuhara, K. M. Kim, and N. H. Osborne. 2021. "Elective Surgical Delays Due to COVID-19: The Patient Lived Experience." *Journal of Medical Care* 59 (4): 288–94. www.ncbi.nlm.nih.gov/pmc/articles/PMC8132560/.

Centers for Disease Control and Prevention (CDC). 2023. "Health Workers Face a Mental Health Crisis: Workers Report Harassment, Burnout, and Poor Mental Health; Supportive Workplaces Can Help." Updated October 23. www.cdc.gov/vitalsigns/health-worker-mental-health/index.html.

Centers for Medicare & Medicaid Services (CMS). 2023. "Publicly-Reported HCAHPS Top-Box Scores, December 2008 to April 2023." In HCAHPS Update Training. Published March 2023. www.hcahpsonline.org/globalassets/hcahps/training-materials/2023-hcahps-update-training-slides.pdf.

————. 2008. "Mode and Patient-Mix Adjustment of the CAHPS Hospital Survey (HCAHPS)." Published April 30. https://hcahpsonline.org/globalassets/hcahps/mode-patient-mix-adjustment/final-draft-description-of-hcahps-mode-and-pma-with-bottom-box modedoc-april-30-2008.pdf (content no longer available).

Cleary, P. D., S. Edgman-Levitan, J. D. Walker, and M. Gerteis. 1993. "Using Patient Reports to Improve Medical Care: A Preliminary Report from 10 Hospitals." *Quality Management in Healthcare* 2 (1): 31–38.

Drapeaux, A., J. A. Jenson, and N. Fustino. 2021. "The Impact of COVID-19 on Patient Experience Within a Midwest Hospital System: A Case Study." *Journal of Patient Experience*. Published December 8. https://doi.org/10.1177/23743735211065298.

Elliott, M. N., M. K. Beckett, C. W. Cohea, W. G. Lehrman, P. D. Cleary, L. A. Giordano, C. Russ, E. H. Goldstein, and L. A. Fleisher. 2023. "Changes in Patient Experiences of Hospital Care During the COVID-19 Pandemic." *JAMA Health Forum* 4 (8):e232766. https://jamanetwork.com/journals/jama-health-forum/fullarticle/2808746.

Ellis, L. 2021. "Developing Learning Health Systems to Navigate the COVID-19 Pandemic." Harvard Medical School. Published March 12. https://postgraduateeducation.hms.harvard.edu/trends-medicine/developing-learning-health-systems-navigate-covid-19-pandemic.

Fiks, A., E. Nekrasova, and S. Hambridge. 2021. "Health Systems as a Catalyst for Immunization Delivery." *Academic Pediatrics* 21 (4): S40–S47. www.academicpedsjnl.net/article/S1876-2859(21)00049-8/fulltext.

French, D. 2022. "What COVID-19 Continues to Teach Us about Hospital Culture." Health Care Innovation Blog, American

Hospital Association. Published August 11. www.aha.org/news/
healthcareinnovation-thursday-blog/2022-08-11-what-covid-19-
continues-teach-us-about-hospital.

Gerteis, M., S. Edgman-Levitan, J. Daley, and T. L. Delbanco (eds.).
1993. *Through the Patient's Eyes: Understanding and Promoting
Patient-Centered Care.* San Francisco: Jossey-Bass.

Irvin, R., M. Venkataramani, P. Galiatsatos, J. D. Hitchcock, N.
Hemphill, M. Dearey, B. F. Bigelow, L. A. Cooper, N. Edwards
Mollelo, K. J. O'Conor, K. R. Page, and S. H. Golden. 2023. "A
Path Forward: COVID-19 Vaccine Equity Community Education
and Outreach Initiative." *Health Security* 21 (2): 85–94. www.
ncbi.nlm.nih.gov/pmc/articles/PMC10079247/.

Keeter, S. 2015. "From Telephone to the Web: The Challenge
of Mode of Interview Effects in Public Opinion Polls." Pew
Research Center. Published May 13. www.pewresearch.org/
methods/2015/05/13/from-telephone-to-the-web-the-challenge-
of-mode-of-interview-effects-in-public-opinion-polls/.

LaVela, S. L., and A. S. Gallan. 2014. "Evaluation and Measurement
of Patient Experience." *Patient Experience Journal* 1 (1): 28–36.

Mazer, S. 2021. "Nurse Burnout and the Patient Experience: The
COVID Crush." *Susan E. Mazer, Ph.D. Blog*, Healing Healthcare
Systems. Published October 1. www.healinghealth.com/
nurse-burnout-and-the-patient-experience-the-covid-crush/.

Muoio, D. 2022. "Leapfrog Group: Patients Report Worse
Hospital Experiences During COVID-19 Pandemic, Raising
Safety Concerns." *Fierce Healthcare.* Published May 10. www.
fiercehealthcare.com/providers/leapfrog-group-patients-are-
reporting-more-potentially-dangerous-hospital-experiences.

Neyra, R. 2023. "The Quiet Decline: Understanding the
Diminished Patient Experience During COVID-19." *Billed Right*

(blog). Published August 29. https://billedright.com/blog/
understanding-the-diminished-patient-experience-during-
covid-19/.

NRC Health. 2024a. Data from HCAHPS surveys administered by
NRC Health.

———. 2022. "A Close Look at Access to Care." *nSight*. Published
December 8. https://nrchealth.com/resource/a-close-look-
at-access-to-care/.

———.2020, 2023, 2024b. *Market Insights Surveys of Healthcare
Consumers*. Lincoln, NE: NRC Health.

———. 2019. Unpublished quantitative survey data.

Best Practices: Case Studies of Dimensions in Action

THE TERM *consumerism* in healthcare is gaining traction. Most organizations are measuring the patient experience to better understand what they can do to improve that experience within the four walls of the organization. Organizations are also focusing on how to attract more patients or consumers to their facilities. What makes the top organizations in the country unique? Why do consumers choose a particular healthcare organization over others that may be closer to home? How are the top organizations implementing the eight dimensions of patient-centered care to create a better patient and consumer experience? This chapter provides answers to these questions from nine high-performing hospitals and health systems across the United States.

The leaders of these organizations share insights on how they are differentiating themselves regarding the consumer experience and how they know they are improving. These leaders understand they have an obligation to be diligent stewards of quality and patient experience, and they ensure that what they ask their staff to do to make improvements aligns with what matters most to their organization and the people involved (consumers, caregivers, staff, and patients). These leaders invest time with their executive teams, organizing their teams' work around what they are trying to accomplish. They then look at key results to demonstrate that they are in fact moving the needle. As these stories illustrate, these organizations are not at the top because of measurement alone; they are at the top in their consumers' eyes because they have provided those consumers with a seat at the table.

The nine case examples that follow are presented in terms of how they address some of the eight dimensions of patient-centered care that were introduced by Harvey Picker and discussed in chapter 1.

LUMINIS HEALTH ANNE ARUNDEL MEDICAL CENTER

Note: This case example was adapted from Perkins (2022).

Picker Dimensions: Involvement of family and friends; emotional support and alleviation of fear and anxiety; respect for patients' values, preferences, and expressed needs; information, communication, and education

Luminis Health Anne Arundel Medical Center has embraced full 24/7 access for patients' families since 2010. The COVID-19–related visitor restrictions were disruptive and harmful to the medical center's patients. In response, a collaboration with the Institute for Patient- and Family-Centered Care (IPFCC) enabled the medical center to adopt processes to facilitate the integration of patient, family, and community partners in the planning and decision-making to reaffirm and reestablish a patient's family as partners—not visitors—during and after the COVID-19 pandemic.

Building on a long history and culture of caring, in 2010 the medical center formally oriented its practice to patient- and family-centered care (PFCC) models. PFCC concepts include respect and dignity, information sharing, participation, and collaboration. The 120-year-old, 453-bed regional health system in

Annapolis, Maryland, with its Magnet-designated teaching hospital known for excellent care in surgery, obstetrics, orthopedics, oncology, and behavioral health, was an early leader in the IPFCC Better Together: Partnering with Families program.

Involvement of Family and Friends; Alleviating Fear and Anxiety

The 2010 work at Anne Arundel began with patient and family advisers (PFAs), initiation of a patient family advisory council (PFAC), and elimination of visiting restrictions. The goal of patient and family advisers is to systematically engage with leaders and staff and hold a mirror to the organization. This work expanded to specialty patient family advisory councils (PFACs) with focus on women and children, behavioral health, emergency care, cancer care, and partnership with the medical center's Latino community. At times, the work has been driven through appreciative inquiry and building on what is working well. Other work has been driven from a problem orientation and seeking to address concerns.

This partnership and family presence is shown to improve many aspects of care experience, safety, and quality (Lamas 2020). The key practice is recognizing family members as partners, rather than visitors or external members in care. Lack of family presence contributes to patient and family harm and caregiver distress. Family presence is linked to reductions in falls, infections, readmissions, excess utilization, care inequities, and caregiver distress, as well as improvement in patient experience and access. Improvements in these constructs align with the seminal STEEEP definition of quality: safe, timely, effective, efficient, equitable, and patient-centered (Institute of Medicine 2001).

With this more than ten-year journey and noted benefits, the abrupt and volatile COVID-19–driven changes in family presence were deeply felt in the hospital. Research studies have demonstrated the negative impact of these policies on rates of delirium and sedation, ICU length of stay, falls, and psychological trauma and moral distress (Gandhi 2022; Valley et al. 2020). Anne Arundel leaders determined the need for a systematic approach to welcome families back to the hospital during COVID (as soon as it was determined to be safe to do so). Their approach was grounded in PFCC principles and a bioethical decision-making model (Dokken, Johnson, and Markwell 2021). The team was led by the hospital president and composed of direct care providers and community members. Lessons learned included recommitment to family presence as evidence-based and inherent to the organizational values and culture; a renewed understanding of the harm to patients, families, and care teams with limited family presence; and the need for a systematic and sustainable approach to drive family presence improvements. Staff, clinicians, and leaders continue to apply this systematic framework to advance their family presence practices.

"Nothing About Me Without Me": Respect for Patients' Values, Preferences, and Expressed Needs; Information, Communication, and Education

The key difference in patient- and family-centered care models is that care is organized through the principles of respect and dignity, information sharing, participation, and collaboration. This partnership yields work focused on "nothing about me without me" and caring "with" and not simply "for or to" (Barry and Edgman-Levitan 2012). Care practices include open family presence or visiting hours, bedside shift reports, and access to electronic medical records.

More important, this model is supported by a foundation that begins with governance practices at the board level that drive leadership structures and processes. At Anne Arundel, the PFACs advise the board and senior leaders on how to make improvements to the model. PFAs have essential roles in work such as medical and nursing staff peer review, root cause analyses, daily safety huddles, COVID-19 incident command structure, quality councils and board committees, approaches to reducing workplace violence and injury, executive job interviews, review of web design and educational materials, hospital bill readability and transparency, patient education material, marketing and website content, well-being strategies, and way-finding content and placement.

The expectations of executives, medical staff leaders, and board members include a commitment to PFCC principles and ensuring accountability of operational leaders to implement practices and achieve results. One fundamental element of success is the very clear and transparent support of leadership as changes have been implemented. Essential to this work was the connectivity of PFAs with board members. The organization's governance structure ensures expectations for PFCC and reporting by PFAs as members at the system-level, seniormost governance quality committee.

In addition, this organization strives to lead on topics of anti-racism and demonstrate their commitment to diversity, equity, inclusion, and justice. The Latino PFAC arose early in the pandemic from a community concern with family access and language barriers during the most limiting phase of family presence. When family members are present, even with a language barrier, rapport is built, care is witnessed, and trust and partnership grow. This same opportunity doesn't exist without family presence. The PFAC acknowledged this gap for family presence and the potential for disparate processes. The yield was strong, with a multi-pronged effort driven through the Latino PFAC; changes included improved interpretation, signage, care planning participation, and financial counseling.

Early in the pandemic when family presence was removed, there was an appreciated ability to just focus on the patient in the midst of such uncertainty. This approach, however, was soon followed by recognition of the clinical harms and caregiver distress generated by lack of family presence. A continued focus has been on team well-being and infection prevention, but with additional focus on support informed by trauma-informed leadership principles (Koloroutis and Pole 2021; Sherman 2021).

Community Impact

This PFCC journey and COVID response have resulted in the engagement of community members beyond patients and families, to the benefit of the organization, patients, families, and communities. In a most poignant example, a longtime community leader, the senior pastor in a church with majority African-American membership, became a key partner in the medical center's COVID-19 response. She remains engaged in the community and serves as a trusted adviser. She was an early voice for COVID-19 vaccination and was recruited to be part of the medical center's recommitment to family presence. The pastor was instrumental in eliciting parishioner input and raising awareness on potential racial disparities related to family presence. She later became a board member. She describes her critical functions as being where the people are, listening to community members and connecting with management, and acknowledging the contribution of "outsideness" she brings with her perspective.

This example and the family presence work being done at Luminis Health Anne Arundel Medical Center demonstrate the importance of developing human understanding, which is achieved when the organization has gained the ability to treat every patient as an individual. The leaders there believe strongly that the more work they do in this area, the better they will be able to connect this work with higher-quality care and improved outcomes.

MASS GENERAL BRIGHAM

Note: This case example was adapted from Edgman-Levitan (2022).

Picker Dimensions: Respect for patients' values, preferences, and expressed needs; coordination and transition; information, education, and communication; access to care; coordination and integration of care

Mass General Brigham is an integrated health system that combined Brigham and Women's Hospital and Massachusetts General Hospital, two of the nation's leading academic medical centers, in 2019. With leaders who had years of experience working with the Picker Institute, the idea of patient-centered care has expanded a great deal since the beginning of the twenty-first century. Today, the concept of patient- and family-centered care has evolved into *person*-centered care, which connects with the human understanding work at NRC Health: how it understands and helps improve all the issues that impact someone's ability to manage and improve their care.

For Mass General Brigham, the concept has expanded in four primary ways:

1. Focus on a deeper understanding of social determinants of health (SDOH) and how the health system can support not just the patients its serves but also the communities where they live, to better coordinate and integrate care.

2. Change the clinical paradigm from "What is the matter with you?" to "What matters to you?" Caregivers want to understand where they have common ground to support their patients' efforts to manage their chronic conditions. Caregivers also want to signal that "what matters to you matters to us" as they respect patients' values, preferences, and expressed needs, and strengthen the trust their patients and communities have in them.

3. Better understand what matters to staff, which is even more critical since the emergence of COVID. If leaders aren't taking care of their staff, the staff can't take care of the patients they serve. This effort includes hiring the right people, orienting them to the values of the organization, and showing how the health system holds them accountable to those values. It's about understanding the "why" for the staff—why they choose to work in

healthcare and in the Mass General Brigham system. Helping people connect with the passion and commitment that motivated them to make a difference in healthcare is critical to reducing burnout. Research done by the health system has shown that the singular commonality of high-performing patient- and family-centered organizations is being a great place to work. That idea is critical for leaders to galvanize behind.

4. Address the impact that racism has on patients, employees, and the broader community. In 2022, the system launched a multimillion-dollar effort, United Against Racism, because the leaders at Mass General Brigham believe that systemic racism is a public health issue. This effort includes initiatives to increase the diversity of the health system's boards, leadership, clinicians, and staff. Leaders are also focusing on policies and work streams to address the structural racism that results in inequitable care by, for example, translating the patient portal from English into eight other languages, increasing access to interpreters, enhancing access for all patients, and improving community health outcomes.

Human Understanding

Mass General Brigham has a unique focus on NRC Health's concept of human understanding, which the health system's leaders believe gets at the culture of the organization and how that impacts the way it delivers care to its patients. This focus connects the "why" for staff with how they partner with patients to understand their needs. From there, staff learn at a much deeper level the interventions and strategies that make sense to the patients, and that is where they target their implementation.

Patient experience surveys are excellent at revealing problems, but not solutions. Patient advisory councils at Mass General

Brigham focus on how patients define the problems and what solutions they would propose. For boards and leadership, this process saves money. In their experience, patients tell the health system exactly what they need, and they will often tell the health system that significant aspects of a system-proposed solution don't matter to them.

To fully leverage the patient advisory councils' feedback, the system uses a human-centered design process that brings together doctors, nurses, practice managers, other care team members, and patients to define the problem and potential solutions, from everyone's perspectives. It is most important to define the problem accurately. Then the possible solutions are whittled down, vetted again from the same multidisciplinary perspective, and then tested and implemented. The system leaders and providers have found this method to be very effective.

Connecting Patient Experience to Outcomes: Respect for Patients' Values, Preferences, and Expressed Needs; Continuity and Transition; Information, Communication, and Education

With the help of NRC Health, Mass General Brigham designs the CAHPS surveys to query patients about the aspects of care that are essential to high-quality care, *through the eyes of the patient.* They focus on the aspects of care that contribute to better outcomes: communication about their diagnosis and medications, coordination with their care team, access to care when they need it, and getting the information they need to manage their own conditions. From this perspective, it makes sense that patient experience scores are directly related to outcomes. This perspective is also the fundamental underpinning of the human understanding approach.

Mass General Brigham leaders also review patient experience data by race and ethnicity and have found that the health system's largest disparities exist for Black and Latino patients. Because leaders stratify the data, they can see where the problems are and then develop targeted interventions to address those patients' needs. Designing culturally sensitive and affirming interventions is also when partnering with patients to help design care becomes even more critical.

To foster more coordinated care and trust in the inpatient setting, primary care physicians make social calls to their patients in the hospital, so the patient knows that their doctor is informed and consulted. Nurses also educate patients about the role of the hospitalist, why they are an expert in inpatient care, why that is important, and how that person is communicating with their ambulatory doctors. Just providing this information to patients has helped increase HCAHPS scores. Many of the hospitalists hand out business cards with their cell phone number on them. They also ask family members to bring photographs of the patient or other objects about him or her to give the care team a sense of who the patient is and what matters to that person. Finally, the hospitalists shadow primary care physicians to gain a better understanding of the primary care physicians' role and relationships with their patients.

In the primary care setting, providers are working to understand how to better engage patients. They use a set of engagement questions about the most important concerns of the patient (usually they are medication, diet, and exercise). Doctors often don't talk much about such concerns, but these are critical aspects of chronic disease management. Doctors who do a better job of discussing these concerns get higher overall ratings from their patients. Primary care providers need training support. The health system is also working to understand how particular problems or conditions can be addressed by specific visit types (e.g., telehealth vs. in person). Leaders are working to create better teamwork and support to address the needs of their clinical staff. For example, when is a pharmacist important? How can community health workers support patient engagement and chronic disease management or substance use recovery?

Connecting Patient Experience with Leadership

Mass General Brigham believes that having patients on the board of directors is critical—people who can bring the patient viewpoint to board discussions. The system has invited patients, family members, and parents to serve on several of the system's boards and committees. They bring invaluable perspectives that often change the care approach. Lay board members who are community leaders do not always represent these perspectives, so it is important to identify people who are committed to providing the views of patients.

Mass General Brigham's governing boards see patient experience and safety data regularly, with an engaged quality/safety committee that can dig deeper. Safety and experience often go hand in hand. Board members are educated about how to interpret the data so that they understand what they are looking at and what questions are important to ask. They start every board meeting with both a positive and a negative patient story, to illustrate their positive impact as well as their challenges. Starting the meeting this way sends a message that patients really are at the core of the health system's purpose and mission.

Every initiative to improve patient experience and quality begins with the patient and family advisory councils—what they think, how they can inform the design and implementation, and how the system should communicate information about improvements to the public. System leaders conducted qualitative research with patients to learn how to explain why providers are asking personal questions such as whether a patient feels safe at home or can afford their medications. Helping patients understand why the providers are asking, what they are going to do with the information, and what kinds of support patients will be receiving has been a game changer.

Access to Care

Mass General Brigham has deep relationships with certain communities where the health system serves as the dominant provider. In Chelsea, which is a small community with the highest number of patients with chronic conditions across Massachusetts, the system created a program called Healthy Chelsea, which is a community group that includes the leadership of the MGB Chelsea Community Health Center, the police chief, the school board chair, the mayor, the town administrator, and the head of probation services, among many others. The system shares its SDOH data with this group, so everyone in it knows where they have housing or education challenges. The health system has similar relationships like this in other communities. Even though Mass General Brigham doesn't provide care to everyone, the work of those community organizations affects everyone who lives there.

In Chelsea, the group learned that there was a high incidence of trauma in children who had witnessed any kind of violence. Through this program, when an incident occurs, a social worker on call meets with the children involved, along with a police officer who is specially trained. The intent is to provide emotional support and to minimize people being afraid of the police. Young children who are part of this program get to know the police officer and social worker over time. Many of these children grow up and decide they want to be a police officer, social worker, nurse, or doctor because of the support they received through this program.

Integrating the Caregiver Experience

Post-COVID, like all health systems around the country, Mass General Brigham was dealing with massive staff shortages and clinician burnout. Human understanding has been critically important to moving the organization forward. To help physicians think more positively about the future, the system engaged with the primary care practices that were hit hardest by COVID through a focused series of events culminating in a retreat. System leaders interviewed staff and doctors and asked: What are the strengths of your practice, and what are the challenges? What is your future vision for your practice? The answers were used to create a draft vision for the practice that was shared during the retreat.

Leaders started each retreat with a "why" exercise: Why are they there, why are they working in healthcare, why is it important, and why are they working in this practice? Physicians and nurses discussed these questions for an hour in a small group of people they didn't normally work with. They got to know one another better, which has helped improve communication and teamwork. Participation in the retreat also showed the clinical staff how committed the leadership is toward making a difference for their patients. Then clinicians participated in an "I CARE" training (communication, advocacy, respect, and empathy), using real NRC Health experience data and comments to show where they were doing well and where they had challenges. Caregivers were asked to define these behaviors: What does good communication, advocacy, respect, and empathy look like to you? Taking clinicians out of their comfort zone helped them look at things through a different lens. The physicians and nurses came up with work plans, and the system leaders helped with process improvement support to develop and implement new workflows.

UNIVERSITY OF CALIFORNIA, SAN FRANCISCO

Picker Dimensions: Coordination and integration of care; involvement of family and friends; respect for patients' values, preferences, and expressed needs; information, communication, and education

The University of California, San Francisco (UCSF) is driven by the idea that when the best research, the best teaching, and the best patient care converge, breakthroughs can be achieved that help heal the world. Following that principle, UCSF's Helen Diller Family Comprehensive Cancer Center combines basic science, clinical research, epidemiology/cancer control, and patient care from throughout the UCSF system to advance the organization's unique holistic cancer program.

Staff members do everything they can to keep the patient at the center of their focus. All care follows a coordinated, multidisciplinary approach to keep patients from having to go multiple places for appointments with different specialists. Bouncing back and forth between offices is typical of cancer care in general, but not at UCSF. There, many subspecialists within cancer treatment—experts in everything from radiation oncology and medical oncology to nutrition and psychology—come together as a care team to treat each patient, and they make sure that the patient's family and friends are involved as much as possible at every step. Doing so helps the patient feel less anxious and fearful, which creates a better environment for healing.

Anticipating the patient's needs has always been at the forefront of UCSF's approach to cancer care. Knowing that patients with cancer typically need to undergo imaging, for example, the facility's designers built 19 types of imaging modalities to keep patients from having to make stressful trips between testing locations. Pain management experts also are on staff, as well as people known as *symptom-management personnel,* who work side by side with physicians to reduce patient suffering. Understanding that patients come from far away to seek cancer care at UCSF and thus have a variety of logistical and emotional needs, the hospital employs psychologists, support group specialists, and social workers, and offers services such as transportation, parking, and assistance with hotels. These services not only take care of the logistics that can cause anxiety for a patient, but they also help meet the patient's emotional needs. This type of service is what sets UCSF apart when it comes to the patient experience.

Coordination and Integration of Care; Involvement of Family and Friends

What patients love most about UCSF is feeling like the entire team is fighting the cancer on their behalf, anticipating problems or challenges, and preventing them if possible. One example of this commitment involved a patient who had head and neck cancer, a difficult cancer to treat. The patient's options were surgery, radiation, or chemotherapy. The team described the side effects of radiation with this type of cancer including an inability to eat, excessive salivation (or drooling), or both. A nutritionist covered nutritional support with the patient and family members so that everyone understood the next steps, including which foods should be avoided (e.g., hard-to-swallow foods) and which foods are beneficial (e.g., calorie-dense, high-protein foods). The nutritional specialists at UCSF have expertise in nutrition for patients with cancer. In this example, the team of specialists were dialed in on the patient's type of cancer and knew how to support the patient and family, both medically and emotionally.

Respect for Patients' Values, Preferences, and Expressed Needs

When the UCSF Helen Diller Family Comprehensive Cancer Center's new building, the Baker Precision Cancer Medicine Building, was designed several years ago, patient preferences were taken into account from the beginning. In the earliest stages of design, the center's leaders conducted journey mapping with patients, projecting how the best possible hospital experience would look and feel from their perspective and translating that vision into the center's architecture and patient flow.

The results of this attention to detail are visible. Beautiful artwork is everywhere in the building, from paintings and hanging quilts to comforting quotes on the hallway walls and in the examination rooms. High-quality furnishings are placed throughout the facility, and color palettes are soothing and harmonious. The result is a relaxing environment, which keeps patients from feeling that the surroundings are sterile, cold, or dull. Even chair positioning is taken into account to keep patients—many of whom spend much time in the same chair over repeated visits—from facing a blank wall, which could lead their minds to wander and provoke greater anxiety. (The importance of surroundings is especially true in the infusion room, where chairs for patients command the hospital's best views of the city and bay.)

Spaces in the center were designed with the same patient focus. Recognizing that some patients prefer privacy, while others enjoy the company of other patients when undergoing treatment, UCSF's leaders built large infusion areas to allow for both private rooms and open spaces. Some spaces are furnished with high chairs at counters where patients and family members can plug in laptops; others have swivel chairs arranged in circles around tables to create a comfortable living-room feeling. Large picture windows overlook the water, adding to the space's sense of serenity. In addition, private consultation spaces have been incorporated into the center just off the waiting areas. Staff members can use these spaces to discuss diagnoses and treatment plans in private, and patients can use them to discuss treatments with their providers or have time alone or with family and friends after receiving a difficult diagnosis.

With all this space (and variety of spaces), one might think it would be difficult to locate a patient. However, UCSF uses an electronic location system. Everyone, from staff members to patients, wears an electronic badge that can be located immediately. Monitors allow staff members to view patients, which allows them to sit or stand wherever they feel most comfortable while waiting to be seen.

Just as patients were involved in the design of the new building, feedback was also solicited from internal customers, faculty, and staff members. Adjustable workstations, with desks that can be raised or lowered for sitting or standing users, allow for flexibility.

Staff members are given multiple computer monitors to increase their efficiency and comfort; receptionists have the best-quality telephones with headsets that allow them greater freedom of movement; and plenty of desk space is provided in team rooms for physicians and other providers to use. Even on-site laundry services are offered to white coat providers to ensure that they don't have to use their days off for work-related chores.

All of this helps create a better work–life balance for UCSF staff, which is important to the organization's leaders. Recognizing that burnout is on the rise among physicians—especially those who work with patients with cancer—UCSF leaders track their engagement throughout the year, following engagement scores, rewarding high-performing areas, and offering assistance to lower-performing areas. Leaders meet with staff members at hiring, as well as at their 60-day mark, to reinforce the mission-driven culture of the organization. Because staff members have made a conscious decision to follow this particular calling, UCSF's leaders are able to emphasize their personal commitment to the work and keep burnout to a minimum.

Interpersonal skills also are essential in this environment. During the highly emotional experience of cancer treatment, patients and their families often make close connections with staff members and express their gratitude to them afterward. Hospital leaders strive to foster such engagement. When patients respond to surveys and write comments recognizing staff members, UCSF leaders send a letter—including the patient's comment—to the staff members thanking them for their contribution. When a patient dies, UCSF makes time and creates safe spaces for staff members to grieve.

Information, Communication, and Education

One of the best ways UCSF keeps the lines of communication open with patients is through its many Patient Family Advisory

Councils (PFACs). There are separate PFACs for Pediatrics and Adult Services, as well as department-focused PFACs, focused solely on the patient experience. Once a year, the PFACs come together at a retreat, where patients are invited to speak directly with the system CEO about things UCSF needs to work on or is doing well. Crucial adjustments to the organization and its processes have come out of these gatherings, including some much needed refinements of the patient portal.

Many organizations outside healthcare succeed with consumers because they are able to bring them to the table and elicit feedback about what they like and don't like. UCSF has embraced this concept with its PFACs and other measures, and it ensures that a consumer voice is always weighing in on everything the organization does. This emphasis has created a culture of accountability within the organization, as well as a lasting and self-reinforcing consumer-centric culture.

MAYO CLINIC HEALTH SYSTEM

Picker Dimensions: Respect for patients' values, preferences, and expressed needs; coordination and integration of care; access to care

Respect for Patients' Values, Preferences, and Expressed Needs

All 76,000 Mayo Clinic employees work together with the sole purpose of putting the patient's healthcare needs first—no matter where they live. As a values-centered culture, anyone at Mayo Clinic can tell you what its primary value is: *The needs of the patient come first.* The origin of that primary value traces back to more than 160 years ago when Mayo Clinic began as a single-physician medical practice on the Minnesota prairie in 1864. In August 1883, after a devastating tornado tore through Rochester, Dr. William

W. Mayo, along with his sons, Will and Charlie, and the Sisters of Saint Francis took care of the injured. Mother Mary Alfred Moes proposed establishing a hospital, with the Mayos serving as staff physicians and the Sisters of Saint Francis providing nursing care.

The uniqueness of the partnership between the Mayos and the Sisters—a partnership of brains and heart—and of the values they espoused set up Mayo Clinic for excellence in two areas: care and service. In 1910, Will Mayo visited Rush Medical Center in Chicago and addressed students in its medical school class, who asked him for Mayo Clinic's secret to success. Mayo told the students, "The best interest of the patient is the only interest to be considered, and in order that the sick may have the benefit of advancing knowledge, union of forces is necessary" (Antiel et al. 2011). Today that translates to Mayo's "institutional core value: The needs of the patient come first" (Mayo Clinic 2024a). This value is carried out through Mayo's "team-based approach, a method that brings together as many specialists as needed for each case, all focusing their collective energy on that one individual patient" (Mayo Clinic 2024b).

A strong culture rooted in the values of the organization is key to a high-performing health system. How do you build such a culture? It starts with the hiring process—making sure the organization is hiring the right person for the right position. Mayo Clinic's leaders ensure that they are hiring the right person by first gaining a better understanding of the candidate's philosophy on teamwork. This is a key to their success; Mayo Clinic focused on team-based care before it became a best practice in the industry. Leaders also make sure that when they consider a candidate, they're not just looking for a person who's a good fit for the organization, but also one for whom the organization is a good fit.

Once hired, the employee goes through the typical orientation and training process that occurs in all health systems, but leaders at Mayo Clinic also make sure to discuss the expectations that come along with its culture, which everyone in the organization lives and breathes. For example, when a physician is paged, they are expected to always answer the page unless they are in an urgent situation with a patient. Before cell phones, the organization had multiple phone stations that were labeled "For Mayo Physician Paging Only." With the ubiquitousness of cell phones, things are easier. Expectations like this allow for strong relationships between physicians and patients, as well as between physicians and their colleagues.

To foster a strong culture, healthcare organizations also need to ensure that the values of everyone in the organization align with those of the organization. You can discern a person's values by asking, "What are your priorities here as part of this organization, and what do you think we could help you with to maximize or optimize those priorities?" This question starts a conversation with people because it demonstrates that they are important to you. It doesn't matter if the employee is in maintenance or the head of the department of cardiothoracic surgery. Similarly, showing patients you respect their values, preferences, and needs begins by thoroughly understanding their chief complaint. However, simply walking into a room and asking, "What's wrong?" does not always resonate well or demonstrate the compassion most patients are looking for. This question can be reworded to make the patient feel that they matter and are in the driver's seat: "What are you most concerned about, and what do you hope that we can help you with?" Questions posed this way set a better tone with patients and their families.

Coordination and Integration of Care

Mayo Clinic also provides excellent coordination for patients throughout the system. Mayo leaders and physicians understand that most patients come to them with highly complex problems. When patients walk in the doors at a Mayo Clinic facility, they say they get the sense that it's different and feel renewed hope. Even when patients cannot be cured, they still leave feeling that staff members have truly listened to them, spent time with them, and done everything they could to help.

Countless interactions take place in a healthcare system, and not all of them are face-to-face. Yet, if you ask consumers, "How do you decide where to receive healthcare?" their decision is often based on recommendations from family members, friends, and other providers. Despite constraints in access or the predominance of technology in today's healthcare landscape, Mayo Clinic's staff members also recognize that a sense of human touch is needed to build great relationships with customers. Whether the customer is a patient, family member, or staff member, every interaction needs to be conducted in an empathetic way, which involves moving beyond "Midwestern nice" to really trying to understand what the person's priorities are.

In a 2019 interview for this book, Dr. Thomas Howell, Medical Director for Patient Experience at Mayo, connected this work on understanding patient priorities with the staff's own personal purpose: "A person's mission at Mayo is to understand how they can contribute to this great organization that provides great care. If you find your personal *why*, that'll be what makes your day at work incredibly meaningful too, because that's why you're in healthcare in the first place. We never want to get the *what* ahead of the *why*. I think when you focus on that *why*, people become engaged on a whole different level."

Access to Care

Mayo Clinic's leaders understand that people travel from all over the world to their hospitals to receive healthcare. When they think about access, leaders think beyond the four walls of the organization. Recognizing that some patients' needs are complex, that the clinic's locations are not always easy to reach, and that wait times for specialists sometimes can be months—a problem that, given the significant provider shortage in the United States, cannot be solved simply by hiring more physicians—Mayo Clinic leaders have looked for ways to leverage technology to help. Starting with the most in-demand medical specialties, such as rheumatology, they began to triage people using electronic consultations to determine which patients need to come in and which might be served via telehealth. This practice is helping the organization maximize its resources and provide even more value to its patients.

Mayo Clinic also understands that consumers today have choices. Furthermore, the organization considers consumers to be everyone—patients, families, their caregivers, their community—and understands that the best way to compete in a consumerist world is through ease of access. Many people, from patients to students and providers, interact with the clinic in distinct ways. None of them expect to be asked the same question seven times and be given different forms every step of the way; rather, they expect integration in their experience. One way that Mayo Clinic is achieving this integration is through its experience relationship management (XRM) group, with the goal of becoming an industry leader in XRM.

Through all this, staff members at Mayo Clinic remain focused on the human connection and keep in mind the importance of each interaction. For example, rather than noting that they have performed hundreds of solid-organ transplantations, staff members focus on the hundreds of lives impacted: the patients who are able to go to their daughter's wedding or their son's graduation or do whatever is meaningful to them. They step back and realize that those 500 transplants aren't just a number; they are people, and Mayo Clinic has helped them live their lives to the fullest.

Mayo Clinic's story illustrates how, in today's culture, a healthcare system can embody many of the Picker dimensions. The organization has shown how a strong culture rooted in values can create a better experience for all. Those values have stood the test of time, and Mayo Clinic has consistently remained one of the nation's top healthcare providers. Some of its earliest best practices—concepts such as team-based care and salaried physicians—were unique when they were adopted, but many health systems across the country have followed suit. Mayo Clinic's success is difficult to replicate because the organization is grounded in a mindset that keeps the patient at its center and that governs its actions according to an internal *why*. In addition, there is an intangible but enduring commitment among dedicated and caring colleagues. The result is a shared purpose that resonates with patients and the public, and it makes Mayo Clinic distinct.

THE JOHNS HOPKINS HOSPITAL

Picker Dimensions: Information, communication, and education; involvement of family and friends; continuity and transition; access to care; respect for patients' values, preferences, and expressed needs; coordination and integration of care; emotional support and alleviation of fear and anxiety

Information, Communication, and Education; Involvement of Family and Friends; Continuity and Transition

The Johns Hopkins Hospital is one of the nation's top hospitals because it is grounded in the mission set forth by one of its first physicians, Dr. William Osler, who said, "It is more important to know what sort of a patient has a disease, than what sort of a disease the patient has."(John 2013). From the beginning, Osler's philosophy of patient-centered care has guided the work of the hospital in its tripartite mission of research, education, and clinical care, serving its patients and the community of Baltimore, Maryland.

Because of its world-class reputation, The Johns Hopkins Hospital serves a diverse population, comprising the residents of Baltimore as well as people seeking care from across the United States and around the world. The Johns Hopkins Hospital not only offers exceptional and leading-edge clinical care but also does so with great compassion.

The providers and staff are passionate about their call to health-care. This type of workforce creates a culture naturally built around the patient and family experience. The Johns Hopkins Hospital regards the patient and family experience as the *complete* journey to receive world-class care; seeking every opportunity "to delight [patients] based on their clinical and emotional interactions with . . . our people, our processes, and our physical setting" (Allen 2018). This definition guides the continuous improvement approach to patient experience.

Another principle guiding the work is person-centered care, including collaboration, information sharing, participation, and respect and dignity. This is accomplished, in part, through tools of shared decision-making. To this end, The Johns Hopkins Hospital provides patient educational materials, trialed and tested with patients and families. Most patients are assigned educational materials of some type (e.g., videos or printed brochures) to help them better understand their condition. Some of these materials are given to the patient at the bedside, while others are accessed through an assigned patient portal, either at the hospital or at home. The patient portal also includes the patient's vital signs, any medications the patient is taking, and instructional materials to go along with those medications. Educated patients and families allow for shared decision-making and better outcomes.

Recognizing the importance of involving family and friends in patients' care outside the hospital, especially in cases involving serious diagnoses in which patients' ability to listen can be affected by their illness or emotions, a patient is asked to identify a caregiver whom staff members ensure is present for important conversations. For example, if a patient needs physical therapy after leaving the hospital, therapy staff will make sure that the patient's caregiver is present when they show the patient the required exercises. In this way, the caregiver understands each exercise and can assist the patient, which helps ensure a safe transition home and appropriate follow-through on necessary at-home care.

Another area of focus is the well-being of providers and staff through a comprehensive wellness program. As an academic medical center, the hospital has physicians who are responsible for the wellness of residents, medical students, and other physicians; it also employs a chief wellness officer and a nursing wellness officer. Support groups are offered for patients with difficult diagnoses as well as for employees and their managers.

Access to Care

As with many hospitals, The Johns Hopkins Hospital has many newer additions and multiple parking lots, and finding one's way can be challenging for patients, visitors, and new staff members. It also can result in increased anxiety and stress. Recognizing this, The Johns Hopkins Hospital staff is always willing to offer people help in finding their way. Part of the organization's strategic plan for the next five years is to "make Johns Hopkins easy" in terms of access. One way it is doing this is by providing a digital way-finding solution.

Respect for Patients' Values, Preferences, and Expressed Needs

The Johns Hopkins Hospital values the inclusion of patients and families at every level of the organization. Through the use of patient and family advisory councils and volunteer advisers, the voice of the patient and family is included in decisions in hiring of executives in the organization and the redesign of buildings and spaces. Patients and families also are involved on key committees. For example, volunteer advisers helped with the selection and implementation of the digital way-finding app, as well as assisted in designing the hospital's new outpatient cancer center.

Patients at The Johns Hopkins Hospital are also asked to evaluate processes throughout the organization—from the check-in process to online appointment bookings—and advise leadership on how they can be improved. Based on their recommendations, the hospital's leaders have implemented self-scheduling in many clinics and outpatient services. Telemedicine is another program that was implemented in response to patient needs. In the past, patients may have had to face long waits—and the ensuing fear and anxiety—to obtain diagnostic results. The patient portal enables quick access to normal results. However, the patient's provider always calls the patient if the results are abnormal.

To better understand consumer preferences, the hospital also has "patient cafes," focus groups in which people from similar backgrounds (e.g., live in the same neighborhood, have similar diagnoses, or speak the same language) are invited to come in and talk about their experiences at The Johns Hopkins Hospital. Acknowledging that its patients come from all over the country, the hospital also hosts virtual patient and family advisory councils, through which individuals provide remote feedback on a regular basis.

Exhibiting this level of respect for the patient's voice creates a more in-depth conversation at The Johns Hopkins Hospital. This dedication fosters improvement in the patient experience, patient engagement, and patient- and family-centered care, and it encourages staff members to be committed to and consistent in valuing the human connection. Positive patient feedback is not only about great clinical care but also about feeling comforted and cared about. It is that human connection that The Johns Hopkins Hospital creates, and it is that human connection that successful organizations never lose sight of.

How COVID Impacted The Johns Hopkins Hospital

For The Johns Hopkins Hospital, COVID revealed the following primary areas of friction: wait times and lack of updates in the emergency department (ED); patients and families in inpatient settings not knowing when or how providers will update them; and patients struggling in the first 48 hours upon coming home. These issues relate to the Picker dimensions of coordination and integration of care; information, communication, and education; continuity and transition; and emotional support and alleviating fear and anxiety. The hospital is now working directly to address these issues. Some were a result of misaligned expectations between patients, families, and clinical teams; hospitalists, nurses, and ED providers are more conscious about this issue now. They are conducting ongoing workshops with their clinical care teams about the most friction-filled experiences and working to build skills as individuals and teams to address those systems and gaps.

Delays, particularly in the ED and then delays transferring from the ED to an inpatient bed, are part of the new fabric of healthcare across the nation. At The Johns Hopkins Hospital, staff most effectively mitigate these delays by updating patients and their care partners on what they are waiting for and why it is important. Staff are doing so electronically, guided by patient and family insight, to better leverage providers' investment in charting in the electronic health record (EHR). Through this new program, the EHR sends consumer-friendly and secure texts to the patients, directly to their smartphones (e.g., "Your CT scan has been ordered," "Your bed is available and someone will be coming to get you shortly"). Gone are the days of nagging busy providers, nurses, and technicians to keep handwritten updates on a whiteboard. Even better, the patient updates via text are more narrowly tailored and reliable in comparison. Sharing information ahead of time also removes surprise and minimizes knowledge inequality such that clinicians can have conversations that are more tailored to the unique needs of each patient.

The Picker dimensions remain highly relevant at Johns Hopkins—particularly emotional support. Reducing the emotional burden of staff has been a priority; providing trusted, trained patient-to-patient and family-to-family supports has been a critical area of investment. The organization is developing a framework for a caregiver support center within Johns Hopkins Medicine that has wraparound external and internal support services—everything from the basics (phone chargers, snacks, lockers, resting areas) to bereavement support and peer-to-peer emotional support networks. A gap analysis of the impacts of this initiative showed it will remove emotional and time burdens on physicians, nurses, and social workers so they can focus their time on their critically ill patients and best inform tough decision-making. Johns Hopkins leaders believe this could result in a competitive advantage for recruiting as well.

Now and going forward in the "kinda after COVID" world, lack of access represents the most significant need for change to meet patients' needs for an improved healthcare experience. Nimble, digital-first approaches integrating apps and pivoting to provision of more care-at-home models are pathways The Johns Hopkins Hospital is seeking—and on which reimbursement models will need to deliver.

CLEVELAND CLINIC

Picker Dimensions: Respect for patients' values, preferences, and expressed needs; access to care; information, communication, and education; coordination and integration of care

Cleveland Clinic has reframed patient experience as the reduction of suffering and care delivered according to the patient's values. Cleveland Clinic is known around the world for exceptional, safe, high-quality, high-value care. The single variable that makes it unique—the reason patients stay with Cleveland Clinic—is its people. Caregivers, as providers are called, provide groundbreaking medical care because of the technical expertise, innovative spirit, and quality of the organization; however, it's the people who make the experience unforgettable for patients. Cleveland Clinic understands that when consumers seek healthcare, they choose not just with their heads, but with their hearts, and caregivers are deeply committed to the patients they serve and believe in treating everyone like family.

Respect for Patients' Values, Preferences, and Expressed Needs

Cleveland Clinic has a five-year strategic vision built around the personalized patient experience. To that end, the organization wants to know its patients intimately—understand their values, preferences, and needs—and then determine how best to make the organization's message and values resonate with them. Cleveland Clinic started on this path 15 years ago when leadership established what has come to be called its "true north," the core concept of "Patients First."

To kick-start the journey toward alignment of patient experience with care delivery, leaders took 40,000 staff members offline for half a day for an event aptly named the Cleveland Clinic Experience. Institute chairs, neurosurgeons, nurses, medical assistants, environmental service workers, and others came together in a roundtable format to discuss the life cycle of caregivers and their patients. Participants asked: What does "Patients First" mean with respect to each individual's role here? What are the values of the organization that everyone wants to rally around, and what are the behaviors associated with those values? During the event, leaders rolled out new workplace language to reinforce the concept that everyone at Cleveland Clinic is a caregiver—they exist to serve, and care for, their patients. A homegrown model of service recovery training was then introduced. Called "Communicate with HEART," it is grounded in empathy and the recognition that when things (inevitably) go wrong in healthcare, caregivers need to use language that is embodied in the acronym HEART: Hear, Empathize, Apologize, Respond, and Thank. For sustainability, the Cleveland Clinic has implemented surveys to gather feedback from patients at the point of service about specific behaviors caregivers should be exhibiting, and these behaviors are built into performance evaluations.

Leadership has since changed, but the organization's alignment with its core concept has never shifted. Caregivers at Cleveland Clinic fulfill patient wishes in every way possible, from hosting multiple weddings and vow-renewal ceremonies to coordinating an on-premises visit of a hospitalized state trooper's beloved horse. Caregivers are relentlessly creative about meeting people where they are, both emotionally and spiritually, and caring for the soul along with the body.

Access to Care

The key to keeping patient experience relevant is hardwiring best practices, as well as innovation. Access is a significant issue for patients. Cleveland Clinic implemented same-day appointments years ago as a means of meeting patient expectations. Today, patients can be seen in scheduled virtual visits or 24/7 express care online for urgent issues, and these modes of access are clearly preferred by patients over traditional appointments. The clinic also adopted Shared Medical Appointments, in which a single clinician sees multiple patients with the same diagnosis at the same time, allowing them to come together and share their experiences. Patients do not want to be defined by their illnesses, and the shared experience of coping with an illness and navigating the journey creates a powerful community. Not only do patients often experience greater satisfaction with shared appointments than with traditional one-on-one appointments, they also have better health outcomes. The reason, of course, is the shared experience: patients together in a room, discussing how they fixed their wheelchairs or how they managed medication side effects. Following tremendous success in this space, Cleveland Clinic is now launching virtual shared medical appointments to create a broader community across the system and expand to less traditional areas, such as bereavement and survivorship programs.

Daily tiered huddles are another new practice. These brief gatherings are held at each level of the organization to discuss issues that matter most to caregivers at that level. The results are reported out to the next level and all the way up to the executive team, which gives everyone in the organization the chance to understand the current state of operations, safety, quality of care, and experience issues, as well as any staffing and caregiver safety needs. Cleveland Clinic has widely adopted Jonathan Bartels's "The Pause," a moment of respect for patients at the time of death and recognition of the privilege to care for them. During the executive-level huddle, leaders pause for a moment of silence after the names of all those who died the day before are read aloud.

Families who have lost a loved one at Cleveland Clinic are also honored in a number of ways. Spiritual care is available for the family within 15 minutes, as is a respectful pause at the bedside to honor the life of the patient, the lives of loved ones, and the caregivers who served the patient. In times of distress, Code Lavenders are also available for patients and their families or caregivers. When called, a team of emergency caregivers arrives to provide moral support and decompression. The Cleveland Clinic knows that there is no exceptional patient experience without caring for the caregivers, who care for patients day in and day out.

To that end, thousands of Cleveland Clinic clinicians have been trained in relationship-centered communication via REDE to Communicate, a homegrown model based on evidence of what works in communication tailored to clinical settings. Dr. Adrienne Boissy, chief experience officer, and colleagues conducted a study that looked at 1,500 physicians who completed communication skills training and a matched group of physicians who did not to determine the impact of the REDE training on patient satisfaction, provider empathy, and burnout (Boissy et al. 2016). The study findings revealed that regardless of the incoming skill set, physician specialty, or years in practice, every physician who underwent training experienced improvement. In addition, a smaller sample demonstrated a significant reduction in burnout, likely because of the community building within the course and empathy modeled to participants. As a result of this study, the REDE model has been adopted by the medical school, is embedded in onboarding, and has been expanded to include microlearnings and complex topics such as opiates, conflict management, and advance care planning.

Designing with the End User: Patients

When patients are partners in their care, they are more likely to engage in care and manage their health. Understanding this, Cleveland Clinic has long had programs focused on listening to patients. In addition to the standard best practices such as bedside shift reports and purposeful hourly rounding, one of the most powerful practices has been to bring physicians, nurses, and patients together for conversations called "plan of care visits" throughout a patient's stay. Questions during these conversations are of the following nature: What needs to happen to get you home? Are we aligned around when that might happen? These discussions don't sound revolutionary, but organizations often drift from including the patient in the care plan on a daily basis; this is the one intervention that has the potential to increase satisfaction across all domains. These visits also allow for greater transparency regarding the day-to-day care of patients and when they might anticipate going home. In addition, call-back programs and telemedicine are dedicated to patients at high risk of returning to the hospital; paramedics are even sent to some patients' homes to check on them.

Cleveland Clinic hears from patients in a multitude of ways, from the classic focus groups, market research, and patient committees to newer programs such as the Healthcare Partners Program. To become a healthcare partner, a patient can be recommended by caregivers or asked directly by the program; alternatively, they can become involved through a portal on the clinic's website. Another exciting way Cleveland Clinic has elevated patients' voices is through executive leadership rounds, which include leaders from across the enterprise, as well as board members and health-care partners. During these rounds, healthcare partners have the opportunity to go out onto the floor with clinic leaders to better understand the current state of the organization and its patients. Consistent board presence on these rounds reinforces commitment at the highest levels of the organization to listening to those they serve, which further humanizes the work of Cleveland Clinic and builds a stronger culture of empathy among its leaders. During leadership rounds, leaders have the opportunity to do the work of caregivers, which enables them to enrich their understanding of caregivers' lives.

Cleveland Clinic has involved patients and family members as cocreators in their improvements and human-centered design projects. An example is the creation of a single digital doorway for the clinic. "My Cleveland Clinic" is a unified app experience that houses online scheduling, EHR functionality for patient portals, a find-a-doctor tool, and more. During development of the app, patients participated in discussions about its design and functionality. Codesign also impacts clinical care, most recently in the areas of pediatric asthma and access improvement.

With an eye for innovation, consistency, and design, the Cleveland Clinic hopes to always make the mantra "nothing for me without me" a reality for patients around the world.

How COVID Impacted Cleveland Clinic

Access, coordination, and teamwork are the key drivers of patient experience, and the Picker dimensions all remain highly relevant concepts with direct intersections in the work Cleveland Clinic is doing to reduce operational friction. Leaders there are now taking a broader perspective, beyond their COVID story to a longer-term evolution of the patient experience that truly began before COVID with a focus on learning from hospitality and retail industries. Patients are learning from those acutely consumer-focused experiences and comparing healthcare unfavorably; Cleveland Clinic leaders consider it their responsibility to step up and meet those expectations.

Cleveland Clinic's historical improvement work based on CAHPS has focused, perhaps too much, on "interactions"—that is, how well the doctors are communicating with patients, whether doctors are making eye contact, and whether nurses are courteous and friendly. While this is necessary work, it has taken place at the expense of focus on the "transaction" side, where much of the frustration takes place.

Since early 2020, the organization has added a custom question to the CAHPS surveys about how easy it is to get care at Cleveland Clinic. More recently it began to apply a large language model (LLM) to translate voice and open-ended responses to this question into meaningful data. The organization learned that delays and waits were more onerous than fully realized or anticipated. The analysis showed that no other question on the survey was more directly correlated with the likelihood to recommend. So, this issue became a significant focus for improvement in 2024.

To alleviate the issue of delays and waits and better coordinate and integrate care, every operational leader has this goal as part of their patient experience improvement plan. For example, in the ED, leaders work as a dyad with an app that aids in triage to "keep the vertical patients vertical" (*vertical* meaning, e.g., those with minor injuries or abdominal pain). The "horizontal" patients (those with serious injuries or conditions) go to an ED bed immediately. However, all patients are evaluated in triage on arrival, regardless of where they are in the ED. If there are no ED beds available, the "vertical" patients receive their tests, and then treatments are ordered in the waiting room, via the app. Many of those patients can be discharged from the waiting room and never need to go to the "back of the house." This system leaves ED beds available for the more serious cases (e.g., sepsis, stroke, heart attack). The new system has significantly reduced waits, delays, and the number of people who have to leave without treatment, all of which have a direct impact on patient experience and Cleveland Clinic's reputation.

Leaders at Cleveland Clinic now think about staffing and roles in new ways as they do not anticipate going back to pre-COVID staffing models. (There will never again be "extra" staff!) One of the key barriers here is EHR documentation. Leaders are looking at potential AI solutions to reduce caregiver burden for documentation, which impacts staffing. A physician or nurse who no longer has to spend two of every nine hours typing into a computer can see six or seven additional patients and leave the ED with a lower stress level. Leaders believe that this use of AI will result in decreased burnout and increased productivity (e.g., for certain high-risk patients in the ED, nurses must conduct and document a mental health assessment every 15 minutes). This change will impact anyone who touches the EHR and has the capability of reducing the burden on any caregiver.

Cleveland Clinic was the first to use the online AI tool Chat-GPT (using an "internal sandbox" that is HIPAA compliant) to interpret hundreds of thousands of voice comments from its CAHPS surveys about the ease of getting care. Using the LLM mentioned previously, the tool has learned to identify the granularity differences of patient voices to conduct demographic evaluations. For example, one site had challenging parking. All patients complained about parking, but the nature of their complaints varied by gender: Men didn't want to walk very far; women feared for their safety. So this finding gave leaders the ability to ask and answer questions and determine the right solutions for that site's parking problem, such as the need for security rovers, escorts, and enhanced lighting, and also helping people with limited mobility who needed other solutions.

The LLM can process written comments as well—and at scale—so that fewer data go to waste and more of it can be translated into real solutions. When it comes to CAHPS, the Cleveland Clinic point of view is that we (as an industry) don't understand enough about the other impacts of care beyond what is on the survey. This is where the opportunities are ripe to learn from hotels and other consumer-focused industries. We must design with empathy, and the organizations that can do this better and sooner will reap the greatest rewards in patient volume and satisfaction.

AKRON CHILDREN'S HOSPITAL

Picker Dimensions: Involvement of family and friends; access to care; emotional support and alleviation of fear and anxiety

Organizational Culture Sets the Tone for Patient- and Family-Centered Care

Patients and families who visit Akron Children's Hospital consistently say it "feels different" when they walk through the doors of any of more than 60 locations in northeastern Ohio. At the heart of this experience is the hospital's warm and friendly culture. New employees are introduced to the organization's culture during orientation on their first day, and it continues to be emphasized throughout their career. The organization prides itself in demonstrating that working at the hospital is more than a job; it's a calling, and promoting this idea from within is one of the many ways the hospital maintains its focus on patients and families. This culture also builds staff and leadership loyalty, creating an environment in which they want to stay.

Since its founding in 1890, the hospital has built its culture around three promises:

1. To treat every child as we would our own
2. To treat others as they would like to be treated
3. To turn no child away for any reason

At Akron Children's, every employee plays a role in creating excellent patient and family experiences. Every interaction makes a difference, whether it's a friendly voice when scheduling a visit, walking a lost family to an appointment, or caring for a sick child for an extended period. Patients and families expect high-quality clinical care, but they want that care to be delivered with respect, dignity, and personalization.

Engaging and Collaborating with Patients and Families

Engaging patients and families through social media, the website, and community programs begins before they enter the hospital.

Each facility is designed "through the eyes of a child" and features children's artwork and colorful walls. The atrium lobby at the Akron campus features the "Incrediball Circus 2," an art installation that catches the eyes of young and old alike. Touches like this set the tone for the holistic care that families can expect at Akron Children's.

Another way the hospital engages patients and families is through family-centered rounds. The healthcare team, including attending physicians, residents, and nurses, partner with the patient and family to develop the plan of care, provide bidirectional communication, and clarify medications and orders. The teams strive to contextualize care by asking, "What matters to you?" and getting to know each patient and family. If family members are unable to attend, the hospital provides whiteboards on which patients and family members can write questions for their providers, and the hospital encourages family members to call any time for updates.

Collaboration with family members is sought, not just in the care of individual children, but also for improvement processes, policies, and design projects for new building structures. Akron Children's has one of the oldest parent advisory councils in the country; it is a group of patients and family members who use the hospital services frequently and want to give back to the organiza-tion. Feedback from these trained volunteers is vital to deliver-ing value-added experience. Parent advisory council members sit on hospital committees, review hospital policies, and advocate for safety and quality. Parent advisers are also members of an interpro-fessional patient/family education committee, which ensures that evidence-based patient education teaching tools and materials are reviewed for health literacy (including clear and plain language), content accuracy, and cultural sensitivity. For patients or family members who want to be involved and provide feedback but find it difficult to do so in person, the hospital hosts an online parent panel with multiple opportunities to share insights.

Feedback from parent advisers and patient- and family-experience surveys and social media is used by the hospital to recognize physi-cians, nurses, and other staff members. These team members are presented with the Chief Moment Officer award, which is given to staff members who have left an impression on a family that reso-nates with the organization's mission, vision, and values. The award is presented monthly at the hospital's leadership meeting.

Access to Care

Access to healthcare is a priority for Akron Children's, so hospital leaders developed a strategy to build regional health centers with primary care and specialty services. Patients and their families do not have to travel far from their homes to receive care. In addition, the hospital has a growing population health program offering case management, interpretive services, and the assistance of commu-nity health workers to at-risk families.

Akron Children's Hospital provides health services in almost every school district within an hour of the organization (68 schools in total). In 2019, it began offering telehealth clinic appointments between school-based clinics and a nurse practitioner located at the hospital or in the clinic. Quickly identifying and addressing the healthcare needs of students decreases their time away from the classroom and enables their parents or other responsible adults to miss less work. The result is better access and enhanced coordination with the hospital.

The hospital also created new healthcare models that provide convenient ways for patients and families with minor health issues to receive care. One such model, Quick Care, allows families who are unable to schedule an appointment with the child's pediatrician to be seen quickly during the day and early evening.

In addition, the hospital has expanded access to care through telehealth. Its "telepsych" program enables patients to go to their primary care office, which may be closer to home than the hospital, for a remote appointment with a psychologist. Having implemented this service successfully for many years, Akron Children's is now expanding it and looking into other telehealth options for the community's low-acute needs, giving consumers more opportunities to choose the location and medium in which they receive care.

Alleviating the Stress of Healthcare

Staff members at Akron Children's Hospital ensure that patients and families are at the center of all they do. Recognizing that comfort and safety lead to healing, they look at the experience holistically and try to make it as pleasant and stress-free as possible. Child life specialists, who are trained in distraction techniques, comfort positioning, and child-specific approaches, are key members of the healthcare team. These specialists reduce patients' fear and anxiety while providing age-specific education and play. They also shape expectations by walking patients through upcoming procedures and allowing patients and family members to look at, and play with, the equipment that will be used.

The hospital offers multiple options for positive distraction, including pet, art, and music therapy. The Doggie Brigade sends animals to visit patients. Occasionally, a visiting pony named Willie Nelson is seen at the bedside. The Emily Cooper Welty Expressive Therapy Center hosts a variety of therapeutic activities and features a recording studio and dance classes for children of all abilities. The Volunteer Services department offers a wide variety of themed activity carts—featuring everything from superheroes to cookies—to help keep children entertained at the bedside.

The hospital also has respite rooms available for families. Both the Reinberger Center at the hospital and the nearby Ronald McDonald House offer services for visitors, including private sleep rooms, showers, consultation rooms, and large kitchens. Because many patients are in the hospital for extended periods, a volunteer-driven hair salon provides services to family members. Various relaxation groups, massages, and mindfulness classes are also offered at respite areas to keep family members relaxed and comfortable.

Family Support

Additional types of support are available to patients and families at Akron Children's Hospital. The Family Resource Center, for example, is staffed by a medical librarian who offers individualized education and specialized kits for families to borrow. To augment the written information, numerous classes (e.g., family CPR and asthma education) are offered with hands-on demonstration in a small group setting.

A Parent Mentor Program, which allows peer-to-peer mentoring for families, pairs trained parent volunteers with those seeking an individual who has gone through a similar diagnosis or experience. Using an online database, a family can search by diagnosis or department, read profiles, and contact mentors they feel might be a good fit for them.

The parent advisory council's coffee cart provides another opportunity for families to connect. This grant-funded cart offers free coffee and snacks to families on inpatient floors, while providing additional information about the parent mentor and adviser programs. Through encounters such as these, parent advisers can comfort other parents who are feeling overwhelmed by their situation. Doing so creates a community in which patients and families can share their feelings.

Finally, parent navigators located within certain specialties meet with parents of children who recently received a diagnosis to help them navigate the system and find needed resources. Many of the specialists also have personal experiences they can draw on to provide support to patients and families.

MOUNT SINAI HEALTH SYSTEM

Picker Dimensions: Coordination and integration of care; emotional support and alleviation of fear and anxiety; continuity and transition; respect for patients' values, preferences, and expressed needs

Putting the Focus on Patient-Centered Care

Patients come from all over the world to seek care at Mount Sinai Health System (Mount Sinai) in New York City, drawn by the hospital's top-notch physicians and its holistic and innovative approach to medicine.

Patients make Mount Sinai their ongoing healthcare provider, not just because of the quality of its physicians but also because of the experiences they have with the entire team of people on staff. The Mount Sinai team shares an empathic, engaged culture built around staff members—both clinical and nonclinical—who are committed to their work. This commitment is evidenced in both the quality of care they provide and in their passion for providing an excellent experience to patients and their families. Patients and families who come to Mount Sinai for medical care have described a sense of comfort and familiarity with the staff members who interact with them. They feel well cared for on a personal level, which is a big factor in gaining patient loyalty.

When Mount Sinai became a health system in 2013, the leadership team understood that to create a cohesive organization from separate hospitals, they would need to promote a cultural transformation that maintained the unique culture and established community ties of each of the hospitals while unifying them as a health system under one set of values.

Initially, Mount Sinai made strong gains in its safety and quality outcomes, but it needed to build on the good work already accomplished to include the overall experience of care. The transformation and focus on experience of care required a shift from physician-centered care, which had long been the orientation of the organization's constituent hospitals, toward a more patient-centered culture.

The leadership team began by partnering with leading experts from outside the organization to understand how similar health systems achieved a patient-centered approach. Recognizing that staff engagement is a significant component of this cultural work, the leadership administered a survey to all staff members to assess their readiness for a cultural transformation. The survey focused on what patient experience means to each staff member and their role, department, hospital, or medical practice. More than 18,000 employees (40 percent) responded, and the results showed that, overall, the staff was ready to embark on this cultural transformation and understood the importance of placing the patient at the center of its work.

Health system leaders also took several steps to communicate with their employees the importance of removing barriers to care and placing patients at the center of everything they do. They held a series of coordinated town halls at the various hospital sites to share survey results and explain next steps. In the months that followed, groups of key individuals—both patient facing and non–patient facing—at all levels of the institution were invited to participate in several sessions to discuss the organization's values and vision. They also worked with a graphic designer to create what would become a visual guide, a colorful and detailed depiction of what the ideal patient experience would look like at Mount Sinai. This visual guide has now become the centerpiece of a four-hour interactive session, the *Mount Sinai Health System Experience*, which brings housekeepers and physicians together to learn what it means to put patients first at Mount Sinai. All 42,000-plus Mount Sinai employees are participating in this session, which helps the organization educate its employees about the mission, vision, and values of the organization.

A renewed focus on engagement and recognition has been another result of the cultural transformation efforts. Several employee recognition programs have been initiated at the various hospitals and ambulatory centers. In addition, staff members from various sites came up with a rallying cry, "Better Together," which reflects the organization's emphasis on partnership and community and celebrates the kind of team spirit Mount Sinai stands for.

Coordination and Integration of Care; Emotional Support and Alleviation of Fear and Anxiety

Mount Sinai's leadership reflects true dedication to the exemplary care the organization provides for its patients, as well as the staff's ability to go beyond simply treating a disease to making patients feel truly *cared for* on a personal level. To do this, the organization focuses on key behaviors that drive the overall patient experience, including responsiveness, compassionate and clear communication, welcoming, and way finding. The organization ensures that staff members spend more time in front of their patients than in front of a computer by using initiatives such as purposeful hourly rounding, which makes patients feel safe and well cared for throughout the day, and leadership rounding, which entails checking in regularly with staff members to learn whether there is anything they need to provide patients with the best experience possible.

Teamwork, reflected in everything from the organization's rallying cry to leaders' responsibility for teaching and role modeling, is the organization's most important tactic in striving for safe, high-quality care. Patients' letters of appreciation often speak to the teamwork they observed among staff members, as well as to the exceptional communication that team members had with one another and with them. This kind of teamwork makes patients feel confident they are in the right place. However, teamwork doesn't happen by chance—there are natural relationship builders and connectors that must be drawn on. Certain technological advancements, such as electronic medical records, have improved the dissemination of information across platforms and institutions. But even such advancements can create a barrier in healthcare by making it easier for people to avoid face-to-face communication. Consequently, a more patient-focused cultural transformation, such as the one happening at Mount Sinai, is imperative.

Mount Sinai employees have reported that they feel like they are part of a family; realizing that this type of emotional connection helps patients with their healing process, they try to convey this sense of family to them as well. Everyone in the organization does this in their own ways, but every job at Mount Sinai—whether it's transporting a patient to radiology or performing heart surgery—comes down to ensuring that patients consistently receive the best care while feeling cared for. The strong connection that employees have to Mount Sinai and to one another enables them to deliver on this promise.

Continuity and Transition

When it comes to care transitions, Mount Sinai focuses on the needs of each patient and their family. Early on, the clinical team works to identify a caregiver for each patient. This individual is included in all important discussions during care and is also engaged with staff to ensure that they understand everything the patient needs to know once back at home. In addition, Mount Sinai is working to make family meetings more commonplace throughout the duration of each patient's care. To that end, the organization has been training staff members to better narrate the care they are providing, so that all questions or concerns are addressed. The staff understands that all patients need clear and simple instructions and messaging pertaining to their illness and the type of care required once they return home. Thus, the staff tries to remain focused on the patient's perspective, rather than being task oriented, and to communicate as often and clearly as possible.

Voice of the Patient

A key component of Mount Sinai's journey toward patient-centered care has been using patient feedback to inform best practices and behaviors. The organization is working toward including patients and family members as partners in every aspect of care in an effort to improve safety, quality, and the overall patient and family experience. Mount Sinai takes a multifaceted approach to incorporating the patient's voice into this work, which includes tracking and trending patient comments on surveys as well as patient complaints and compliments. In addition, the organization recently implemented a Patient and Family Partnership Program to support and expand on some of the work underway involving recruitment and training of patients and family members to serve as partners with staff at the hospital and medical practice level in efforts such as workflow redesign, patient education, and continuous improvement initiatives. Staff members who work with patient and family partners report that they are more meaningfully engaged in their work and feel that they have a greater impact in the helping and healing process. This work exemplifies the sentiment of "Better Together."

JEFFERSON HEALTH

Authors' note: Jefferson Health, now an 18-hospital system with more than $9 billion in revenue, became central to Greater Philadelphia's response to the COVID-19 pandemic. Several reviews have established that Jefferson took care of the largest number of COVID patients, helped in part by its years of preparation, its integration of resources, and its geographic spread that included the southern part of New Jersey. The case example that follows demonstrates how Jefferson's 2013–20 decisions were effective during the early years of the pandemic and have prepared the system for success in the future.

Picker Dimensions: Coordination and integration of care; continuity and transition; access to care; involvement of family and friends; information, communication, and education

In 2013, Jefferson Health started a new chapter in its storied history. Founded in Philadelphia by the grandson of a Revolutionary War general, Jefferson initially became known for Dr. George McClellan's great innovative idea in 1824: Medical students should participate in the care of patients during their school years, not wait until after medical school, as was the "practice" at the time.

By 2013, Jefferson was known for its medical school, a historic nursing school, and other health profession schools. It worked closely with the top-ranked Thomas Jefferson University Hospital in a multicorporation governance arrangement. However, that year, the trustees of both institutions decided to combine the university and hospital, and they hired the first modern-day combined president and CEO—Stephen K. Klasko, MD, MBA—as a change agent to move the historic institutions into the future.

At the time, Jefferson consisted of two hospitals in downtown Philadelphia, an attached third hospital for neurosciences, three boards, six colleges, 12,000 employees, and approximately

$1.5 billion in revenue. The separation of the university and hospitals even extended to the e-mail and payroll systems.

Although each of these institutions scored well in national rankings, the trustees believed they were ill prepared for future change in both healthcare and higher education. As president and CEO, Dr. Klasko moved quickly to combine the governing boards and outline a plan for values-driven change that would prepare Jefferson to be a consumer-facing institution (Governance Institute 2017; Voosen 2016).

Dr. Klasko proposed to the board that Jefferson commit to pursuing two key strategies:

1. **Differentiation:** Jefferson would differentiate itself from the other six academic medical centers in Philadelphia by elevating innovation essentially to the level of a mission and adopting the following values: Put People First, Be Bold and Think Differently, and Do the Right Thing. The vision statement became: Reimagining health, education, and discovery to create unparalleled value.

2. **Proactive jump to the future:** Dr. Klasko's guiding idea was that Jefferson would understand what will be obvious a decade from now and commit to doing it today. The core of that transformation would be seeing patients and students as human beings seeking health and education where *they* are.

Healthcare, he believed, would become like everything else—digital and mobile. It needed to be "healthcare at any address."

Both higher education and healthcare delivery face four problems that Jefferson set out to tackle:

1. They both cost too much, with sunk costs in legacy facilities.

2. Patients need to be able to "own" their own medical records (as they do their financial records), and students

need to be able to easily track their progress academically using some of the same tools that they now use to track their fitness.

3. Both the traditional academic and healthcare ecosystems have difficulty with transparency and explaining to students and patients how costs correlate with outcomes.

4. Both are ill prepared for a digital future: The "Fourth Industrial Revolution" will change the future of work, while offering revolutionary opportunities to resolve issues such as health disparities and access to care.

Jefferson's new vision of reimagining health and higher education essentially meant getting a "195-year-old academic medical center to act like a start-up company," Dr. Klasko stated. In healthcare, that meant transitioning from a business-to-business model, in which providers sell themselves to physicians and insurers, to a business-to-consumer model, in which providers sell themselves to consumers. Just as important, Jefferson recognized that people do not view themselves as "patients" until they are ill. Jefferson hoped to attract people into its digital services who want to thrive without having health concerns get in the way. Through that model, those people will already be part of the "Jefferson health club," making Jefferson easier to access when they need a service.

This vision of people as people, not "patients," became the heart of the idea of "health assurance" as articulated by Dr. Klasko and coauthors Hemant Taneja and Kevin Maney in the book *UnHealthcare: A Manifesto for Health Assurance* (Taneja, Maney, and Klasko 2020). In the book, and in Jefferson's partnership with Taneja's General Catalyst, they described using the tools of a digital and mobile lifestyle to help people with issues of wellness, mental health, and fitness—integrated with the sick care provided by traditional providers of care.

As a result of these changes in philosophy, Jefferson in 2021 was a radically different entity from the hospital and university of 2013.

What had been an independent teaching hospital with two ancillary hospitals and about $1.5 billion in revenue became the largest provider of hospital beds in Greater Philadelphia, with more than $9 billion in revenue. Jefferson Health had become an 18-hospital system, including an insurance provider renamed Jefferson Health Partners, and proposals for more growth in the near future. Thomas Jefferson University merged with Philadelphia University in 2017, offering a range of professional degrees, focused on world-leading initiatives in the design of the human experience.

To that end, Jefferson embarked on four distinct strategies to differentiate itself from the competition, as detailed in the sections that follow.

Strategy 1. Healthcare at Any Address

Just as they shop and bank from the comfort of their homes, consumers want to obtain their healthcare digitally, with no fixed address. To accomplish this, Jefferson Health has launched a variety of programs to better address care coordination and integration, as well as access to care and involvement of family and friends, including the following:

- **Virtual visits:** Telehealth will soon become like "telebanking." Although no one uses the term *telebanking*, everyone understands that most banking is done online, except for specific tasks that require a visit to a branch office. Healthcare will be much the same—done online, with fewer tasks that require the consumer to find a building and parking. Jefferson organized its telehealth activities by launching JeffConnect, which provides easy and convenient access to a physician through virtual appointments. This program quickly led to an 18 percent increase in new patient referrals, with the largest gains occurring among younger patients. To get physicians on board, Jefferson changed the way it compensates clinicians, offering incentives for those who embrace telehealth. As a result, Jefferson Health by 2019 boasted perhaps the largest telehealth practice driven by its own faculty across all specialties.

- **Teletriage:** Almost all nonambulance patient visitors to the ED at Thomas Jefferson University Hospital were set up to speak to a physician immediately via telehealth. The system was critical to handling the 80 percent increase in ED visits in the summer of 2019, when a nearby safety-net hospital in Philadelphia went bankrupt, and Jefferson took on a substantial portion of the diverted emergency load. In its self-insured employee population (35,000 patients and their families), a variable deductible program was established ($500 if you come to the ED and $0 if JeffConnect sends you to the ED), resulting in an almost 50 percent reduction in ED visits through telehealth, urgent care, and next-day appointments; $5 million in savings; and increased employee satisfaction and productivity.

- **Virtual inpatient rounds:** Jefferson began a pilot with a video conferencing company to allow family members to participate virtually in inpatient rounds and discharge planning. The same service was used to update family members on their loved one's well-being immediately after surgery.

- **Preventive/screening appointment reminders:** Jefferson automatically sends reminders to a patient's smartphone or smartwatch when it is time to schedule an appointment, such as for a colonoscopy or a mammogram. Such reminders greatly increase the likelihood that the patient makes the appointment and ultimately receives the needed service.

As part of this effort, Jefferson has changed the way it markets to consumers to improve information, communication, and education. The new approach segments consumers and then targets identified cohorts in distinct ways. For example, a 65-year-old with a smartwatch and a sleep tracker will respond to online tracking through JeffConnect, while a patient with cancer who is not digitally savvy has a phone ambassador. The goal was to give consumers the information they need to make good decisions about their health, and then help them connect with the healthcare community. Once they connect, Jefferson seeks to inspire long-term loyalty by providing true value for the money, including a single point of contact and a seamless experience across the continuum.

As the decades progress, Dr. Klasko believes a growing proportion of the population with chronic conditions will rely on virtual health assistants to promote wellness and ongoing care management. By 2030, a majority of healthcare interactions will be virtual or at home, and the majority of these interactions will involve artificial intelligence or machine cognition applications.

Strategy 2. Scale Through the Hub-and-Hub Model

Unlike other academic medical centers, Jefferson did not pursue a hub-and-spoke model where the goal is to funnel patients from outlying communities to a tertiary or quaternary hub in the city. Rather, Dr. Klasko articulated a hub-and-hub model with the goal of providing patients access to care in their local communities. To that end, Jefferson completed five mergers and acquisitions with community hospitals in four years, allowing merged entities to participate in governance through board seats at an equivalent number to that for legacy Jefferson board members. This unique "governance as currency" model promoted a board that adopts a community mindset and single-board mentality.

Strategy 3. Culture Change

Building a consumer platform in a traditional academic medical center can be an arduous process because academic leaders have been trained in an autonomous and a hierarchical atmosphere. Overcoming these biases requires engagement through every "moment of truth." To accomplish a working environment in which innovation and creativity are emphasized as much as traditional academic and clinical skillsets are, Jefferson launched an institute, and several leadership development programs played a critical role in spearheading cultural change throughout the organization. They included the following:

- **Jefferson's Onboarding and Leadership Transformation (JOLT) Institute:** Each year, 40 emerging leaders completed the nine-month JOLT program, which integrates classroom instruction, a project/sketch assignment, and executive coaching. Selected candidates went through an application process and were sponsored and received executive approval to participate. JOLT graduates experienced a 325 percent improvement in their ability to handle difficult issues and scenarios.

- **Jefferson Leadership Institute:** This initiative "reprogrammed" physicians by focusing on competency development and improving readiness for leadership roles through specially designed projects that included participant and sponsor feedback. The goal was to change long-standing belief systems, overcome perceived limitations and selection/education biases, reduce resistance to change, and avoid burnout. As discussed in previous chapters, reports of physician burnout continue to increase, and most burned-out physicians remain disengaged from their organization. By contrast, capable and engaged physicians tend to be more productive and feel as though they can make a difference.

Strategy 4. Going "All-In" on Innovation

At a February 2017 retreat, Dr. Klasko gave Jefferson leaders a choice with regard to pursuing innovation. The first option was to pursue incremental improvement in the clinical and academic environments, supported by philanthropy, and to pursue innovation and partnerships as a secondary concern. The second option was to make innovation and strategic partnerships the core and driver of the health system's strategic vision and its main differentiator from the competition. Jefferson's leaders chose this second approach, and the management team that oversees the clinical and academic enterprises has been charged with making this vision a reality.

To date, Jefferson has embarked on many strategic partnerships. In aggregate, they account for 25 to 30 percent of Jefferson's entire profits, making them critical to the financial health and vitality of the organization. These profits stem from Jefferson's insistence on taking equity stakes in new projects, not just serving as a pilot site for others. Beyond the financial benefits, Jefferson's leaders ensure that these innovations improve clinical or academic performance, such as bending the cost curve, improving revenue cycle performance, and redefining the patient experience. At the same time, beyond the reputational and revenue aspects of these partnerships, they have allowed physicians and nurses to develop critical skills, such as creating equitable access and improving SDOH, and turn population health from a philosophy to an everyday practice (rather than innovating for the sake of innovation itself). Examples of these innovative partnerships include the following:

- **JeffDesign:** Jefferson is the first medical school to integrate design thinking into its curriculum. Medical students are accepted into the program without taking the Medical College Admission Test, and they participate in a comprehensive design thinking cohort that explores upstream solutions to acute problems and develops products for market. In addition, to build the medical toolbox, the students join CoLab PHL (Philadelphia), a redesigned Airstream trailer that goes into neighborhoods to engage communities in a design thinking exercise to improve conditions that contribute to the SDOH.

- **Livongo:** This consumer digital health company focuses on the treatment of chronic diseases. The technology-driven continual interaction with patients has shown strong initial results for type 2 diabetes care, including a 28 percent reduction in ED visits and a 39 percent reduction in inpatient admissions.

- **Digitally powered transportation services:** Through this joint venture, Jefferson extends its "healthcare with no address" philosophy by bringing JeffConnect and other patient services directly into patients' homes, while using "AI-directed" transportation services when patients need care in the office or hospital.

- **Human-centered medical education:** Jefferson is home to the decades-long research that resulted in the Jefferson Scale of Empathy, a validated 20-item scale that focuses on the cognitive skills of empathy and the power it has to improve patient care and experience and allay burnout in clinicians. The goal is to teach health professionals to be ready for when machines can remember data, but clinicians must be the humans in the room, even if that room is virtual.

- **Nurse safety:** Jefferson recognized an increasing problem related to behavioral health and patients who were perceived as threatening to nurses and other health professionals. Jefferson co-owns and partnered with a digital/GPS company to develop Strongline, which enables a nurse to signal concern for their safety by pressing a small button that silently alerts anyone within the area to come to their aid.

How COVID Impacted Jefferson

The strategies outlined in the Jefferson story became critical to Jefferson Health's response in caring for the largest number of patients suffering from COVID. The university's joint work in Italy permitted Jefferson to receive prepublication information about COVID from Milan, Italy, leading to immediate orders to mask up. A prescient infectious disease professor at Jefferson had stocked personal protective equipment in anticipation of a disaster. As a result, Jefferson had very low levels of employee deaths from COVID, and among the nation's lowest numbers for in-hospital transmission of the deadly virus.

The pandemic intensified the integration of Jefferson Health's hospital systems. For example, the multiple ethics committees became one, helping physicians make consistent decisions about the allocation of ventilators.

Dr. Klasko immediately commenced a weekly letter to all employees that thanked them for their work and contained a playlist of songs pertinent to the issues at hand. As other events occurred, such as the nationwide protests against police brutality following the 2020 murder of Black citizen George Floyd by a white police officer during an arrest, the vehicle of music allowed Dr. Klasko to address any topic in an emotional and considerate way through lyrics. Throughout 2020, the response to those letters was unusual and gratifying, showing how much the employees of so many new hospitals looked to the CEO for leadership.

REFERENCES

Allen, L. 2018. "The 4 Values of a Positive Patient Experience." Johns Hopkins Medicine. Published October 18. www.hopkinsmedicine.org/-/media/international/documents/partners-forum/lisaallen_the-four-values-of-a-positive-patient-experience.pdf.

Antiel, R. M., J. C. Tilburt, F. W. Hafferty, M. D. Brennan, and P. S. Mueller. 2011. "Whose Best Interest?" *Minnesota Medicine* 94 (12): 47–49.

Barry, M. J., and S. Edgman-Levitan. 2012. "Shared Decision Making—The Pinnacle of Patient-Centered Care." *New England Journal of Medicine* 366 (9): 780–81.

Boissy, A., A. K. Windover, D. Bokar, M. Karafa, K. Neuendorf, R. M. Frankel, J. Merlino, and M. B. Rothenberg. 2016. "Communication Skills Training for Physicians Improves Patient Satisfaction." *Journal of General Internal Medicine* 31: 755–61. https://link.springer.com/article/10.1007/s11606-016-3597-2.

Dokken, D. L., B. H. Johnson, and H. J. Markwell. 2021. *Family Presence During a Pandemic: Guidance for Decision-Making.* McLean, VA: Institute for Patient- and Family-Centered Care. www.ipfcc.org/events/IPFCC_Family_Presence.pdf.

Edgman-Levitan, S. 2022. "Human Understanding: Digging Deeper with the Board." *BoardRoom Press* 33 (4). Published June by The Governance Institute.

Gandhi, T. K. 2022. "Don't Go to the Hospital Alone: Ensuring Safe, Highly Reliable Patient Visitation." *Joint Commission Journal on Quality and Patient Safety* 48: 61–64.

Governance Institute. 2017. *One Jefferson: Accelerating Reinvention of Academic Medicine Through Growth, Integration, and Innovation.* Lincoln, NE: Governance Institute.

Institute of Medicine. 2001. *Crossing the Quality Chasm: A New Health System for the 21st Century.* Washington, DC: National Academies Press.

John, H. 2013. "From Osler to the Cone Technique." *HSR Proceedings in Intensive Care and Cardiovascular Anesthesia* 5 (1): 57–58.

Koloroutis, M., and M. Pole. 2021. "Trauma-Informed Leadership and Posttraumatic Growth." *Nursing Management* 52 (12): 28–34.

Lamas, D. L. 2020. "Families Are Central to Critical Care: But the Waiting Room Is Empty." *New York Times*. Published August 17. www.nytimes.com/2020/08/17/opinion/coronavirus-hopsitals-visitors.html.

Mayo Clinic. 2024a. "Mission and Values." Accessed September 22. www.mayoclinic.org/about-mayo-clinic/mission-values.

———. 2024b. "The Needs of the Patient Come First." YouTube video, 7:10. Accessed September 22. www.youtube.com/watch?v=lBgdd7nolQg.

Perkins, S. B. 2022. "Human Stories: COVID Lessons on the Importance of Family Presence." *BoardRoom Press* 33 (5). Published October by The Governance Institute.

Sherman, R. O. 2021. "Using a Trauma-Informed Leadership Approach." *Nurse Leader* 19 (4): 321–22.

Taneja, H., K. Maney, and S. Klasko. 2020. *UnHealthcare: A Manifesto for Health Assurance*. Self-published, Lulu.com.

Valley, T. S., A. Schutz, Mt. T. Nagle, L. J. Myles, K. Lipman, S. W. Ketcham, M. Kent, C. E. Hibbard, E. A. Harlan, and K. Hauschildt. 2020. "Changes to Visitation Policies and Communication Practices in Michigan ICUs During the COVID-19 Pandemic." *American Journal of Respiratory and Critical Care Medicine* 202 (6): 883–85.

Voosen, P. 2016. "Is It Time for Universities to Get Out of the Hospital Business?" *Chronicle of Higher Education*. Published May 31. www.chronicle.com/article/Is-It-Time-for-Universities-to/236643vv.

PART III

Building a Consumer-Centric System

CHAPTER 7

Consumer-Centric Leadership

WHEN THE PROVERBIAL alien visits from intergalactic space, healthcare delivery in the United States will truly be a mind-boggling conundrum. Some features of this conundrum are well known: an immensely wealthy country where health outcomes for its population fall behind those of less wealthy countries. A country where longevity is falling for the first time—many children will live shorter lives than their parents.

But there is a deeper conundrum in healthcare delivery. It is the contrast between the passion, knowledge, and dedication of the American healthcare workforce and the confusing, fragmented, tedious, and inequitable delivery of care to patients. As the examples in chapter 6 demonstrate, healthcare organizations that emphasize the Picker dimensions of patient-centered care, every day for every patient, can transform the consumer experience. But many organizations have not yet found the courage to forge ahead on this urgent path. The consumer revolution in healthcare is nothing less than people understanding that the system itself is sick, and that moving from a focus on "sick care" to "health assurance" will be necessary for the traditional healthcare ecosystem in much the same way as convenience and cost pressures transformed the retail industry.

This revolution includes the use of technology to make everything that is difficult today easier. Organizations will be rewarded if they can effectively and appropriately use technology to help individuals and their families thrive, while those that remain focused on sick care will go the way of retail organizations that ignored the Amazon revolution. These changes require us to revise our understanding of healthcare so that people are supported at all times, where they are, when they need it, including at home. The revolution places the human at the center of the healthcare journey.

This revolution also includes the fight for health consumer citizenship: the right to understand the costs and outcomes of a treatment plan, the right to own one's own medical records, and the right to access care itself.

Finally, the revolution will be fought by both outsiders and insiders. On the outside, the healthcare delivery industry, dominated by legacy institutions, faces competition from retail medicine, private equity and health plan purchasing of physician groups, telehealth, the shift to outpatient care for numerous procedures that used to require a hospital bed, and the so-called millennial skimming companies that offer instant digital access to services that once required patients to sit, sometimes for long periods, in the waiting rooms of physicians' offices.

The insider revolutionaries are ready, too. Today's medical students are increasingly diverse and deeply committed to social justice. They are keenly aware that social and lifestyle factors account for much more of the long-term outcomes for their patients compared with what they as new physicians can offer in episodic sick care.

In educational circles, the crisis of complex care is front and center. Educators are aware that they are preparing students in disciplinary silos, when what's really needed are teams that treat complex problems spanning mental health, social health, and physical health. In fact, we know that the solution to the rising national bill for healthcare is to solve the problem of complex care: The 5 percent of patients who account for 50 percent of the cost of healthcare in the United States are most often in need of complex care.

This chapter looks at the revolutionaries who can lead America's great academic health institutions, with digital technology companies envisioning consumer-based healthcare delivery. More of us can join the revolution—if we embrace it and the role of leadership in making it happen.

This chapter also suggests that hope is not a strategy, as legacy institutions face the need to become nimble and consumer focused and decide how to meet consumers where they are.

THE CEO AS CHIEF CONSUMER OFFICER

Today's CEOs face the same concerns the public faces—partisan divides that mean any election could switch healthcare policy overnight. We are living in the twilight zone between value-based payments and fee-for-service.

But what remains true is that regardless of how a hospital is reimbursed, it must develop into a consumer-facing institution that creates loyalty by eliminating the fragmentation and confusion felt so often by patients. As a result, a CEO must become an institution's guide to a new future by elevating innovation as a mission, encouraging creativity as a core value, and building the data capacity that allows design thinking to succeed.

A CEO's job starts with their trustees. Every leader needs a strong, courageous board. It takes a bold group of trustees today to look beyond the obvious accounting measures of revenue over expenses and instead look at investment in the future, culture change, innovation, and commitment to the community.

Healthcare trustees must appreciate and act on the balance between the old math and the emerging new math. Academic medical centers have relied on a traditional formula of patient care collections, tuition and fees, and sometimes research grants. This isn't "bad" math. But it is under enormous pressure because of the inability to charge patients more, or charge students more. In contrast, the new math includes innovative partnerships to build a consumer platform, as well as an expanded relationship with the community expressed in philanthropy. There isn't a shortage of money from donors; there is a shortage of bold ideas that will pay off in social change. We would argue that this drive to impact social change puts mission-driven, not-for-profit provider organizations in a better position when compared with the for-profit, non-mission-based entrants into the market. As the industry shifts from traditional charity, donors—the new donors—will want to see results. Both partners and donors want one thing: genuine change. Physician Jaan Sidorov argues for harnessing the small-group dynamic of generative wisdom by leading trustees through "problem-based learning sessions," borrowing from medical education's success with problem-based learning. Sidorov (2016) wrote:

> Truly insightful boardroom meetings are still the result of an alchemy that is difficult to create on-demand. When complicated issues arise, every process and skill . . . is still no guarantee against resorting to obsolete heuristics, circular reasoning, over-attention to detail, or dominance by a strong-willed individual . . . that fails to recognize a new value proposition or misses an emerging enterprise risk.

The wisdom of groups can work. It requires trustees willing to commit to a future-facing strategy in which money invested in an integrated consumer-facing platform becomes preeminent, and where CEOs are held accountable for progress in addressing community needs. The leader has to make sense of what is happening—indeed, the leader has to bring to life a growth-affirming innovation narrative.

George Day and Greg Shea (2018) of the Wharton School of Economics argue that four levers are most effective for leaders in healthcare. The first lever is to invest in people: create a leadership academy and hire team leaders and project directors who value innovation. An organization needs so-called changemakers, individuals who see an opportunity or obstacle and have the gravitas and support to enlist others to follow their lead and look at creative and flexible means to overcome the obstacle or embrace the opportunity.

Formal leadership training works. It starts with self-awareness and builds to seeing how to be effective in changing an organization. It works especially well when it targets midcareer professionals, people who have learned some of the ways things are done and are ready to be insiders in the revolution. Pay attention to good people who are uncomfortable with the status quo. Do not dismiss their complaints. They will show you the future.

The second lever, according to Day and Shea (2018), is to encourage prudent risk taking. The boss who punishes a bad idea creates an organization averse to creativity.

The third lever is to adopt a consumer-centric innovation process: build the data sets you need to treat individuals as consumers. Doing so may involve a much deeper dive into strategically gathered information about your current and prospective customers.

The fourth lever is to align metrics with innovation: reward learning over scorekeeping.

These four levers speak to a critical need in the pursuit of innovation: invest in building an in-house capability to generate and maintain deep data sets into the interactions between the institution and its customers. These data are key to decision-making at every level, from the handling of test results to the making of appointments.

CHANGING THE DNA OF HEALTHCARE

The educational pipeline also must change. Several universities, as well as health systems that have sponsored new medical schools, realize that we must change the DNA of healthcare delivery itself— we need students prepared for the age of artificial intelligence (AI) and ready to deliver value to communities.

Medical education remains trapped between two historic standardized tests, forcing students to compete for relative advantage based on their ability to succeed at test taking. Using Medical College Admission Test (MCAT) scores predisposes medical schools to select, unfortunately, relatively privileged individuals whose greatest skill is sitting alone and absorbing data. But admissions committees are also trapped: Because the Step One board examinations determine whether a student will be accepted to a prestigious residency, admissions committees often argue that accepting students who do poorly on the MCAT is a false promise because they will likely do poorly on the Step One examinations and be unable to pursue the specialty of their choice.

However, some medical schools have resisted the trap. They are using emotional intelligence, leadership, and empathy as criteria to select more diverse students. Boston University has been a leader in using holistic admissions to double diversity in its medical school. According to Robert A. Witzburg and Henry M. Sondheimer (2013), "Students from groups underrepresented in medicine now make up approximately 20 percent of the entering class, as compared with 11 to 12 percent before the adoption of holistic review."

Other schools have used emotional intelligence and leadership skills as criteria twinned to a curriculum that supports them. Thomas Jefferson University pioneered the Jefferson Scale of Empathy, with decades of sustained data supporting it, and which many observers believe should be an admissions criterion for health professional schools.

We still have a long way to go on this point, which may be impacted by the 2023 US Supreme Court decision resulting in dissolution of affirmative action in college admissions—and that makes it all the more important for medical schools to adopt holistic admissions. The Association of American Medical Colleges (AAMC) reported a total of 22 percent of medical students being from racial or ethnic minorities in the 2022–23 academic year. While the AAMC data set shows other signs of increasing diversity, including more women and a more varied socioeconomic status of medical students, this does not represent significant movement since the 2012–13 academic year (AAMC 2022). In fact, it is time to question whether the "one-size-fits-all" medical education model continues to serve society in light of the fact that it can easily take one individual past the age of 30 to finish.

On the one hand, we need physician scientists who can manipulate cells at the back of the eye to stop an aggressive cancer. On the other hand, we desperately need physicians with maturity and emotional intelligence who can earn the trust of their communities to convince a patient to undergo an early eye examination, before the cancer becomes uncurable. Both kinds of skills are needed, at the same time.

The traditional focus on memorizing information must end. Within a few years, it will be absurd to select medical students based on memorization skills, multiple-choice test results, and organic chemistry grades, which fail to create physicians who are empathetic, communicative, and creative. Today, physicians have some type of AI next to them that is better than any human at memorizing the myriad genomic and scientific formulas. What that artificial brain cannot do, however, is *be* human. We need medical students prepared to answer when a patient asks, "What does this mean, doctor?"

Perhaps the most pressing crisis in healthcare is the inability of the workforce to handle complex care. In the current healthcare environment, providers in siloed disciplines and departments treat a costly group of patients who may have multiple chronic illnesses, coupled with learning disabilities, mental health issues, and social or economic challenges. The solution requires schools to collaborate even beyond today's interdisciplinary education to create true community laboratories that develop research-based curricula and build teams for treating complex care. Those who study complex care report that simple solutions can unravel complex problems. But today's reimbursement models don't pay for simple solutions, thereby creating a cycle of high costs as patients seek routine help from the emergency department (ED). For example, at Jefferson

Health, a concept called "hotspotting" has been deployed whereby medical students and nursing students communicate with the 5 percent of patients with chronic illnesses who utilize the most resources. In many cases, these efforts have resulted in the trifecta of increased patient satisfaction and better outcomes at a fraction of the cost of ED and physician visits.

So, what's the solution? Throughout this book, we have written about the need to provide more personalized care while at the same time caring for the needs of the population. This need for "consumer segmentation" can be extrapolated to student segmentation. We need students who will be physician scientists and are selected and educated in the traditional manner based on MCAT exams, multiple-choice tests, and academic/scientific rigor. We need students who will be great clinical "healers" chosen based on self-awareness, empathy, communication skills, and cultural competence who can take advantage of the fact that their iPhone can answer many of the facts that former generations of students had to memorize. And we need medical students who will help develop the generative AI and other technologies and lead the technology revolution.

Just as important, we need to develop young doctors and nurses who understand the basics of and can keep pace with the incredible transformations that will occur related to generative AI, large language models, robotics, and other fourth industrial revolution technologies so that they are not victims but rather proponents of these new technologies. We wouldn't consider training a cancer specialist without educating them about CAR-T or immunotherapy, and we wouldn't train a radiologist who could not interpret MRIs or CT scans. It will be equally tragic if the healthcare providers of the next few decades are not trained in and totally comfortable with these game-changing technologies.

Perhaps the greatest challenge and opportunity is integrating the machine into the team. As Jack Ma, a teacher who became the founder of AliBaba, said at the World Economic Forum (2019),

"How can we teach kids to be more creative and do things that machines cannot do? Machines have chips, but human beings have hearts ... Education should move in this direction." The key will be creating a future where machines do what they do best (memorize and analyze large segments of data) and have human caregivers do what we should do best (show understanding and empathy toward our patients) and not try to get humans to outmemorize the robots or pretend that generative AI will be as understanding and empathetic as the best of human caregivers. One way to look at this is that it took us years to get doctors and nurses to work together in "centers for interprofessional education," and now we have to get doctors and robots to understand each other, perhaps in "centers for intersentient education"!

The key is that patients and consumers will always want another human being to answer the question we've emphasized elsewhere in this book; namely, "Doctor, what does this diagnosis or lab test mean to me and my family?" That is why training a new generation of health professionals along with generative AI in a team approach must be an integral part of this new future. In fact, now that we have developed computer and AI entities that can memorize and analyze better and more data points than any human on the planet, human wisdom, empathy, and ability to ask the right question become much more important traits for doctors and nurses than knowing the right answer.

ANCHOR INSTITUTIONS: A FALSE PROMISE?

The failure to integrate mental, physical, and social health points to a more acute issue: the false promise of "anchor institutions." Many cities, such as Chicago, Baltimore, and Philadelphia, boast of their "eds and meds," and each is rich with historic academic health centers and universities. But each of these cities also ranks among the nation's worst in the longevity gap between zip codes—more than 20 years between their richest and poorest neighborhoods. The consumer revolution must cut across income levels.

The ideas of population health, including addressing the social and economic determinants of health, have not yet taken hold through the academic medical continuum, from selection and training to research and clinical practice. Jennifer E. DeVoe and colleagues (2017) issued a call for action to academic medicine:

> To build world-class, 21st-century infrastructure for improving health, [academic medical centers] can renew investments in primary care, strengthen ties with public health, create sustainable community laboratories and classrooms, envision multidisciplinary research centers, and build strong community–academic partnerships for facilitating bidirectional teaching, learning, innovation, and discovery.

Our collective experience with COVID-19 makes this call for action more acute. The most negatively impacted groups of consumers were in counties with higher rates of minorities and lower socioeconomic status—people who were already severely impacted by the social determinants of health (SDOH) and had less access to affordable healthcare because of lack of coverage, lack of providers, lack of transportation, or lack of ability to take time off work without losing pay (American Academy of Family Physicians 2024). Moreover, qualitative research conducted by The Governance Institute from 2022 to 2024 revealed a stark decline in dedicated staffing and strategic/leadership focus not only on continued investment in initiatives to address SDOH but also on new investment to expand such programs. At the same time, many health system CEOs who have spoken with The Governance Institute as a part of this research have doubled down on the importance of a successful anchor institution as an economic engine in many communities that are struggling financially because of inflation and higher costs of living (Governance Institute 2024).

EMBRACING DIGITAL HEALTH TECHNOLOGY

We overestimate technology in the short run but underestimate it in the long run. Nowhere is this truer than in healthcare delivery. Yet when a traditional medical center partners with a Silicon Valley firm, medical outcomes can actually improve—sometimes dramatically.

One key conundrum for healthcare delivery involves type 2 diabetes. Occasionally an individual with this disease has an acute issue requiring great scientific knowledge. However, for the majority of encounters, the science is not remote: Weight and age have overwhelmed the body's ability to handle glucose, and the resulting inflammation attacks every organ. The difficulty lies in helping that individual with sustained complex care—the physical sequelae of the disease, the depression that accompanies it, and the struggles arising from any plan to lose weight consistently without surgery. The social complications are immense: depression can lead to job loss, which leads to a loss of insurance, and so forth.

But a Silicon Valley company, Livongo, founded by people who themselves have diabetes, had an immediate impact on members' hospitalization and emergency department visits, resulting in a dramatic drop in acute care encounters (see the case study on Jefferson Health in chapter 6 for more information).

The lessons learned from digital health firms are many, including the following:

- In many instances, the data gathered by our current electronic health records (EHRs) are insufficient to help individuals maintain a healthy lifestyle at home. They do their job—record medical encounters—but they don't provide the knowledge needed by the patient.
- Constant contact through an electronic concierge works. However, we do not yet have a system for patients that even parallels the continuous monitoring of automobiles sitting in garages. In the near future, wearable devices,

robots, and AI will constantly monitor vital signs and other parameters and notify you and your caregiver when there is a need for intervention. The static snapshot approach to EHRs in the physician's office will be replaced by 24/7 monitoring, with information transmitted through phones, voice assistants, and so forth.

- Some companies have found that patients prefer to "talk" to a computer about mental health issues rather than visit a therapist, and, as a result, they can obtain help anytime, anywhere. This change will be especially relevant for younger patients who often relate better to "bots" than humans, particularly about sensitive issues and if the "bot" looks more like them than the human does.

Machine learning is not a gimmick in healthcare, although its early applications seem to be little more than toys. But technology's potential to monitor thousands of individuals at once, and to provide real-time help and guidance, is unparalleled. For problems such as heart disease, diabetes, depression, and even compliance with cancer care, using machine learning to help patients can create major breakthroughs in medical outcomes themselves.

THE SWITCH FROM PATIENT TO CONSUMER: GAINING HUMAN UNDERSTANDING

From changing the DNA of healthcare to embracing digital health technology, the CEO as chief consumer officer must finally explore the connection between leadership and the human experience of healthcare: a personal journey of which providers are the guardians. NRC Health defines human understanding within the context of healthcare as providers' ability to understand the people they care for with greater clarity, immediacy, and depth, as well as to appreciate what matters most to each patient to ease their journey. Human understanding encompasses the Picker dimensions and has a deeper purpose—to view patients as more than stakeholders, target audiences, and populations—to know patients as *human beings*. The following is an exploration of these three aspects of human understanding.

1. **Clarity** involves the ability to illuminate the critical moments to improve the patient's treatments, outcomes, and overall experience.

2. **Immediacy** is the ability to capture what people think and feel about their care in real time and over time, to enable providers to build on what is working and resolve problems with greater speed and personalization.

3. **Depth** explores a patient's experience through a multidimensional lens. A provider must understand the totality of their interaction with every patient—before, during, and after care—to comprehend the patient's personal journey toward well-being.

NRC Health research on human understanding and its impacts focuses on whether everyone treated the patient as a unique person during their care encounter. The Human Understanding Metric (HU^{me}) was developed through several national market studies with a total of more than 85,000 participants, a series of diverse focus groups, and field tests across a range of high-performing health systems. The decision to reference "everyone" in this metric is a result of views expressed within the focus groups and national surveys. The vast majority of people expect that everyone, not just the care team, should treat them as a unique person. Through its *Market Insights* survey, NRC Health found that 63 percent of patients and consumers believe that being treated as a unique person is important in healthcare, double that of other services or activities such as banking and hospitality; in the same survey, 38 percent of patients said this is actually happening (NRC Health 2022a).

This research also shows a direct impact of human understanding on the net promoter score (NPS), a widely used indicator across industries of how likely someone is to recommend your business or service to others. Specifically, patients who answer a 10 ("Yes, everyone treated me as a unique person") are 12 times more likely to be a "promoter" on the NPS scale; patients who answer 0 ("No one treated me as a unique person") are 13 times more likely to be a "detractor." This metric positively impacts patient and consumer loyalty as well, with 86 percent of people who were treated as a unique person by their top-of-mind hospital professing loyalty to that organization (NRC Health 2022a).

Connecting this research back to the equity and SDOH problem in healthcare, this research also shows that human understanding is integral to health equity. Black patients are less likely to report being treated as unique than white patients are, and Asian patients are the least likely to report being treated as unique (NRC Health 2022a).

What we know now through this research is that patients are asking providers to *join them* in their health journey, rather than trying to "engage" patients in what providers are trying to do. Human understanding capabilities can be achieved through sophisticated data collection and real-time reporting mechanisms, including transparent reporting of physician performance to the physicians themselves, collection of intelligence about the local market such as community perceptions and preferences, and competitive analysis. Also necessary are outreach, coaching, and comprehensive improvement plans for midlevel managers and frontline staff. However, the most important piece of the puzzle is building a consumer-centric culture, where everyone in a provider organization lives and breathes human understanding. Accomplishing this requires strong messaging and support of these efforts (by means of leadership encouragement and guidance, resource investment, and staff development) by executive leaders and, ultimately, the board.

With human understanding as the ultimate aim, healthcare leaders can go beyond patient-centered care to strategically address the consumer revolution, which will improve our ability to help many more patients. The revolution will fuel performance improvement in healthcare, just as it has in other industries, by transforming this illogical system from one that is confusing, fragmented, tedious, and inequitable to one that meets consumers where they are and is grounded in the *human* at its center.

REFERENCES

American Academy of Family Physicians. 2024. *Impact on Health Systems from COVID-19 and the Role of Social Determinants of Health*. Published March/April. www.aafp.org/pubs/fpm/issues/2024/0300/covid19-health-disparities.pdf.

Association of American Medical Colleges (AAMC). 2022. "Diversity Increases at Medical Schools in 2022." Press release, December 13. www.aamc.org/news/press-releases/diversity-increases-medical-schools-2022.

Day, G. S., and G. P. Shea. 2018. "Grow Faster by Changing Your Innovation Narrative." *MIT Sloan Management Review.* Published December 10. https://sloanreview.mit.edu/article/grow-faster-by-changing-your-innovation-narrative/.

DeVoe, J. E., S. Likumahuwa-Ackman, J. Shannon, and E. S. Hayward. 2017. "Creating 21st-Century Laboratories and Classrooms for Improving Population Health: A Call to Action for Academic Medical Centers." *Academic Medicine* 92 (4): 475–82.

Governance Institute. 2024. *One Impact Campaign to Address the Financial Health of Patients and Communities* (qualitative research; case studies and publication forthcoming). Lincoln, NE: Governance Institute.

NRC Health. 2022a. "Patient Perceptions of Human Understanding." *nSight*. Published August. https://nrchealth-2. infogram.com/1te94me7p4w83ltw1x0zypdzx1cq8kk36q6.

Sidorov, J. 2016. "Using Problem-Based Wisdom to Transform Governance Oversight to Insight." *Healthcare Transformation* 1 (3): 154–63.

Witzburg, R. A., and H. M. Sondheimer. 2013. "Holistic Review—Shaping the Medical Profession One Applicant at a Time." *New England Journal of Medicine* 368 (17): 1565–67.

World Economic Forum. 2019. "Do Sleep, Don't Have Doubts: Jack Ma's Guide to Sanity and Success." Published January 23. www.weforum.org/agenda/2019/01/do-sleep-dont-have-doubts-jack-mas-guide-to-sanity-and-success/.

CHAPTER 8

Internal Talent Needs

To PUSH HEALTHCARE to new heights and achieve the bold prop-osition of human understanding, consumer-centric leadership is only the beginning. Far beyond the C suite, within the sprawling halls of the average hospital, hundreds, if not thousands, of feet are on the ground (our potential insider revolutionaries): nurses, phy-sicians, physicians' assistants, nurse practitioners, midwives, secu-rity guards, janitors, and so forth. These employees are the testing ground for any vision or strategy, and success or failure depends on them.

Engaging employees is far from easy. Across all industries, US worker satisfaction has remained relatively low in the years since the Great Recession of 2008–9. The COVID-19 pandemic and the Great Resignation of 2021–22 didn't help. The Pew Research Center reported a 51 percent satisfaction rate overall among US workers in 2023, but healthcare ranked the lowest, compared with 27 other industries (Menasce Horowitz and Parker 2023). For too many healthcare workers, time is spent doing administrative tasks such as typing, filling out forms, and filling in the electronic health record, often at night when they are supposed to be done with work (Burky 2023).

An engaged employee is in such demand (more than 4,800 hos-pitals and health systems across the country, plus countless other types of healthcare corporations, are seeking practitioners), an entire industry has sprouted solely to help organizations engage their employees. However, accomplishing this goal may be difficult without truly defining what is meant by an engaged individual.

> *Employee engagement* is the emotional commitment the employee has to the organization and its goals.

This emotional commitment means engaged employees actually care about their work and their company. They don't just work for a paycheck or for the next promotion but work on behalf of the organization's goals, which they share (Kruse 2012).

What if we took a step back and looked at what it means to be an engaged individual in society? For that, we turn to Abraham Maslow, an American psychologist who studied human needs. He devised a hierarchy, an ascending level of needs from the most basic to the most desirable and difficult to attain. These rungs are sometimes referred to as "Maslow's Mountain" because, much like climbing a real mountain, it can be difficult, if not impossible, for many people to reach the top (see exhibit 8.1).

EXHIBIT 8.1: Maslow's Hierarchy

Source: McLeod (2024).

Most of us take for granted our basic physical needs, such as food and water, until we are faced with situations in which we are deprived of them. As we move up the mountain, our needs become more emotional. Not everyone has friends or feels a sense of connection. Many who do still lack self-esteem or don't feel recognized by others in their lives. The summit is self-actualization. This, Maslow argued, is the fulfillment of one's purpose. It's also incredibly rare for one to achieve sustained self-actualization.

Where does work fit in this hierarchy? Surely, as overworked Americans, we find some connection between our needs and our jobs. In chapter 4, we discussed the calling of healthcare and the emotional connection many caregivers feel toward their work. But do we gain friendships, self-respect, and even self-actualization in our jobs?

THE DOWN-MOUNTAIN EFFECT OF COVID

There's no denying that the COVID-19 pandemic brought into focus startling new realities for virtually all Americans. Simple freedoms and pleasures evaporated as the nation grappled with fighting off a deadly new virus. A simple trip to the grocery store became riddled with caution and anxiety, yet it was necessary and one of the few escapes from home for many people. But for healthcare workers, the setting didn't change, and the horrors and fatigue created a warlike environment. Needs such as safety, security, and health were challenged in new ways. Breath, perhaps the most foundational of Maslow measures, was stolen from so many victims. The realization of what COVID took away, which continues to this day, has left immeasurable pain and sadness behind. Much of that pain was absorbed by healthcare's front lines.

COMPASSION FATIGUE

Among healthcare workers, burnout and fatigue were serious concerns long before they were exacerbated by COVID. Historically, no industry has put an emotional strain on its workers quite like healthcare. Like other industries, healthcare has plenty of unengaged employees. But lack of engagement can be much more dangerous in healthcare. For example, nurse engagement is the number one variable correlating to patient mortality, more than the nurse-to-patient ratio (Aiken et al. 2002). Disengaged employees call in sick more often, pay less attention when they are at work, and tend to leave their jobs faster, causing higher staff turnover. An emergency department that is understaffed or staffed with distracted, detached workers is a recipe for disaster.

Compassion fatigue is defined as the "physical and mental exhaustion and emotional withdrawal experienced by those who care for sick or traumatized people over an extended period of time" (Merriam-Webster 2024). In healthcare, compassion fatigue is an issue for all members of the care team. Physicians suffer from burnout in especially high numbers, according to one study designed to provide a representative snapshot of physicians and the general US working population (Sternberg 2016). Nearly half of physicians (49 percent) meet the definition for overall burnout, compared with 28 percent of other US workers. A more detailed analysis revealed that more than 54 percent of physicians have at least one symptom of burnout (Alexander and Ballou 2018). Emotional exhaustion and depersonalization among physicians is also more than one-and-a-half times greater than among the general working population. Physicians work a median of 50 hours per week, and their satisfaction with the work–life balance is far lower than that of other workers: 36 percent versus approximately 66 percent (Comparably 2020; Westgate 2014). Researchers in another study found that increasing a nurse's workload by one surgical patient was associated with a 7 percent increase in a patient's odds of dying within 30 days of admission. Boosting the workload from four to six patients resulted in a 14 percent increase in a patient's risk of dying, while increasing the workload from six to eight patients resulted in a 31 percent increase in a patient's risk of dying (Ball et al. 2018).

According to a survey of nearly 8,000 surgeons published in the *Annals of Surgery*, 9 percent of respondents stated that they had made a major medical error in the past three months. Approximately 70 percent attributed these perceived errors to a personal issue such as fatigue, stress, or a lapse in judgment. The worse the surgeon's burnout, the more likely the surgeon was to report having made a medical error. Specifically, each 1-point increase in a surgeon's score on a scale of emotional exhaustion was associated with a 5 percent increase in the odds of having reported an error, while a 1-point increase in a surgeon's depersonalization score was tied to an 11 percent increase (Shanafelt et al. 2010).

Many observers believe that the Great Resignation had much to do with the fallout of fighting a pandemic and needing a reset. In healthcare, this may be broadly true, but for many workers, the itch to switch jobs had been roiling beneath the surface for many years. The average traveling nurse didn't decide overnight to pack up and ship out to another hospital. And so our fatigued workforce, even more drained from fighting COVID, has tried to find itself in other spaces and places. Has it worked? No. Recent studies show that workers who quit their job during the Great Resignation are significantly less satisfied than their colleagues who stayed (Brewer 2024). Regardless of whether employees stay or go, they need to be engaged wherever they are. The findings point to the need to pay attention to employee engagement all the way to the top of the organization.

Hiring, helping, and proactively retaining employees should be on every hospital CEO's short list of priorities. Bringing the human understanding lens to employee engagement work can be impactful: a 2023 Harris-Kumanu poll found that workers who agreed with the statement "My organization tries to understand my personal purpose for working" were 70 percent more likely to remain with their current organization, compared with 35 percent of workers who disagreed with that statement (Strecher 2023). The workers who agreed were also more highly engaged, 59 percent versus 16 percent (Stretcher 2023). However, a 2018 survey showed that just 26 percent of organizational leaders consider employee engagement "very important" (Dale Carnegie & Associates 2018). The same survey also found that 31 percent of managers strongly agreed that their companies make employee engagement a top priority, while 16 percent "somewhat or strongly disagreed." Yet, 41 percent of senior leaders strongly agreed that they are supporting their managers in efforts to engage employees, and only 8 percent disagreed. Clearly, senior leaders believe they are supporting employee engagement more than do their direct reports. This gap could be one reason for the disconnect among employees on the ground.

One common myth is that healthcare is a bustling, growth-generating industry that naturally pays well and therefore has higher employee engagement. In the context of work, does money buy happiness? Princeton University researchers studied this connection and found a link between an increase in salary and an increase in engagement; however, they found that every 1 percent increase in employee satisfaction required a 10 percent increase in salary (Kahneman and Deaton 2010). This one-to-ten ratio means that hefty raises would be required to even modestly boost employee satisfaction. This finding may even shed light on why people who flocked to higher salaries at new organizations during the Great Resignation are still finding themselves stuck and unhappy. While money certainly isn't unimportant, it doesn't seem to hold the key to an engaged healthcare workforce.

MEASUREMENT

How, then, can we boost employee engagement in healthcare? Nearly every hospital and health system conducts annual engagement surveys, and the results of these surveys flood into human resources departments. Many of these surveys are long: Every department has questions to include, and often there is a stack of legacy questions that cannot be abandoned for fear of severing a trend on an important issue. The result is a deluge of data for human resource managers to comb through and analyze in order to find actionable results. To say their backs are against the wall is an understatement. NRC Health's employee engagement study provides additional context (see exhibit 8.2).

Another issue is data integration—comparing and sharing the perspectives of employees and patients to reveal areas of strength and opportunity as well as to identify deeper issues that may threaten the organization in ways that are not readily apparent.

INTERNAL NET PROMOTER SCORE

The net promoter score (NPS), a staple of measuring loyalty in business, asks people to rate an organization based on their likelihood to recommend its products or services to family and friends. The idea is that people will only recommend an organization if they are committed to the organization themselves. When we zoom in on employees in particular, their loyalty to the organization that employs them becomes an even more important litmus test as to how they feel about their employer. According to NRC Health's employee engagement studies, large swaths of healthcare workers are not advocates for their organization (NRC Health 2018). On a standard 11-point NPS scale, only 32.0 percent of employees were engaged (a score of 9 or 10), while 29.2 percent were disengaged (a score of 0–6). The largest segment of employees—38.8 percent—had a score of 7 or 8 and were considered passive. If we calculated an NPS for the average healthcare organization, it would receive a paltry 3 out of a possible 100, a very similar score to that for the average cable company (see exhibit 8.3).

The same NPS structured question was asked of healthcare employees in terms of the organization and specifically how it

EXHIBIT 8.2: Reasons Managers Give for Dissatisfaction with Annual Employee Surveys

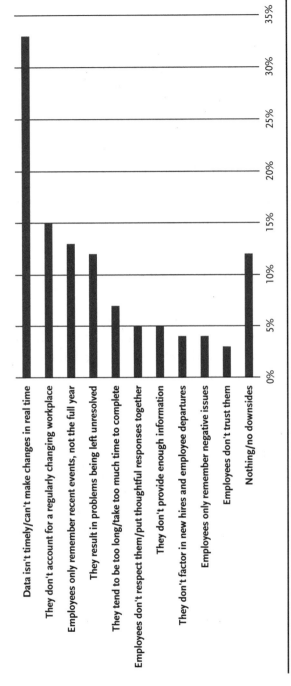

Source: NRC Health (2018).

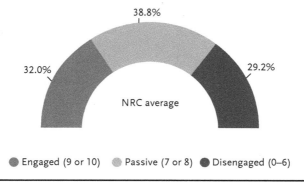

38.8%

32.0%

29.2%

NRC average

● Engaged (9 or 10)　◌ Passive (7 or 8)　● Disengaged (0–6)

Source: NRC Health (2018).

delivers on the patient experience. Are organizations ready to engage their patients? As shown in exhibit 8.4, the results were only slightly better than those for employee engagement: 41.0 percent of employees gave their organization a score of 9 or 10 on engagement, 21.7 percent reported that the organization was disengaged (a score of 0–6), and 37.3 percent stated that it was passive (a score of 7 or 8).

These numbers reveal a problem inside the healthcare organization and in the minds of employees. We often don't believe in ourselves enough to deliver excellent patient care. If we can't engage our own employees, how do we hope to engage patients and consumers who will be our future patients?

Interestingly, healthcare employees and healthcare consumers are on common ground here. Both groups set a high bar for how healthcare should be, and neither believes it is measuring up. When was the last time we tried to compare employee and consumer perspectives? We usually keep them separate within our many silos. Employee research is housed within human resources, and consumer research is housed within the marketing department. Both departments spend plenty of time researching their respective audiences, but never the twain shall meet.

EXHIBIT 8.4: Average Net Promoter Score for Organizational Engagement by Employees

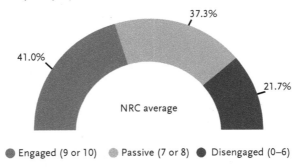

37.3%

41.0%

21.7%

NRC average

● Engaged (9 or 10)　● Passive (7 or 8)　● Disengaged (0–6)

Source: NRC Health (2018).

EMPLOYEE EXPERIENCE + CONSUMER EXPERIENCE

We know this much: When employees are engaged, they deliver a better patient experience. And when employees are not engaged, it's not just a human resources problem. Patient experiences suffer from disengaged employees, and patients are well aware when a decline in employee engagement occurs (see exhibit 8.5).

Thus, increasing employee engagement becomes a patient-centered imperative. Since 2010, NRC Health has been diligently tracking the organizations that are trying to improve employee engagement while keeping an eye on patient ratings. It's clear that the two move in concert with each other (see exhibit 8.6).

Why don't more organizations tie the two together? Much like the rest of healthcare, each department is incredibly busy and dealing with its own dashboard of metrics—many tied to their paychecks—which keeps the blinders on and prevents collaboration across departments. However, this type of movement is precisely what is needed to make big changes to an organization and ultimately deliver a patient experience to which everyone is contributing and owning.

EXHIBIT 8.5: Organization Engagement and Patient Satisfaction

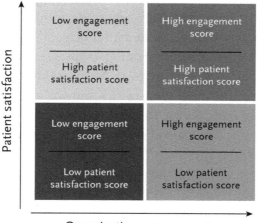

Source: NRC Health (2018).

EXHIBIT 8.6: Patient Ratings Increase with Engagement Ratings

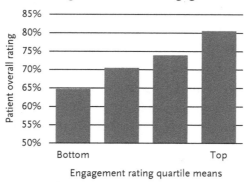

Source: NRC Health (2010–2016).

As we try to find a way to bring these areas together, we return to the original Harvey Picker work and the eight dimensions of care (introduced in chapter 1). For 30 years, we generally have thought about these dimensions in terms of patients only. But for the dimensions to be delivered, caregivers must be educated and engaged in each dimension. For "access to care" to be delivered, the person who answers the phone must exhibit a good attitude and a problem-solving approach. For "physical comfort" to be delivered, a caregiver needs to display a human touch and an empathetic ear.

NRC Health has been training employees in Picker's eight dimensions for more than 15 years. Most healthcare organizations assume employees know these tactics, but the evidence we present indicates that most either do not know or have forgotten them. Employees often complain of not having enough training and support in the things they *didn't* learn in school. In the aftermath of COVID, these employees are deeply hungry for new training, support, and knowledge. But it must come from somewhere, and all signs point to leadership.

THE STORY OF UNIVERSITY OF ILLINOIS MEDICAL CENTER

The healthcare industry and its leaders make a lot of assumptions about what its employees know. For instance, internal culture and branding efforts are intended to reflect an organization's mission, build a vision for the organization, and instill values in employees that will translate into day-to-day behaviors.

The University of Illinois Medical Center (UIMC) had similar assumptions about its employees when it attempted to build an external brand for consumers. As one of several academic medical centers in Chicago, including the University of Chicago, UIMC was in a challenging position. It is physically located on the campus of the University of Illinois at Chicago, and its name was constantly being confused with the University of Chicago. Its leaders recognized that internal brand confusion existed, and they sought a way to remedy it. Most organizations considering a brand refresh hire a creative firm and head straight to the marketing and advertising concepts to spread awareness of the brand and boost their image to consumers. But what about awareness and willingness to recommend among UIMC's own employees? Often, brand messaging flies right over their heads. When an employee sees a brand message for the first time on a billboard in the midst of other commuters, that employee can be resentful and feel left out.

UIMC wanted to avoid this trap by looking at these two audiences—consumers and employees—together. What if employees were treated like consumers? It seems radical to not assume your employees know your brand inside and out, but the results can be fascinating.

The medical center discovered that many employees lacked knowledge about the brand and struggled to recall basic concepts about the organization's mission, vision, and values. Much like external consumers, they were unable to point out exactly what made the organization different from competitors and had trouble conveying ideas about the brand's future direction. Some employees even went so far as to say they may not use UIMC as their provider of choice.

UIMC was open to the results, and the marketing team and branding firm decided to suspend any new external advertising to focus first on employees. An internal branding campaign took shape, with the main goals of first acknowledging that employees didn't know enough about UIMC and then giving them the knowledge and tools to learn more and become brand advocates.

Leaders launched this internal branding campaign with a ribbon-cutting event and through information fairs in which employees could learn about the organization and its benefits, much like a would-be job applicant. They created a robust employee-friendly physician directory and posted additional primary care resources, including extended appointment hours, intended for both internal and external use. Fair organizers also included testimonials so employees could hear from others like themselves about the organization. All events and resources had a strong C suite presence.

EXHIBIT 8.7: Consumer and Employee Decision Models

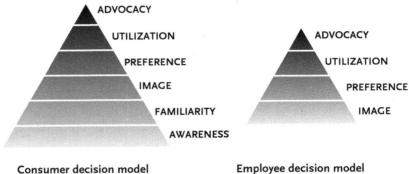

Consumer decision model: ADVOCACY, UTILIZATION, PREFERENCE, IMAGE, FAMILIARITY, AWARENESS

Employee decision model: ADVOCACY, UTILIZATION, PREFERENCE, IMAGE

Source: NRC Health.

The results were clear: After six months, employees had a knowledge boost and a better understanding of the brand. They were more aware of UIMC's offerings and—just as is the goal with consumers—more likely to choose and recommend UIMC for care in the future (see exhibit 8.7).

By launching an internal branding campaign first, UIMC leaders were able to gather feedback and home in on the right message for external consumers. Once in the market, they saw better results in overall brand awareness among consumers, just as they had with employees. By using employees as a testing ground, they built internal and external brand advocates.

In the end, employee engagement and patient and consumer experiences are linked in virtually every healthcare organization. Clearly, there is room for improvement in engaging both key audiences. However, what predates the experience is the *perception* of the experience. Among employees, this perception pertains to how they feel about their jobs each and every day—if they feel they can deliver the brand promise while maximizing their talents and achieving fulfillment in their role. These important personal beliefs don't show up on an organizational chart and aren't reflected in titles; they are closely held by the individual and in need of nurturing by the organization to which they give so much of themselves.

EMPLOYEE ENABLEMENT

The future of employee engagement requires the separation of traditional engagement drivers from the resources that employees desire but never seem to get. Managers often work within the confines of the employee's role, pay and benefits, interaction with other employees and their roles ("org-charting"), leadership rounding, teamwork, respect and recognition, and development opportunities. These are boilerplate management duties that every employee expects from a manager. Although vital, they are not key to enabling employees to fulfill their potential and climb Maslow's mountain.

What is needed is a separate structure to promote employee empowerment through coaching, additional role resources, expanded training opportunities, collaborative efforts (cross-functional projects), volunteer opportunities, and other off-role responsibilities that employees greatly appreciate (see exhibit 8.8). For example, employees want their managers to provide career planning and development services, but many managers see career planning as a threat. They don't want to run a training program for their competition if and when employees are ready to move on. But this reluctance is the opposite of what most employees need. They need help from their managers to envision their future with the organization. The average American spends only 1.5 hours a year on career planning. By comparison, Americans spend an average of 946 hours on leisure activities and sports and 400 hours on household activities. Without support from their employer, employees aren't going to feel as if they have a plan, and when they become disgruntled, they will be more likely to quit, leaving healthcare organizations with holes to plug in the organizational chart. While this exodus seemed to happen in larger numbers during the Great Resignation, healthcare is constantly facing an uphill climb to keep employees engaged, or simply to keep them at all.

When employers are willing to separate some of these "hard" and "soft" responsibilities, they have a better chance of connecting

EXHIBIT 8.8: Improving the Culture: Engagement and Enablement

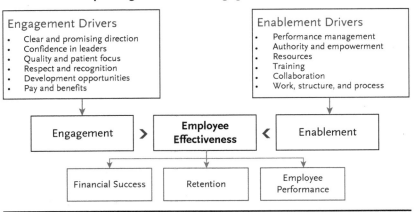

Source: NRC Health (2018).

with managers in the job areas that keep them fired up and engaged. For example, if an employee wants to volunteer more and the manager not only allows the employee to take time off to do so but also inquires about the experience, devotes a few minutes in a team huddle for them to report on it, and extends the offer to volunteer to other direct reports, a feeling is generated among employees that managers aren't just complying with their request but actually caring about them when they aren't at work. Employees may notice the increased attention from managers who are truly invested in their future. This recognition of the attention, in turn, could create a more driven workforce ready to fulfill their potential in their existing roles and beyond. As Brandon Jones of Carillion Clinic shared during his appearance on NRC Health's Patient No Longer podcast (August 4, 2023), "We have caregivers that we must take care of so that they can show up every single day to take care of their communities. . . . Without our care teams . . . we don't have a mission, we don't have a vision, we don't have values, we don't have anybody to take care of anybody."

When healthcare workforces are mobilized to fulfill their potential, the ultimate beneficiary is the patient. It is impossible to envision patient-centered care without activated and empowered employees who, perhaps, have recaptured the powerful inspiration—the calling—that brought them to healthcare in the first place.

REFERENCES

Aiken, L. H., S. P. Clarke, D. M. Sloane, J. Sochalski, and J. H. Silber. 2002. "Hospital Nurse Staffing and Patient Mortality, Nurse Burnout, and Job Dissatisfaction." *Journal of the American Medical Association* 288 (16): 1987–93. https://jamanetwork.com/journals/jama/fullarticle/195438.

Alexander, A. G., and K. A. Ballou. 2018. "Work–Life Balance, Burnout, and the Electronic Health Record." *American Journal of Medicine* 131 (8): 857–58.

Ball, J. E., L. Bruyneel, L. H. Aiken, W. Sermeus, D. M. Sloane, A. M. Rafferty, R. Lindqvist, C. Tishelman, P. Griffiths, and RN4Cast Consortium. 2018. "Post-Operative Mortality, Missed Care and Nurse Staffing in Nine Countries: A Cross-Sectional Study." *International Journal of Nursing Studies* 78: 10–15.

Brewer, K. 2024. "Great Resignation Workers Less Satisfied than Before." *Journal of Accountancy.* Published June 5. www.journalofaccountancy.com/news/2024/jun/great-resignation-workers-less-satisfied-than-before.html.

Burky, A. 2023. "Healthcare Ranked Lowest for Employee Satisfaction, Qualtrics Survey Finds." *Fierce Healthcare.* Published January 19. www.fiercehealthcare.com/health-tech/qualtrics-survey-finds-only-half-healthcare-employees-think-they-are-paid-fairly.

Comparably. 2020. "Survey: Two-Thirds of Employees Are Satisfied with Their Work–Life Balance." Updated January 13. www.

comparably.com/news/survey-two-thirds-of-employees-are-satisfied-with-their-work-life-balance/.

Dale Carnegie & Associates. 2018. *Employee Engagement: It's Time to Go All In; Making Engagement a Daily Priority for Leaders.* White paper. New York: Dale Carnegie & Associates.

Kahneman, D., and A. Deaton. 2010. "High Income Improves Evaluation of Life but Not Emotional Well-Being." *Proceedings of the National Academy of Sciences* 107 (38): 16489–93.

Kruse, K. 2012. "What Is Employee Engagement?" *Forbes.* Published June 22. www.forbes.com/sites/kevinkruse/2012/06/22/employee-engagement-what-and-why/.

McLeod, S. 2024. "Maslow's Hierarchy of Needs." *Simply Psychology.* Updated January 24. www.simplypsychology.org/maslow.html.

Menasce Horowitz, J., and K. Parker. 2023. "How Americans View Their Jobs." Pew Research Center. Published March 30. www.pewresearch.org/social-trends/2023/03/30/how-americans-view-their-jobs/.

Merriam-Webster. 2024. "Compassion Fatigue." *Merriam-Webster.com Dictionary.* Accessed June 26. www.merriam-webster.com/dictionary/compassionfatigue.

NRC Health. 2010, 2011, 2012, 2013, 2014, 2015, 2016, 2018. *Employee Engagement Studies.* Lincoln, NE: NRC Health.

Shanafelt, T. D., C. M. Balch, G. Bechamps, T. Russell, L. Dyrbye, D. Satele, P. Collicott, P. J. Novotny, J. Sloan, and J. Freischlag. 2010. "Burnout and Medical Errors Among American Surgeons." *Annals of Surgery* 256 (6): 995–1000.

Sternberg, S. 2016. "Diagnosis: Burnout." *U.S. News & World Report.* Published September 8. www.usnews.com/news/

articles/2016-09-08/doctors-battle-burnout-to-save-themselves-and-their-patients.

Strecher, V. 2023. "Harris-Kumanu Poll: US Full-Time Employees, January 2023." Presentation at Governance Institute Leadership Conference, April.

Westgate, A. 2014. "Eighteen Work–Life Balance Tips for Physicians." *Physicians Practice*. Published July 30. www.physicianspractice.com/view/eighteen-work-life-balance-tips-physicians.

CHAPTER 9

Removing Barriers

"In the end, the only thing that really matters is creating patient-defined value."

— *Arlen Meyers, MD, MBA, president and CEO, Society of Physician Entrepreneurs*

ONCE HEALTHCARE ORGANIZATIONS activate and empower employees to recapture their inspiration for human understanding, they have a tremendous opportunity to turn that inward transformation outward to help shape the communities around them. Every neighborhood in the United States leans on the local hospital as a bedrock of the community and a provider of lifesaving care to residents. Once employees are engaged, enabled, and mobilized to live the mission of the organization, the next frontier becomes transforming the patient experience itself through the eight dimensions of patient-centered care developed by Harvey Picker (discussed in chapter 1). After all, without patients there would be no hospitals, no physicians, no nurses. However, as our research has revealed, far too often the road to patient-centered care is littered with distractions and barriers. These hurdles wear down care providers and create malaise among employees. No one suffers more from bad care than patients. So what, exactly, keeps getting in the way?

RESPECT FOR PATIENTS' VALUES, PREFERENCES, AND EXPRESSED NEEDS

The mission of healthcare organizations is to serve all who come through the doors, but that means people from many walks of life with a variety of expectations regarding their care. Organizations that want to better understand their consumers must start with a shift on the inside: Staff members must fully understand the diverse health beliefs and practices among patients, as well as the ethnic and cultural groups in their specific patient population. They need to ask questions of the patient population to better understand their needs and beliefs. This means adding new and different questions on patient intake forms (e.g., gender identity, how they prefer to receive certain information from their provider) and then ensuring that the data are stratified by stakeholder groups to enable targeted, meaningful changes. Care providers also need to view and treat patients holistically—mind, body, and soul (the human understanding piece we have been discussing in this book). Staff members should ask more questions about therapeutic decisions that can affect patients' lives. For example, ask the patient if they prefer to be treated with medication or possibly with alternative therapies. Allowing patients to heal in the way they prefer can result in better outcomes.

Many organizations are providing patients with direct access to their medical records, which allows them to view all the episodes and decisions that make up their care journey. Some top-performing organizations allow patients to interact with their providers through electronic communications protected by the Health Insurance Portability and Accountability Act. Organizations also provide educational materials in the medical record so patients can conduct their own research by visiting reliable websites and accessing high-quality content about their condition, medications, and possible side effects.

Other important activities include comprehensive planning and services focused on the particular needs of cultural groups and diagnostic groups. Such personalization can be achieved through virtual or in-person support groups composed of patients with similar conditions and family members or through education (e.g., a nutrition guide for patients with diabetes).

COORDINATION AND INTEGRATION OF CARE

As hospitals have grown into health systems and the front doors to care have multiplied, the confusion patients feel has increased. This confusion is not limited to access but also pertains to the patient experience itself. Consumers often feel as though their care is uncoordinated and haphazard, creating a chaotic journey overall. When healthcare providers don't work together in an attempt to integrate a patient's care, this unsettling patient perspective becomes reality. Therefore, caregivers must make a concerted effort to provide coordinated care.

For example, giving patients written and visual information about the members of their care team can help create a bond between patient and caregiver. Explaining each caregiver's role and how the caregivers' roles connect around the patient, and identifying the clinician in charge, can fill in a patient's educational gaps and boost their confidence early in the experience.

Many organizations throughout the United States are using team-based care to help with the coordination of patient care. Team-based care enables patients to feel confident that the team is communicating and working together. Similarly, team-based care is effective in the clinic setting when all specialists are in one location for a patient's visit. Rather than needing to go to multiple facilities for treatment, patients can experience streamlined care without challenging transitions.

But what about when things go wrong? While it's always important to stay on top of errors and service gaffes, it's even more important to plan for them. Giving patients and their families realistic expectations about wait times, expected levels of discomfort, possible adverse effects, and other factors germane to care delivery can help staff prepare patients for things that may go awry. A patient who is told at the outset that the provider is running late or that a procedure isn't always perfect will be far less frustrated than a patient who finds out after the fact.

INFORMATION, COMMUNICATION, AND EDUCATION

Information needs to be conveyed via multiple vehicles so it is accessible to all patients. Top-performing organizations use their Patient and Family Advisor Councils to review educational materials and ensure that the content is understandable to patients and families, rather than loaded with medical jargon. They also rely on feedback from these councils to ensure that information is communicated in various ways (e.g., video, written materials, support groups). The increasing number of digitally savvy consumers makes it vital to include information in electronic medical records. When patients can review important data while still in the hospital and then review it at home as they get back to daily life, the result can be less friction during the recovery process. Having "to do" items such as reading educational material or watching a video provides patients with reliable information when they go home. Most patients don't believe they have enough information when they are discharged.

Beyond individual patient interactions, healthcare organizations must determine how they can systematize education across their patient population. Educational workshops for all staff members—including employed physicians—can result in improved communication with all patients. These workshops often involve role-play and action planning, with an emphasis on how to combat the most common challenges that patients face. To be most effective, these workshops must draw on actual patient feedback.

Asking patients about their health-related goals—the "why" behind wanting to get better—is vital to providing the right information at the right time. Does a patient want to attend their child's graduation or wedding? The conversation might shift to when the patient may be able to travel again or gain full mobility. Does a patient want to ride horses again? If so, the conversation might shift to risks involved if further injury occurs. These conversations provide realistic expectations, a reasonable timeline, and a better understanding of what may happen after a patient leaves the hospital.

More and more organizations are focusing on population health issues. In so doing, they are essentially writing "wellness prescriptions." These prescriptions allow for an organization to list nutritional guidelines and the exercise level the patient needs to maintain when leaving the hospital. Recall from chapter 2 that many patients are open to using these types of services when offered—and find it particularly appealing if their healthcare provider offers them directly. Organizations are also evaluating patients in terms of food insecurities and providing food prescriptions for their food pharmacy. They understand that if the patient does not have food to eat in the future, they will not take a medication that must be taken with food. Another potential question to ask patients is whether they have working electricity in their home; if a medication needs to be refrigerated, does the patient have a way to keep it cold? Healthcare organizations are asking patients with asthma if they have clean, properly filtered air in the home, and, if not, they are working with social service agencies to help find solutions.

PHYSICAL COMFORT

Among all patient needs, perhaps none is more basic than physical comfort. There is nothing worse than being unable to sleep in the hospital because of constant interruptions and distractions. Hospitals can be quite uncomfortable. Scheduling the many routine but necessary procedures—blood draws, regular doses of medication, changing dressings, bathing, weighing, daily radiographs, and so forth—can mean long days and nights for patients, and longer checklists for care providers. However, striving to schedule these tasks during waking hours and allowing patients to rest as much as possible at night is vital. Little acts of thoughtfulness such as providing shelf space and bulletin boards in patients' rooms to permit them to personalize their space can make a world of difference. Keeping patients comfortable and safe should be on every checklist.

Healthcare organizations can also enhance physical comfort by furnishing waiting areas with movable tables, chairs, and sofas to allow visitors to create their own comfort zones. Many organizations now have multiple waiting areas with several types of furniture to suit visitors' varying preferences. Televisions and areas for laptop use also add convenience and comfort to waiting areas.

EMOTIONAL SUPPORT AND ALLEVIATION OF FEAR AND ANXIETY

The patient journey can be one of the most emotionally taxing experiences of a person's life. Just as an emotional connection is vital to employees delivering on an organizational mission, it is essential for the organization's caregivers to acknowledge the emotional needs of patients and to nurture them. But they shouldn't have to do this alone. Healthcare organizations can develop a network of patients and family members willing to share their experiences with newly diagnosed patients and their families. Top-performing organizations provide support groups for patients as well as for staff and managers, closing an important feedback loop of internal and external emotional support. For example, a staff member diagnosed with cancer can attend a support group as a patient, but they can also be part of a support group whose aim is to understand what it means to be a caregiver with cancer. Support groups are also available for managers who have staff members with cancer so they can better support them, personally and professionally, on their journey.

Creating customized experiences also helps the patient heal. Ask the patient about something they enjoy or a nickname they like to be called. If the patient loves a certain college sports team, for example, a staff member can note this in the chart, and caregivers can mention the score of a recent game when they come into the patient's room.

Some organizations are relying more on volunteers to help ease patients' anxiety. Volunteers can sit with anxious patients in the waiting room to help calm their nerves. If a provider knows a particular patient tends to be nervous when coming to the office, this is a perfect opportunity for a volunteer to provide emotional support for the patient in the waiting area (Institute for Healthcare Improvement and NRC Health 2019).

INVOLVEMENT OF FAMILY AND FRIENDS

We have mentioned family and friends in several chapters, but this is an aspect of the patient experience that, surprisingly, can be easy to ignore. Family and friends can make a crucial difference to patients as they receive care and are on the road to recovery. To that end, healthcare organizations need to have respite rooms for families so they can remain in the facility while their loved one receives care. Family members may not want to be far from the patient, but they also need rest so that they will be able to care for the patient when the patient returns home. Care providers must make sure the family knows where the respite rooms are located.

Ask the patient who will be the family member or friend serving as their designated caregiver. Then, when staff members are having important conversations with the patient, make sure this caregiver is present. If the caregiver is not present, a staff member should ask if there is a more convenient time for the caregiver to attend or provide a line for the person to call in and receive updates about the patient. Alternatively, provide an e-mail address or a website URL that will enable the caregiver to transmit a message via an online portal (many organizations are now providing a physical or virtual space for family members to leave questions). Access to an online portal or to a whiteboard in a patient's room also allows family members to write down questions, which can be particularly helpful if they forgot to inquire about something during a meeting with the care team.

Family members also like to connect with family members of other patients in the hospital. One way for these families to connect is through a nonalcoholic "happy hour," which enables them to establish their own informal support network. Not only will patients and families want to stop by, but staff members look forward to connecting with volunteers and family members. When healthcare organizations are responsive to the needs of family and friends, their power to heal the patient becomes even stronger.

CONTINUITY AND TRANSITION

The actual patient care journey is rarely as flawless as depicted in PowerPoint presentations at healthcare conferences or on websites of healthcare providers. As we discussed in chapters 2 and 3, most consumers are plagued by disjointed experiences and confusion at every turn. Even if they work for a hospital, consumers often begin a healthcare journey without enough information to confidently navigate their care. It is easy to pin this lack of education on the consumer, but healthcare's complexity poses a challenge for patients with varying degrees of knowledge about the industry. Hospitals and their employees must bridge the complexity gap and provide coordinated patient care, which starts with human-to-human interaction and education.

As noted previously, the patient must have a designated caregiver at the outset of the care journey. Top-performing organizations integrate this person into all essential components of the care journey, including conversations about medications and what to expect when going home. If the patient needs physical therapy when transitioning home, the hospital ensures that the designated caregiver is present for the exercise education so the caregiver will know how to assist the patient and recognize when the exercise is done correctly or not.

Begin discharge education during admissions by providing important information on the intake form. Nurses can then discuss relevant discharge details throughout the patient's hospital stay to enhance understanding and set expectations (e.g., present some of the acronyms the patient may hear and explain what they mean, as they will be part of the care plan to ensure that the patient is healing and able to go home). Bedside educators are trained to make sure that patients understand all their conversations with and instructions from nurses and physicians. If they do not understand something, the educator rephrases the information to help ensure a smooth discharge process (Zablocki 2015).

Because patients have individual needs, the organization should consider distributing customized discharge instructions including a copy of the discharge summary, medication cards, educational videos of the discharge process, and any other videos that might be beneficial to the patient back at home. Give patients a chance to ask any final questions, and make sure they don't leave the building until all their questions and concerns have been addressed.

Finally, don't let patients go without reaching out. Like an attentive restaurant server who makes sure the customer is satisfied with the meal, the organization should schedule phone calls within the first day or two after discharge to ensure that the transition home goes as expected and all questions have been answered. If nurses or other care providers are too busy to call, consider setting up an automated system to make postdischarge calls to ensure that no patients are left out.

ACCESS TO CARE

Before patients ever come through one of our doors, they are increasingly likely to find us through a screen—a cell phone, tablet, computer, or other convenient device, as we've chronicled in previous chapters. As a result, healthcare organizations must eschew the temptation to provide information and access when convenient to them and instead offer it when and where the consumer wants it. Doing so starts with being transparent about provider reviews and comments, as well as posting educational materials about various conditions on the organization's website. Consumers are turning to Google and accessing WebMD regularly to research their own conditions. Providing reliable educational materials allows the health system to share the knowledge the consumer is seeking; in turn, the consumer is highly likely to seek care at your institution because they consider it the expert on their condition. Ignoring patients' digital first steps can limit a healthcare organization's ability to influence patients and start the patient journey on the right foot.

Healthcare organizations must be increasingly "off campus" and more involved in the community so that consumers recognize the brand in their daily lives and not just when they are sick. Offering telehealth services to school nursing offices initiates a partnership from the beginning. If a sick child is in the nurse's office, the nurse may conduct telemedicine if the parent signed up for this program when registering the child for school. Doing so allows the child to receive a visit with their own physician while in the school nurse's office. When the parent picks the child up, the provider has already phoned in any needed prescriptions, relieving the parent of the need to take the child in for care, wait for the appointment, and then wait for the prescription to be called in to the pharmacy and filled. This convenience can make a big difference to patients and families as they ponder their accessibility to the care they need.

ADDRESSING COMPASSION FATIGUE

We can remove all the aforementioned barriers and improve the patient experience across the board, as long as our organization's caregivers are up to the challenge. As we explored in chapter 8, caregivers are the conduit of the patient experience, but they can become a blockage. What happens when a nurse is drained of the ability to be nice or a physician can no longer answer another question? What happens when the spirit that drove a caregiver into medicine in the first place seems to be getting crushed? (For a discussion of compassion fatigue, refer back to chapter 8.)

How do organizations resolve this issue? An important place to start is human understanding. Our lessons learned from COVID now require us to see every provider, caregiver, and staff member at our institutions as unique, in addition to every patient—the concept of human understanding can also be applied to the workforce. Do healthcare leaders have a deep understanding of why their staff continue to show up every day, despite the long and difficult hours, and myriad other employment opportunities that pay equally well and come with less stress and risk? People who have a strong sense of purpose are not only healthier overall but also are less likely to experience burnout in their job (Strecher 2016). When employers try to understand their employees' personal purpose for working, they are almost four times more engaged and twice as likely to stay with their current employer (Strecher 2023). Human understanding can help get the entire workforce and senior leaders back to that sense of purpose that drew them to the profession in the first place.

According to NRC Health's Physician Engagement National Survey, conducted from 2015 to 2017, physicians want to spend more time with their patients. They want to be sure that their patient loads are not so heavy that they do not have enough time to fully discuss the patient's medical condition, necessary tests, and treatment options with the patient and family members. Creating more team-based care is important to physicians to enable better communication throughout the care team and organization. Physicians also want more rigorous systems of checks and balances to prevent medical errors in the hospital. Moreover, they like to work for organizations that keep up with the latest advancements in medical equipment and technology.

Another way to combat physician caregiver fatigue is to assign a mentor—someone the physician can trust, develop a rapport with, and contact when struggling.

Many top organizations conduct rounds on their staff, and effective staff rounds have been shown to help combat compassion fatigue (Thompson 2013). Staff rounds enable leaders to make sure that staff members have everything they need from a clinical standpoint to do their job, as well as a manageable workload. Staff members understand that there will be times of high census, but this is when it is crucial to provide extra recognition for those who go above and beyond in their day-to-day duties.

Keep in mind that things sometimes go wrong in healthcare, and those incidents can be a matter of life or death. Healthcare organizations must provide a safe space for staff members to grieve when they lose a patient. Many organizations have a code that when called allows for food or something soothing to be brought to the care team to comfort them and give them a moment to grieve. Quiet rooms are also available for staff members to use when a patient dies or when they need to recharge. Some organizations hold monthly sessions for hospital staff to discuss what went well and what went wrong with difficult cases. In addition to the medical issues, staff members discuss the emotional impact of the case, so they all can share in the experience.

Patient- and family-centered care week is another activity many hospitals and health systems offer. During this week, former patients and family members share their stories. They tell staff members how much they affected their lives and that they will always remember them. Such words of appreciation help recharge caregivers when they need it the most.

Recognizing staff throughout the year for exemplary service is important. However, if employees are only recognized for improvement, the result can be a vicious boom-and-bust cycle of improvement.

Finally, in today's world, generative AI and large language model (LLM) tools are becoming more prevalent and, when applied in the right situations, remove or reduce the mundane, repetitive work of physicians and nurses, freeing up that precious time for direct patient care and reducing fatigue and burnout. These solutions are discussed further in the subsequent section on technology-based solutions.

BREAKING THE CYCLE OF IMPROVEMENT

In healthcare, improvement is a marathon, not a sprint. If too much emphasis is placed on improvement, and leadership becomes infatuated with boosting scores, the result can be similar to compassion fatigue. By its nature, sustainable improvement must be slow and steady. Rapid jumps in scores are difficult to sustain, and scores that go up and down too much can create frustration, and even apathy, regarding the pursuit of improvement.

Leaders in top organizations are aware of this pitfall and support a methodical and measured approach to performance improvement that enables the hospital to avoid boom-and-bust cycles and improvement apathy. By shifting the conversation from "How does this impact the bottom line?" to "How does this impact the consumer's experience?" healthcare providers can ensure that they are implementing initiatives that have a positive impact on patients, families, consumers, and caregivers; maintain focus on the mission and on the patient; and ultimately overcome the barriers described in this chapter.

TECHNOLOGY-BASED SOLUTIONS

While the earlier discussion demonstrates human-based solutions to remove the barriers to a consumer-centric healthcare experience, providers today also have an ever-expanding collection of technology-based solutions at their fingertips. Admittedly, there is much concern around the risks and pitfalls of AI tools—the wrong tools being used, or the right tools being deployed for the wrong reasons or at the wrong times, or the tools' potential to exacerbate inequity—yet many of these tools present real, demonstrated solutions that can alleviate fatigue, burnout, staffing shortages, and other problems.

Generative AI and LLMs Working to Solve the Healthcare Workforce Crisis

Generative AI is moving intelligence from an "automation copilot" to a pilot performing human and empathetic tasks, allowing the human capital of the healthcare ecosystem to perform the tasks needed for their level of expertise. For example, Hippocratic AI presented "Rachel" at a conference—its AI "nurse" being "paid" less than a dollar an hour that can make thousands of calls a day around preoperative or postoperative routine check-ins and even combat loneliness among seniors (Hippocratic AI 2024). According to its presenter, Rachel is indistinguishable from a human, reacts almost instantaneously, and is almost impossible to flummox. In a demonstration, the patient was told by Rachel that he would need someone to drive him home after his colonoscopy. Not knowing anyone in that area, he asked Rachel if he could go on Craigslist to find a post-op ride. Rachel immediately suggested that "finding someone in your church or synagogue might be a better alternative because Craigslist could be unreliable!"

At the University of California, San Diego, AI is being used to reduce the sepsis mortality rate in its emergency rooms, with initial results showing a reduction by 17 percent (Anderson 2024). Using a deep learning model named Composer, which is trained to search for more than 150 variables including demographics, vital signs, and medications, it can determine whether a patient is at risk of sepsis much sooner than traditional methods have been able to do, and it sends an alert through the electronic health record (EHR). The university hopes to expand this tool to be used to detect postoperative sepsis as well (Anderson 2024).

Other examples of generative AI being applied to healthcare include risk stratification to aid in care coordination and chronic disease management (Kennedy 2024); enhancing and streamlining nursing scheduling and nursing recruitment, reducing the staff hours required for such tasks (Burky 2022); and various tools that automatically transcribe verbal notes into the EHR to significantly reduce the amount of time physicians need to spend documenting after a full day of seeing patients.

Using AI-Powered Social Work to Address Determinants of Health

AI is increasingly being integrated into social work to address economic and social determinants of health (SDOH). These determinants include factors such as income, education, employment, housing, and social support, which significantly impact health outcomes. Following are some notable examples of how AI is being used in this context:

- AI, particularly natural language processing (NLP), is being used to extract SDOH data from unstructured

EHRs, which allows for a more comprehensive understanding of patients' socioeconomic conditions, which in turn can inform better healthcare interventions (Patra et al. 2021).

- Some of the most exciting applications are predictive analytics for health outcomes based on SDOH, enabling proactive interventions. For example, AI models can predict which beneficiaries are at risk of dropping out from health information delivery programs, allowing for targeted interventions to improve maternal and child health outcomes (Teamcore 2024).

- AI-powered tools are being developed to provide direct support and interventions for individuals facing social and economic challenges. For example, Woebot is a therapeutic chatbot that uses AI to simulate therapeutic conversations, providing mental health support through cognitive behavioral techniques and other therapeutic methods (Reamer 2023).

- For those in the field, AI tools are also being integrated into social work education to better prepare future social workers and support current ones. For example, the University of Kentucky's College of Social Work uses virtual reality and AI in child welfare investigation simulations, providing students with realistic practice scenarios (Barnes 2023). The Crisis Contact Simulator, developed in partnership with Google.org, is a tool that simulates digital conversations with LGBTQ youths in crisis, helping counselors practice and improve their skills before engaging in real-life scenarios with actual young people who identify as lesbian, gay, bisexual, transgender, queer, or questioning about their sexual or gender identity (Reamer 2023).

AI-powered social work offers significant potential to address the economic and social determinants of health by improving data extraction, providing direct support, enhancing education, and addressing systemic biases. However, it is crucial to approach these technologies with a critical lens, ensuring ethical use and mitigating risks such as algorithmic bias and privacy concerns. By leveraging AI responsibly, social workers can enhance their ability to serve and support vulnerable populations effectively.

The New Role for the "Human in the Middle"

As online and offline merge through technology, how we select and educate medical students and other health professionals will radically change. It seems ridiculous that we concentrate on science grade point average, organic chemistry grades, and Medical College Admission Test results and then demonstrate amazement when doctors are not more empathetic, communicative, and creative. It will be crucial to segment our nursing student and medical student classes so that the "traditional parameters" are used to develop new physician scientists but criteria such as self-awareness, empathy, communication skills, and cultural competence become increasingly important for those physicians and nurses who will be practicing in direct patient care. Simply put, "Rachel" and other AI physicians and nurses will be better than any human at memorizing the Krebs cycle or recognizing the genetic abnormality of a newborn, but an AI entity will never understand that when the pregnant person is asking "What does this mean?" it is not about the chromosomes but about that patient's image of a "perfect baby."

Predictive Analytics, Social Determinants, and Health Equity Moving from Philosophy to Mainstream

While health systems and payers in the traditional healthcare ecosystem and technology providers have all acknowledged the scourge of healthcare inequities and access gaps as well as the fact that food, education, housing, and other social determinants are the main harbingers of health, most efforts in the past have resulted in making the wealthy healthy through direct-to-employer models and direct-to-consumer or commercial insurer efforts. As there is more payer–provider alignment, we are beginning to see examples where it makes financial sense to solve "problems at home." For example, if your health system has risk-based first-dollar contracts, for a patient with multiple emergency department admissions for asthma who has a house with a mold problem, it makes more financial and social sense for the health system to hire "mold removers" than to continue to care for the patient's recurrent health emergencies associated with the mold.

THE ROLE OF HEALTHCARE LEADERS IN APPLYING NEW TECHNOLOGIES AND REDUCING FRAGMENTATION

Especially with regard to implementation of generative AI and LLM tools, a robust system of enterprise AI governance must be put in place in health systems, with equity leaders and other important stakeholders at the table. Establishing AI use policies and guardrails, along with ongoing evaluations of upside opportunities and downside risks of each AI use case, will be essential. Successful selection and integration of AI capabilities into strategic plans will require the ability to identify those with the greatest strategic value. And they must keep the consumer at the center—the AI tools used must be fueled by equitably representative data and unbiased algorithms that seek to identify and ameliorate health disparities (Graham, Anderson, and Kiesau 2024).

Traditional healthcare system leaders need to avoid going too far in acting like a start-up tech company, while at the same time carefully adhering to the charitable mission to improve health.

Healthcare leaders can leverage these new technologies and AI to reduce fragmentation and improve care coordination for consumers in five key ways:

1. Utilizing AI algorithms to analyze patient data from multiple sources and identify potential gaps in care or conflicting treatments. This information can help prioritize interventions and facilitate better coordination among specialists involved in a patient's care (Medtronic 2024).

2. Employing predictive analytics and machine learning models to identify patients at high risk of fragmented care or adverse outcomes. Doing so allows for targeted interventions and personalized care plans (Daugherty 2024).

3. Expanding telemedicine capabilities and integrating remote patient monitoring devices to provide continuous care and reduce unnecessary in-person visits. Doing so can help maintain continuity of care and prevent fragmentation, especially for patients with multiple chronic conditions (Tateeda 2024).

4. Developing unified digital platforms that integrate various point solutions and provide a single access point for patients to manage their health information, appointments, and communications with providers. This unification of platforms can help reduce the fragmentation caused by multiple disconnected apps and portals. For example, Paul Meyer, a digital health pioneer, is cofounder of a public benefit corporation called the Smart Health Network, which operates in conjunction with payers, providers, and health systems to "defragment" the paperwork, fragmentation, and cost by making it easier for people to check in and connect with

their multiple providers and health plans (Smart Health Network 2024).

5.   Using NLP to analyze clinical notes and extract relevant information, making it easier for providers to quickly understand a patient's complete health story and reduce fragmentation in communication (Siwicki 2024).

A common theme in this book has been the importance of humans and technology synergistically solving the fragmentation issues and non-consumer-centric delivery of healthcare. By implementing these technologies and AI-driven solutions, healthcare leaders can significantly reduce fragmentation, improve care coordination, and ultimately enhance the overall patient experience. However, it's crucial to maintain a balance between technological innovation and human-centered care, ensuring that these solutions augment rather than replace the essential human elements of healthcare delivery.

THE FUTURE OF HEALTHCARE LOOKS BRIGHT

Dr. Stephen Klasko has been a health system CEO and leader for more than 30 years and has commented in several of his national talks that the rate of change in healthcare has been outpaced by every other sector of the economy. For years at conferences the same problems and same stale solutions were being offered, with little change for the consumer in the way that they were able to access and improve their health. We hope that, as you have gotten this far in the book, wherever you are in the healthcare ecosystem (after all, we are all patients at some point), you are already feeling the momentum toward a much more optimistic healthcare delivery future. If you reread this book a few years from now, here are a few of the transformations you now view as routine.

From Apple Watches and Oura Rings to Seamless Data and Wearables

In many ways, we are in the "iPod" stage of the "iPhone" revolution when it comes to wearables. More and more Americans now wear devices such as Oura Rings and Apple Watches, which help self-assess their readiness score, exercise, number of daily steps, and other health-related information. These devices require little coordination with a physician or other caregiver. The future wearables will be "implanted" and always on. They will monitor pulse, blood pressure, temperature, cardiac arrythmias, voice fluctuations, and other functions and seamlessly mesh with the patient's providers. Under this model, no one will die from atrial fibrillation at night because the patient will be notified immediately when their heart rate changes and will receive a communication from the on-call provider.

Consumer Segmentation

When you see a billboard that says "We are patient-centered at Pleasantville Health System," what does that really mean? Are they referring to a 58-year-old with three wearables checking their steps every day, or a 35-year-old disconnected person, or a 75-year-old with cancer who only uses their phone to FaceTime with their grandchildren? The retail industry has figured out how to communicate with us in a *very* personalized, segmented manner. Health systems will need to learn from the success of other industries and create a seamless, customized experience across the continuum.

Democratization of Clinical Trials

Simply put, clinical trials—a lifeline for people with cancer, dementia, and many rare diseases—have seen huge progress in available drugs and modalities, but the provision of clinical trials is still antiquated. Billions of dollars are spent by pharma in fragmented enrollment drives hospital by hospital. Adding to that problem is that once again, money matters. A well-resourced person can take the time and money to fly or drive to a National Cancer Institute cancer center while others are unable to leave their community. New AI and tech models such as Paradigm are putting less burden on the physician so that the latest clinical trials become more accessible and can be performed in most cases by community oncologists. That will also require actionable data owned by the patient. Companies such as Health Ex are providing patient-owned data repositories so that patients retain control and potentially are "rewarded" with an honorarium when their data is used for a clinical trial.

From Hospitals as Brick and Mortar to Hospital at Home to "Healthcare at Any Address"

The definition of a health system is changing. Although our organizations changed our names from "hospital systems" to "health systems," we have traditionally defined our address by where we fail to keep people healthy. The new world healthcare order will have the hospital's address always changing and the health system brand based on its care and caring. When Dr. Klasko was the CEO of Jefferson Health, he had a sign in his office that said, "I hope five years from now when someone asks where Jefferson is, you can't define it . . . but it certainly won't be where our sickest patients are"—even though that will always be part of our mission.

Bringing It Back to Human Understanding

Creating a strong foundation for this modern, consumer-centric healthcare delivery system must prioritize human understanding at every touch point. The following is a "short list" of universal strategies to reframe attention on what matters most, identified by experience leaders from almost 100 healthcare organizations in a series of summits hosted in 2022 by NRC Health's Human Understanding Institute (NRC Health 2023):

1. **Alignment and Buy-in**
   - Broaden the conversation to recognize that experience extends beyond any one clinical encounter and beyond the care setting in general.
   - Position experience as shaped by how we do everything—not "one more thing to do."
   - Illustrate connection to other strategic priorities: quality, safety, loyalty, revenue.
   - Focus on patient comments to humanize improvement opportunities.

2. **Human Connection**
   - Make human connection an expectation for standard work in all interactions with patients, families, and colleagues.
   - Leverage tools that help make behaviors authentic and systematic. Examples include engaging in purposeful rounding and summarizing patient context in the EHR.

3. **Frontline Focus**
   - Demonstrate that experience is important on both sides of the stethoscope by focusing on what matters to employees as individuals.
   - Develop a comprehensive strategy to address employee well-being and foster mutual respect.
   - Adjust workflows and workloads—with frontline input—to make it easier to do the right thing.

The idea is to engage, collaboratively, with patients, consumers, communities, physicians, nurses, and staff, to foster a culture of inclusivity that can generate valuable insights. This inclusive culture, in turn, enhances the organization's capacity to create solutions that enable consumer-centered care.

REFERENCES

Anderson, M. 2024. "How UC San Diego Health Used AI to Reduce Its Sepsis Mortality Rate." *Healthcare Brew*. Published April 18. www.healthcare-brew.com/stories/2024/04/18/how-uc-san-diego-health-used-ai-to-reduce-its-sepsis-mortality-rate?mbcid=35092930.102736.

Barnes, C. C. 2023. "Karen Magruder, UK College of Social Work DSW Student, on Researching Use Cases of AI Technology in the Field of Social Work." *College News, Student Spotlight. UK College of Social Work*. Published February 14. https://socialwork.uky.edu/social-work-innovation-in-the-era-of-chatgpt-and-ai/.

Burky, A. 2022. "From Finding the Right Candidates to Keeping Them, How Hospitals Are Using AI to Address Workforce Needs." *Fierce Healthcare*. Published November 23. www.fiercehealthcare.com/ai-and-machine-learning/finding-right-candidates-keeping-them-ai-aiding-healthcare-industry-meets.

Daugherty, A. 2024. "Top 8 Trends Revolutionizing Healthcare in 2024, According to Experts." *Business of IT* (blog), SHI Resource Hub. Published February 9. https://blog.shi.com/business-of-it/top-8-trends-revolutionizing-healthcare-in-2024-according-to-experts/.

Graham, G., B. Anderson, and T. Kiesau. 2024. "How to Leverage AI to Advance Health Equity and Mitigate Risk."

Chartis. Published June 3. www.chartis.com/insights/ how-leverage-ai-advance-health-equity-and-mitigate-risk.

Hippocratic AI. 2024. "Hippocratic AI Announces Collaboration with NVIDIA to Develop Super-Low-Latency 'Empathy Inference' for One of the World's First Generative AI-Powered Healthcare Agents." News release, March 18. www. globenewswire.com/news-release/2024/3/18/2848236/0/en/ Hippocratic-AI-Announces-Collaboration-with-NVIDIA-to- Develop-Super-Low-Latency-Empathy-Inference-for-One-of-the- World-s-First-Generative-AI-Powered-Healthcare-Agents.html.

Institute for Healthcare Improvement and NRC Health. 2019. *Mass Customization in Healthcare Delivery.* Webinar. Presented July 1.

Kennedy, S. 2024. "Exploring the Role of AI in Healthcare Risk Stratification." *Xtelligent Healthtech Analytics.* Published May 8. www.techtarget.com/healthtechanalytics/feature/ Exploring-the-role-of-AI-in-healthcare-risk-stratification.

Medtronic. 2024. "Five Healthcare Technology Trends in 2024." Published January 3. https://news.medtronic.com/ five-healthcare-technology-trends-in-2024-newsroom.

NRC Health. 2023. *2023 Experience Perspective.* Lincoln, NE: NRC Health. https://nrchealth.com/4ty1dsx-2/#fundamentals-first.

Patra, B. G., M. M. Sharma, V. Vekaria, P. Adekkannatu, O. V. Patterson, B. Glicksberg, L. A. Lepow, E. Ryu, J. M. Biernacka, A. Furmanchuk, T. J. George, W. Hogan, Y. Wu, X. Yang, J. Bian, M. Weissman, P. Wickramaratne, J. J. Mann, M. Olfson, T. R. Campion Jr., M. Weiner, and J. Pathak. 2021. "Extracting Social Determinants of Health from Electronic Health Records Using Natural Language Processing: A Systematic Review." *Journal of the American Informatics Association* 28 (12) 2716–27.

Reamer, F. 2023. "Artificial Intelligence in Social Work: Emerging Ethical Issues." *International Journal of Social Work Values and Ethics* 20 (2): item 05. https://jswve.org/volume-20/issue-2/item-05/.

Siwicki, B. 2024. "AI in 2024: Welcome to the 'New Normal' in Healthcare." *Healthcare IT News.* Published January 4. www.healthcareitnews.com/news/ai-2024-welcome-new-normal-healthcare.

Smart Health Network. 2024. "Making It Easier to Check-In and Connect with Your Healthcare Network." Accessed September 23. https://smart.health/.

Strecher, V. 2023. "Harris-Kumanu Poll: US Full-Time Employees, January 2023." Presentation at Governance Institute Leadership Conference, April.

———. 2016. *Life on Purpose: How Living for What Matters Most Changes Everything.* San Francisco: HarperOne, an imprint of HarperCollins.

Tateeda. 2024. "Top-17 Healthcare Technology Trends in 2024." *Healthcare and Medicine* (blog). Published January 21. https://tateeda.com/blog/healthcare-technology-trends.

Teamcore. 2024. "AI for Global Health and Public Health." Harvard School of Engineering and Applied Sciences. Accessed July 16. https://teamcore.seas.harvard.edu/ai-social-work.

Thompson, A. 2013. "How Schwartz Rounds Can Be Used to Combat Compassion Fatigue." *Nursing Management* 20 (4): 16–20.

Zablocki, E. 2015. *Bryan Health Educates Patients One Discharge at a Time (Part One).* Picker Institute Patient-Centered Care case study. NRC Health. Published July. https://nrchealth.com/wpcontent/uploads/2016/10/CS_Bryan-Health-Part-One.pdf (content no longer available).

CHAPTER 10

Nonpreferred and Preferred Future

ECONOMISTS USE HARD measures of reality to poke holes in our views of a utopian healthcare system. The problem is when they're right. If you ask a health economist to predict American healthcare delivery in ten years, they will remind you of some hard numbers. The cost of care to the nation is rising as a percentage of gross domestic product. Within states' budgets, spending on healthcare rises in proportion to a decline in expenditures for education: Healthcare is the Pac-Man that is chomping through the budget.

And most important, by many measures, the United States continues to have one system for the wealthy and one for the poor, with fewer middle-class people feeling secure in their insurance plans.

This is perhaps the most brutal reality, and there is an urgent need to solve health disparities. But looking at America's major cities, now home to 50 percent of the population, we find gaps in longevity based on zip code that are among the worst in the world. In a country as wealthy as the United States, it is an indictment on the entire healthcare system that one's zip code is more important than one's genetic code.

This book focuses on the very real, and very needed, consumer revolution. And it is not just about the technology. The key will be how we use these new technologies and digital transformations to benefit not only those who can afford fancy electronics but also those who are the most vulnerable because of social and socioeconomic factors. So let's look backward in time, and then forward, to seek some answers to crafting a new future.

If we were writing this book 30 years ago—back when physicians blamed managed care for burnout, we might have asked three questions:

1. There seems to be a huge problem with health inequities, both in American cities and around the globe. Why can't we address them?
2. Physicians seem to respond poorly to change and often want to accept the status quo. How do we get physicians to be more creative, adaptable, and optimistic about a changing future?
3. My bank just got an ATM. Why can't healthcare do cool consumer things like that?

Those same questions could be asked today. Health inequities are just as serious; physicians are still afraid to change; and although you can now do all your holiday shopping online, if you have a stomachache, in all likelihood you are getting on the phone and listening to 11 options just to get an appointment within a few days. Medicine, it appears, is still caught in the "iron triangle." As Dr. William Kissick wrote some 30 years ago in *Medicine's Dilemmas: Infinite Needs, Finite Resources*, the iron triangle of cost, quality, and access means that one cannot be increased without decreasing another. Dr. Kissick argued that to break the iron triangle, we have to disrupt the system itself, and disruption by definition is painful (Kissick 1994). The Institute for Healthcare Improvement (2024) makes a similar argument with its Triple Aim. We cannot work toward advancing one goal without advancing the others at the same time. But to date, redistributing resources to tackle inequity and reducing waste in healthcare have been beyond our political will.

There is no such thing as nondisruptive disruption. In other words, if we want to transform and democratize the US healthcare delivery system, those entrenched ways of doing things will not survive. Think about the difference between how Target and Walmart handled the Amazon revolution versus how Circuit City and Sears ignored the changes in the oncoming retail revolution.

Is this an unsolvable problem? Is healthcare doomed to be the global exception to the consumer revolution? Or will it undergo disruption? Will that disruption occur because the traditional healthcare ecosystem finally gets it? Or will start-up companies and venture capitalists pull consumers into rational, friendly, and accessible platforms, with hospitals, insurers, and pharmaceutical companies being left at the station?

It's time to look ahead.

John Sculley, the former Apple CEO, tells a famous story about his early days working with Steve Jobs. Sculley told Jobs he needed a business plan to assure backers and partners. He talked about the business plan that Jobs created for Apple. This was at a time when the computer industry was stagnating. While Sculley was expecting a consultant-driven, glossy, 60-page strategic and financial plan, the entire three-year blueprint for strategic action was written on a single page—actually half a page:

- Year 1: First, we change.
- Year 2: Then, we change the industry.
- Year 3: Then, we change the world.

Steve Jobs recognized that the computer world was going through a once-in-a-lifetime change from a desktop/laptop industry to a digital lifestyle. He disrupted how the company selected, paid, and motivated employees ("we change"); he diverted dollars from the development of PowerBooks and desktop computers toward iPods and digital instruments ("we change the industry"); and, with the iPhone and iTunes store, he started the global mobile revolution ("we change the world").

Not everyone understood the strategy, either within or outside the company. Much has been written about Gateway (missing the digital computer revolution), Blockbuster (missing the streaming revolution even though it initiated it), Kodak (missing the digital camera revolution even though it invented the first portable digital camera), and traditional retail megastores underestimating the Amazon revolution.

Which brings us to healthcare. We are going through a once-in-a-lifetime disruption from a business-to-business model to a business-to-consumer model—from physician and administrator as the boss to the patient as the boss—in other words, a radically new type of health experience that works as simply and easily as most other consumer experiences. This new model is so different from the old one, we can't even call it healthcare. That label is tied to the past and is incorrect in the first place. Anyone in healthcare will tell you that we're really in a "sick care" industry designed primarily to take care of people only after they develop health problems.

We need a new term that captures the spirit of a developing concept: *health assurance*. Health assurance encompasses some of the key themes of this book:

- It gives people "health citizenship," including the right to own their medical records and the right to access care.
- It fundamentally reimagines the business of healthcare delivery to focus on health, with the services and technology aimed at ensuring that we stay well, so we need as little sick care as possible.

This jump, from the past to the future, will be disruptive, and it may be painful for some people. However, in an industry in which technology has advanced light-years for individual patients, healthcare delivery, the patient experience, and social determinants of health remain in the precomputer age.

YEAR 1: WE CHANGE

We are witnessing two parallel revolutions. On the one hand, people are asking for and demanding better treatment as customers of a cumbersome legacy system. On the other hand, technology, artificial intelligence (AI), and genomics will fundamentally transform how and where healthcare is provided. Real-time genomic-based decision support is already commonly used in writing drug prescriptions. Soon, many people with chronic conditions will be relying solely or in large part on virtual health assistants for wellness and management. And within ten years, a majority of all healthcare services will be delivered virtually, at home or remotely, involving AI or machine cognition applications.

To fix ourselves, we must replace the iron triangle of cost, access, and quality with a patient "diamond" of health assurance: the ability to thrive without health challenges getting in the way; the development of health-related human relationships when needed; easy navigation of one's own healthcare; and the ability to understand options that balance cost and outcomes.

At the same time, we must fix the way we select and train healthcare providers. We cannot continue to choose medical students based on their science grade point average, multiple-choice test results, and organic chemistry grades and hope that physicians will be more empathetic, communicative, and creative. Rather, choosing students based on their self-awareness, empathy, cultural competence, and communication skills is the *only* way to ensure that the "human in the middle" (the provider) is adding value to the "human at the center" (the patient) of healthcare. We need to transform the medical school experience, from the selection process to mentorship to reducing the length of study.

We also need to recognize that it will take a major cultural change for physicians to accept the fourth industrial revolution (including AI, 5G, the internet of things, robotics, digital twin technology that creates virtual models of physical objects, etc.).

It took years to get physicians and nurses to work collaboratively through interprofessional institutes and models. Soon we will need to develop "intersentient" education models between humans and nonsentient AI robots.

YEAR 2: WE CHANGE THE INDUSTRY

Our industry, although lifesaving for many people, is contributing to some of society's greatest challenges. Healthcare organizations are too expensive within local, state, and federal tax and revenue structures. We contribute to inequity by perpetuating health disparities. In addition, we burden families caring for older adults, in part because providers treat the end-of-life stage as a disease to be fixed and in part because we haven't designed simpler and less expensive ways to ensure healthy aging.

As Millennials and Gen Zers age, they will fight the system. Why? Because there is little chance that, in the one-click world in which they were born and raised, these younger generations will accept an archaic healthcare system. There is even less chance that they will accept long waits in the waiting room, nontransparent costs and outcomes, and the inability to track and manage their own health in the same way they shop, travel, and handle every other aspect of consumer life. Before long, our current hospital-centric industry will seem as outdated as going to a bank to get money.

Here's one view of a future driven by health assurance: A company offers a subscription service to a technology-plus-human package that becomes the first layer of healthcare, a kind of pre-primary care. An individual signs up for the service and allows it to access their data, both static (e.g., DNA) and real-time (e.g., heart rate from a smartwatch, sleep patterns from an app). All these data will be analyzed through an AI-driven predictive analytic platform that keeps track of the person's health and then observes and learns from his patterns. The technology is running in the background, constantly keeping an eye on the individual's health. If the AI spots something unusual—the person isn't sleeping, their heart rate is up, or some other combination of events—it might send a text message asking some basic questions. The answers first go to an AI bot. Perhaps the person decides that not much is wrong, they're just stressed about a big decision at work. However, if the AI suspects something more, it sends the dialogue to a human physician, one who has time to talk with the person. In this way, the AI is taking over some of the low-level work that used to suck up the physician's day. The physician can then get on a video call with the individual and investigate their health issues. For example, Nvidia, in collaboration with Hippocratic AI, is working to develop empathetic AI healthcare agents that enable super-low-latency conversational interactions. This collaboration aims to create digital human avatars that can call patients, follow up on care coordination tasks, deliver preoperative instructions, and perform postdischarge management (Hippocratic AI 2024). The missing link is the creation of FDA-approved continuous sensors across a variety of parameters. All.health (2024) is developing a wearable system that collects and analyzes 24/7 data on a person's biometrics while screening for a variety of chronic diseases. It will not be long before the sensor-wearable technology of companies like All.health seamlessly integrate with the avatar-human coordination of companies like Hippocratic AI.

In the very near future, providers will be paid on the basis of quality, cost, patient experience, and outcomes; hospital stays will be commoditized; physicians and nurses will coexist (and ideally cooperate) with deep learning, machine cognition entities; we will select and educate humans (medical students) to be better humans than the robots, not better robots than the robots; and population health, predictive analytics, and social determinants will move to the mainstream of medical education and clinical care.

Moreover, technology and digital transformation will be pervasive in healthcare, and like banking, travel, and retail, most healthcare interactions will take place at or close to home. When that occurs, we truly will have "healthcare with no address."

YEAR 3: WE CHANGE THE WORLD

Changing the world is the most important part of the strategic plan, and it will require the most discussion and innovation. Spending 80 percent of our healthcare dollars on the areas that affect 20 percent of a person's health is unacceptable. Food, education, housing, prevention of chronic conditions, and combating climate change *are* healthcare! In the outdated sick-care model in which the hospital was the center of the universe, they were only part of an academic exercise. In the new health assurance model, these things become *the* most important determinants of health. Healthcare policy, healthcare incentives, and salaries will be tied to creating a healthcare system that works to prevent chronic conditions, with the patient as a partner, with technology monitoring in the background, and with most healthcare interactions happening at home. The real test for AI engineers, technology entrepreneurs, and the healthcare ecosystem is this: Can we marshal the trillions of dollars spent in healthcare not just to develop an improved magnetic resonance imaging unit or robotic surgical arm, but also to understand how to prevent childhood obesity, eradicate smoking, prevent drug abuse and overuse of opioids, create a clean environment, and, in essence, take a no-limits approach to eradicating noncommunicable diseases? It is a future where health policy, population health, and personalized medicine converge.

CALL TO ACTION: A FRAMEWORK FOR BUILDING A CONSUMER-CENTRIC HEALTHCARE SYSTEM

Consumers want access, engagement, and value. The eight dimensions of patient-centered care identified by Harvey Picker's team (described in chapter 1) are as relevant today as they were 30 years ago. We know that our healthcare delivery system is not being transformed fast enough and in the right ways. Our action framework laid out in this book for healthcare leaders involves the following changes and investments (both physical and philosophical) to remove barriers, change the DNA of healthcare, and build a consumer-centric healthcare system:

- **View the CEO as chief consumer officer.** Elevate innovation as part of the mission, encourage creativity as a core value, and build the data capacity that allows design thinking to succeed. Leverage the collective knowledge and passion of the board to further the cause of building a consumer-centric culture from the top down.

- **Live the dimensions.** Know your care for every patient and identify areas in which caregiving falls short of the eight dimensions of patient-centered care.

- **Look through the consumers' eyes.** Keep consumers at the center of improvement efforts. Get out from underneath measurement overload. Measure what you must to comply with value-based purchasing contracts, but spend the most time determining which metrics will get at what matters most to consumers (through direct feedback) and will help move the needle most effectively. Next, ensure that what is measured is translated into actionable and sustained improvement.

- **Be transparent.** Help consumers know what to expect along the entire journey of care, including treatment options, expected outcomes, and costs. Help them make decisions in the same way you would for your own family members.

- **Embrace technology.** Build competencies and capacity to gather the data you need, when you need them, and use those data, which span all eight dimensions of patient-centered care, to achieve transformational improvements in access, engagement, and value.

- **Innovate.** Determine how to meet consumers where they are. Behave like the healthcare delivery system of the future, now.
- **Gain human understanding.** Understand your patients, families, caregivers, and other consumers with greater clarity, immediacy, and depth, and ease their journey.

THE COURAGE TO ACT

When the path isn't obvious, you need a mindset and attitude that are open, nimble, determined, and committed. Jason Booher was a US Navy SEAL and innovator, trainer, and leader of hundreds of missions for 23 years. To Jason, *impossible* really is just a word. For healthcare executives, Jason has lessons for the action phase we need now (Klasko and Booher 2024).

Navy SEAL Team operations teach us solutions to today's healthcare challenges, including how the SEALs attract, retain, and develop top-performing talent and how leadership and global operating models are constructed. But a deeper look reveals an organization that is courageous enough to pivot and change when needed. The SEAL Teams, and the greater 10,000-person Naval Special Warfare Enterprise, have repeatedly transformed themselves over the past 80 years to stay relevant—to stay effective. Much like healthcare systems, organizational innovation in the government is extremely hard, even in the world of Special Operations. Change takes time, energy, and resources. It takes a clear understanding of why the change is needed, and it takes focus on the long-term vision and sheer determination to guide people and teams through that change—often with rotating leadership and ever-competing agendas.

The most critical lesson: Do not continually focus on the 1,000 reasons something can't be done. Find the one way to make it happen and lead the teams to complete the mission. To do that, you first have to *believe* it can be done. That optimism and laser focus on mission accomplishment, coupled with the courage to act, allowed the SEAL Teams to succeed where others failed. Having the courage to believe and then apply the correct planning, preparation, and leadership—to act—was the differentiator. Courage to act made the difference.

The American healthcare system is broken, fragmented, expensive, and inequitable. That is not an opinion—it is fact. We also have the greatest resources and minds available to translate our elite status in research and specialty care into a consumer-centric model wherein we recognize that most people, even those with chronic diseases such as diabetes or cancer, want to be able to thrive without health or finances getting in the way. That is the American dream. The $4 trillion we spend is enough, our great healthcare workers are talented enough, our pharma companies are the leading drug developers in the world, and the sheer data and intelligence that the payers and others have stored is immense. The same revolution in science and clinical care for single patients with formerly incurable diseases through treatments such as CAR T-cell therapy for cancer, GLP-1 agonists for diabetes, various RNA vaccines (notably for COVID-19 to ease the recent pandemic), and others is now happening in the healthcare delivery world with generative AI, virtual reality, large language models, natural language processing, drone technology, and sensors.

There is no shortage of great ideas. However, the sheer number of players in the US healthcare system creates enormous complexity. It's difficult to identify where to take tangible action; action that will prove to add value where it's needed most—with the patients, people, and communities we are supposed to serve. Where the *rubber meets the road.* We must identify where and how to incentivize these various players whose changes—a transformation in their industry—will ultimately lead to real value-creation. We must incentivize them to embrace change and disruption in their systems. Then, we must each have the courage to act.

In 2021, the Adidas company launched the "Impossible Is Nothing" campaign. It was inspired by a famous quote attributed to Muhammad Ali, "Impossible is just a word thrown around by small men and women who find it easier to live in the world they've been given than to explore the power they have to change it" (Rovell 2016). Impossible is potential. If anyone tells you that creating a significantly better healthcare delivery system is impossible, we hope you will smile, put on your running shoes (Adidas or otherwise), and play Sia's 2020 hit song "Courage to Change." This should be *the* anthem and overriding motto for all of us who want to create a better and healthier healthcare system in the United States.

REFERENCES

All.health. 2024. "We Enable the Most Advanced, Continuous Healthcare—Whenever and Wherever You Need It." Accessed September 23. https://all.health/.

Hippocratic AI. 2024. "Hippocratic AI Announces Collaboration with NVIDIA to Develop Super-Low-Latency 'Empathy Inference' for One of the World's First Generative AI-Powered Healthcare Agents." News release, March 18. www.globenewswire.com/news-release/2024/3/18/2848236/0/en/Hippocratic-AI-Announces-Collaboration-with-NVIDIA-to-Develop-Super-Low-Latency-Empathy-Inference-for-One-of-the-World-s-First-Generative-AI-Powered-Healthcare-Agents.html.

Institute for Healthcare Improvement (IHI). 2024. "Triple Aim and Population Health." Accessed August 23. www.ihi.org/Engage/Initiatives/TripleAim/Pages/default.aspx.

Kissick, W. 1994. *Medicine's Dilemmas: Infinite Needs Versus Finite Resources.* New Haven, CT: Yale University Press.

Klasko, S., and J. Booher. 2024. "The Courage to Act: A Strategy for Designing the Future When the Present Is Daunting." *E-Briefings* 21 (1). Published January. www.governanceinstitute. com/page/EBriefings_V21N1January2024.

Rovell, D. 2016. "Muhammad Ali's 10 Best Quotes." ESPN.com. Published June 3. www.espn.com/boxing/story/_/id/15930888/ muhammad-ali-10-best-quotes.

Index

Depth: human understanding and, 196, 197

DeVoe, J. E., 194

Diabetes management: digital health technology and, 195–96

Digital health firms: lessons learned from, 195–96

Digital health technology: embracing, 195–96. *See also* Technology

Digital twins, 253

Dimensions of patient-centered care: access to care, 12, 17, 99; continued relevance of, 99, 100, 200; continuity and transition, 12, 99; coordination and integration of care, 11, 99; COVID-19 pandemic and, 109–12; defining through the eyes of the consumer, 114–21; emotional support and alleviation of fear and anxiety, 12, 13, 17, 99; information, communication, and education, 13, 99; involvement of family and friends, 13–14, 99; physical comfort, 13, 99; Picker Institute's outline of, 12–14; respect for patients' values, preferences, and expressed needs, 13, 99; training and supporting employees in, 215. *See also* Case studies of dimensions of patient-centered care in action

Dimensions of patient-centered care, defining conceptual framework for, 99; conclusions, 113–14; qualitative methodology, 100–1; qualitative results, 102–4, *104*; quantitative methodology, 101–2; quantitative results, 105–9, *107–8*

Discharge education, 229

Disruptors to healthcare industry, 69–74

Diversity: medical school admissions and, 190

Doggie Brigade (Akron Children's Hospital), 163–4

Ebola public relations fiasco in Texas, 55

Economic determinants of health, 194

Educational workshops: for staff members, 225

Electronic health records (EHRs), 30, 33, 151, 157, 159, 235, 243

Electronic medical records (EMRs), 30, 33; bedside documentation and, 33; Mount Sinai Health System and, 168; shift to electronic health records, 30, 33

Emily Cooper Welty Expressive Therapy Center (Akron Children's Hospital), 164

Emotional commitment, 202

Emotional exhaustion, 204

Emotional intelligence: medical school entrance criteria and, 190; need for physicians with, 191

Emotional support and alleviation of fear and anxiety, 13, 17; at Akron Children's Hospital, 160; comparison of historical and recent qualitative feedback on, 102, 103, *104*; comparison of historical and recent quantitative feedback: dimension level, 107, 109, *108*; COVID-19 pandemic and, 17, 112; defining through the eyes of the consumer, 117–18; dimension comparison (historical and current), 95, 97, 98; as dimension of patient-centered care, 13, 99; at Luminis Health Anne Arundel Medical Center, 126; at Mass General Brigham, 136; in Mount Sinai Health System, 167–68; qualitative research results on, 90; removing barriers to, 226–27; at The Johns Hopkins Hospital, 151, 152

Empathy: at Cleveland Clinic, 153, 156, 157, 160; medical school entrance criteria and, 190; at Jefferson Health, 178; at Mass General Brigham, 137; need for physicians with, 192

Employee enablement, 215–17, *216*

Employee engagement: definition of, 202; future of, 215; importance of, 205–6; internal net promoter score and, 207–9, *209, 210*; linked with patient and consumer experiences, 210–12, 214, *211*; measurement of, 88, 206–7; as patient-centered

HCAHPS. *See* Hospital Consumer Assessment of Healthcare Providers and Systems

Health: consumer engagement with, 38; social and economic determinants of, xii, xviii, xxiii–xxiv, 194, 235, 237, 238, 252, 255

"Health assurance": future driven by, 253–56; General Catalyst and, 71–72, 172; at Jefferson Health, 172; moving from "sick care" to, 185; themes related to, 252

Healthcare: boosting employee engagement in, 206–7; as a calling, 79, 216–17; changing the DNA of, 189–93, 196, 257; choosing, 79–81; consumer revolution in, 185–86; consumers' expectations for, 12, 16, 38–39, 60, 60, 60–61; four effective levers for leaders in, 188–89; limited consumer knowledge about, 52–53; rise of choice and, 65–67; use of "consumerism" in, 125

Healthcare consumers: CAHPS programs and needs of, 8, 9; challenges faced by, 38–39; common ground with healthcare employees and, 131, 209; COVID-19 pandemic's effect on, 17; how quality is defined by, 39–40, 42–44; limited knowledge of, 28, 52–53; most valued attributes of care, *44*; online, average age of, 36, 59; rise of, 27–47. *See also* Consumers

Healthcare delivery: consumer revolution in healthcare and, 91, 185–87; embracing digital health technology, 195–96, 257–58, 259; robust digital tools and, xxi–xxii, 252, 259

Healthcare employees: common ground with healthcare consumers, 131, 209

Healthcare expenditures: as percentage of US gross domestic product, 15, 57, 249; rise in, xix

Healthcare industry: compassion fatigue and, 204–6, 231–33; measurement overload and, 81–82, 90, 257; shift to business-to-consumer model in, 172, 252

Healthcare organizations: consumer engagement and, 38; consumerism mindset and, 33; counternarrative needed by, 55; defensiveness of, 61; internal net promoter scores within, 198, 207–9, *209*, *210*; mission of, xxvii, 216; "off-campus" involvement of, 230. *See also* Case studies of dimensions of patient-centered care in action

Healthcare Partners Program (Cleveland Clinic), 156

"Healthcare with no address": attaining, 255–56; at Jefferson Health, 178–180

Health consumer citizenship: fight for, 186; health assurance and, 252

Health disparities and inequities, 28, 45, 134, 172, 249, 254

Health Insurance Portability and Accountability Act, 222

Health maintenance organizations: advent of, 29

Helen Diller Family Comprehensive Cancer Center, University of California, San Francisco, 138, 139

HHS. *See* US Department of Health and Human Services

High-deductible arena: frustration with price opacity and, 58

High-deductible health plans, xviii, 27, 28, 58, 117

Hilton Hotels: digital key introduced by, 62

Hippocratic oath, 80

Home monitoring devices, 32–33, 239

Hospital Compare website (Centers for Medicare & Medicaid Services), 40

Hospital Consumer Assessment of Healthcare Providers and Systems (HCAHPS), 15, 21, 65, 81, 85, 89, 90; Affordable Care Act and, 84; COVID-19 and, 109; first public reporting of survey results, 9; government mandate of, 17, 18, 42; independent *vs.* system hospital performance on, *43*; main goals in shaping of, 24; measurement overload and impact of reporting by, 81–84; modernizing, calls for, 91; questioning approach of, 84, 86; reduction in metrics and, 87–88

Respite rooms, 117, 164, 227, 228
Results: difficulty in sustaining, 90–91
Retail clinics, 17, 18, 120
Retail medicine: consumer revolution and, 186
Retail revolution, 251
Robotic medicine, xxiii, xxix, 4, 113, 192, 253
Robotics: physicians and, 192, 253
Role-playing, 225
Roosevelt, Eleanor, 10
Rush Medical Center, Chicago, 143

Safety needs: in Maslow's hierarchy, 202
Salary and employee satisfaction study, 206
Sculley, John, 251
SDOH. See Social determinants of health
Sears, 251
Secure messaging, 151
Self-actualization: in Maslow's hierarchy, 202, 203
Self-advocacy: qualitative research findings on, 103
Sensors, 32, 255, 259
Shared Medical Appointments (Cleveland Clinic), 154
Shea, Greg, 188, 189
Shkreli, Martin, 55
"Sick care": COVID-19 and, xviii; moving to "health assurance" from, 185, 186, 252, 256
Sidorov, Jaan, 188
Sisters of Saint Francis: Mayo Clinic partnership and, 143
"Six Degrees of Kevin Bacon," 51
Six degrees of separation in consumer–provider relationship, 51–67; consumer expectations, 60, 60–65; healthcare as ignored industry, 52–54; healthcare spending, 57–58; infinite information, 59–60; media and "healthcare is broken" narrative, 54–57; rise of choice, 65–67
Smartphones: apps, xii, 62, 63, 113, 174; emergence of, 30, 36
Social determinants of health, xii, xviii, xxiii, xxiv, xxv, 131, 194, 235, 237, 238, 252, 255

Social media, xxiii, xxvii, 33, 59; access to care and, 36; average age of users, 59; patient and family engagement, 161–62
Sondheimer, H. M., 190
Southwest Airlines, 56, 61
Staff rounds: combating compassion fatigue and, 232
Stakeholders: aligning around the same goals, 20; data on, 222; new technologies, fragmentation, and, 238–40; patients as more than, 197; patients vs., 55
States' budgets: healthcare's impact on, 249
Step One board examinations, 190
Strategies: for refocusing on human understanding, universal, 243–44
SullivanCotter's executive compensation survey, 85
Support groups, 115, 119, 138, 149, 224, 227; virtual, 223
Supreme Court. See US Supreme Court
Surgeon burnout: medical errors and, 205
Surgery: "best and worst of" vignette, 3–7
Surprise billing, 16, 40
Surveys: annual employee, manager dissatisfaction with, 206–7, 208; results and modes of, 100–1, 113
Symptom-management personnel: at University of California, San Francisco, 138
Systemness, 87–90

Tablets, 30
Taneja, Hemant, 172
Target, xxix, 251
Team-based care: coordination of patient care and, 223–24, 232; Mayo Clinic Health System and, 143, 146
Technology, xxi–xxix, 196, 197, 253–56, 259; communication using, 31; consumer access points via, 39, 239; consumer revolution in healthcare and, xi, xxii–xxiii, 36, 186–87, 252; embracing, 195–96, 257; at Jefferson Health, 178; leveraging new, 239–40; at Mayo Clinic, 145, 146; medical students and development of, 192;

mobile, 60; patient use of, as active care team members, 32–34; qualitative and quantitative studies and, 113; solutions for patient care, 233, 234–38, 240; Southwest Airlines failure, 56–57; trust and, xxvii; wayfinding at The Johns Hopkins Hospital, 149; wearable, 32, 59, 196, 241, 255. *See also* Artificial intelligence; Electronic medical records; Large language models (LLMs); Predictive analytics, Smartphones; Social media; Telehealth; Telemedicine

Telehealth, 31, 32, 186, 230; at Akron Children's Hospital, 162–63; COVID-19 and, xx, xxi, xxiv, 31, 111; dimensions of patient-centered care and, 113–14; at Jefferson Health, 173–74; at Mayo Clinic, 146

Telemedicine, 32, 239; at Cleveland Clinic, 156; COVID-19 and, 31; at The Johns Hopkins Hospital, 150; in schools, 230

Teletriage: at Jefferson Health, 174

Thomas Jefferson University, 173, 190

Thomas Jefferson University Hospital, 170, 174

Through the Patient's Eyes (Gerteis et al.), xxviii, 12, 21, 101, 102

Tiered huddles: at Cleveland Clinic, 155

To Err Is Human (Institute of Medicine), 8

Transition and continuity. *See* Continuity and transition.

Transparency: in consumer-centric healthcare system, 156, 254, 257; consumer need for, 40, 116, 117, 129; difficulty with, traditional academic and healthcare ecosystems, 172; electronic medical record systems and, 30; HCAHPS survey and, 17; lack of, in healthcare, 40; price, 40, 102–3; provider reviews and comments and, 230

Transportation services: digitally powered, Jefferson Health and, 178

Triple Aim: as a framework for optimizing health system performance, 18; patient-centered care and, 27; patient engagement and, 19;

reducing health inequities, 250; universal acceptance of, 34

Triple Aim, consumer edition, 34–40; access (consumer aim 1), 35–37, 35; engagement (consumer aim 2), 37–39; overview, 34–35; value (consumer aim 3), 39–41

Trust: infinite information issues and, 59–60; online reviews and, 116; technology and, xxvii

Uber, xxv, 61, 62–63

UCSF. *See* University of California, San Francisco

UIMC. *See* University of Illinois Medical Center

United Against Racism: program at Mass General Brigham, 132

University of California, San Francisco (UCSF), 137–42; coordination and integration of care at, 139; involvement of family and friends at, 139; information, communication, and education at, 141–42; overview, 137–38; Picker dimensions, 137; respect for patients' values, preferences, and expressed needs at, 139–41

University of Chicago, 212

University of Illinois at Chicago, 212

University of Illinois Medical Center (UIMC): internal branding campaign of, 212–14

Urgent care clinics, 37, 68, 120; post-COVID future of, xxviii

US Department of Health and Human Services (HHS), 8

US Supreme Court: dissolution of affirmative action programs, 190

Value-based care, xviii, 9, 16, 17, 70

Value-based payments: government emphasis on, 9; transition from fee-for-service payments to, 187, 257

Value-based purchasing: Affordable Care Act and shift to, 81, 85

Value-Based Purchasing (VBP) program: percentage of patients reporting positive overall experience for all hospitals *vs.* hospitals in, 2008–2014, *82*

About the Authors

Ryan Donohue serves as a strategic adviser to NRC Health, the largest surveyor of healthcare consumers in the United States. Ryan is a thought leader in the realm of healthcare consumerism and has an extensive background in consumer decision-making, brand preference, and loyalty in healthcare. Since 2006, he has conducted specialized research on the effects of consumerism on the US healthcare industry. His mission is to inspire and persuade physician, hospital, and health system leaders to embrace and engage the healthcare consumer.

Donohue has authored several publications on healthcare consumerism, brand strategy, and effective marketing tactics. He also serves as an adviser and faculty member for The Governance Institute and is a regular contributor to the *Boardroom Press* newsletter and other Governance Institute publications. He speaks regularly at Governance Institute leadership conferences and many other healthcare leadership events. On the heels of this book, Ryan launched a popular podcast by the same name: *Patient No Longer*.

NRC Health is one of the preeminent research firms in the US, specializing only in healthcare. Donohue has worked with many top health systems and hospitals to understand the opportunities generated by a more consumer-centric healthcare climate. Representative clients include Mayo Clinic, Trinity Health, Baylor Scott & White Health, New York–Presbyterian Hospital, Providence, and Partners HealthCare. Donohue continues to research how everyday people make decisions and how providers can move toward their patients to build lasting relationships and a healthier world.

Stephen K. Klasko, MD, DSc, MBA, is a preeminent innovator and advocate, pursuing his passion to bridge traditional academic medicine with the emerging world of generative AI, digital medicine, and entrepreneurship. His focus on building radical collaboration has led to numerous new partnerships. In 2018, he was recognized by *Modern Healthcare*, tying for second place on its list of the most influential individuals in healthcare. In 2024, he was named one of healthcare's "Great Leaders" by *Becker's Hospital Review*.

His career has been driven by his vision for a revolution in healthcare and higher education, as dean of two medical colleges, as a health system CEO, and as a university president. As an author, he has used creativity through music, science fiction, and storytelling to develop what he sees as "heretical optimism" in creating institutions that are friendly and equitable and that develop healthcare and education "at any address."

About the Contributors

Megan Charko, MAM, is the former content marketing manager at NRC Health. In this role, she worked closely with all teams at NRC Health to manage high-touch reference relationships across the NRC Health customer base. Previously, Ms. Charko was the program manager of pediatrics at NRC Health. As such, she collaborated with pediatric organizations across the country and in Canada to coach executive leaders on best practices that support the organizational alignment of strategic initiatives with customer-focused improvement efforts. Ms. Charko authored a nationally released white paper, *Challenging Convention: Millennial Parents' Expectations of Pediatric Care*. She has extensive knowledge of the Centers for Medicare & Medicaid Services (CMS) Consumer Assessment of Healthcare Providers and Systems (CAHPS) programs, value-based purchasing comparative reporting, consumerism trends, and facilitating organizational relationships with various demographic groups such as patients along the entire healthcare continuum, payers, physicians, and staff.

Ms. Charko is a graduate of Nebraska Wesleyan University in Lincoln with a BS in communication studies. She earned a master of arts in management with an emphasis on leadership from Doane University in Crete, Nebraska.

Katherine Johnson, PhD, is former senior director of research and analytics at NRC Health, where she led teams of researchers and analysts across the organization while engaging in research in the area of healthcare customer loyalty. Dr. Johnson also led NRC Health's quality and corporate compliance efforts to advance patient-centered care and ensure that the organization and its partners were operating in accordance with the protocols and guidelines set forth by CMS for all CAHPS surveying. Dr. Johnson has cultivated a talent for blending scientific rigor with real-world business needs, and she strives to make research accessible and actionable for colleagues and customers.

Dr. Johnson received her doctoral degree in sociology from the University of Nebraska–Lincoln, where her primary areas of focus were criminology and quantitative/qualitative methodology. She has published research briefs for NRC Health, as well as peer-reviewed journal articles and book chapters in the area of health and mental health among homeless and runaway youth.

Jona Raasch is the former CEO of The Governance Institute, the leading provider of governance knowledge and solutions for CEOs and directors of hospitals and health systems. Ms. Raasch has been involved with hospitals and health systems at all levels for the majority of her career. As the chief operating officer for NRC Health (The Governance Institute's parent company), Ms. Raasch spent 22 years helping hospitals and health systems measure and improve in the areas of quality, communication, education, and client satisfaction. She also has worked closely with a panel of industry experts whose focus is on developing and implementing initiatives to improve the patient experience.

Ms. Raasch is a member of the NRC Health advisory board and has served as an adviser to the board of the Picker Scandinavia, Germany, and Switzerland offices.

Kathryn C. Peisert has worked in healthcare governance educational development since 2003 and, as the editor in chief and senior director, is responsible for all The Governance Institute's print and online publications, video programs, webinars, and e-learning courses. In this role, she researches and identifies key healthcare governance challenges and issues for the nation's hospital and health system boards. She researches national healthcare governance structure, culture, and best practices and also develops The Governance Institute's annual education agenda. She works with The Governance Institute's parent company, NRC Health, to develop educational publications for healthcare leaders in patient experience, cross-continuum care delivery, and consumer perceptions in the healthcare marketplace.

Previously, she served as editor with The Governance Institute and before that was a permissions and copyright editor for Roxbury Publishing Company, now a division of Oxford University Press. She has authored or coauthored articles in *Health Affairs*, *Journal of Health & Life Sciences Law*, *Prescriptions for Excellence in Health Care*, and *Healthcare Executive*, as well as numerous articles, case studies, and research papers for The Governance Institute.

Ms. Peisert has a bachelor's degree in communications from the University of California, Los Angeles, and a master's degree in music from Boston University.

Jennifer Volland, DHA, RN, FACHE, MBB, CPHQ, NEA-BC, is former vice president of program development at NRC Health. She has worked in healthcare for more than 30 years, starting in the pediatric intensive care unit at Children's Hospital in Omaha, Nebraska. Prior to joining NRC Health, she was vice president of nursing at Cancer Treatment Centers of America in Zion/Chicago. She also led the healthcare practice at Juran Institute (founded by the world-renowned "Father of Quality" Dr. Joseph Juran) and created its healthcare product materials at a time when Six Sigma was shifting into healthcare. Dr. Volland has certified Six Sigma Green, Black, and Master Black Belts in the United States, England, Ireland, and Canada. She was the first individual to train and certify individuals in Six Sigma and Lean at the national level for the National Health Service in the United Kingdom. Dr. Volland is known as an industry expert on quality and driving accelerated improvement, having conducted numerous best-practice topic webinars and authored or coauthored many peer-reviewed publications, professional organization articles, and white papers.

Dr. Volland is a past president of the Nebraska and Western Iowa Chapter of the American College of Healthcare Executives (ACHE) and a past ACHE Regent for Nebraska and Western Iowa. She also has served multiple terms on the ACHE Regents Advisory Council for Nebraska and Western Iowa. In addition, she has served on the ACHE Examination Committee and Programs, Products, and Services Committee and received the ACHE Regents (Senior-Level Healthcare Executive) Award. As an American Nurses Credentialing Center content expert, she participated on the team that reviewed and updated the NEA-BC (Nurse Executive Advanced–Board Certified) national board certification examination.

Dr. Volland has a BA in psychology from the University of Nebraska, a BS in nursing from Creighton University, an executive MBA from the University of Nebraska, and a doctor of health administration degree from Central Michigan University.